"Khan's timely collection of essays helps us understand the true losses children, youth, and their caretakers are forced to reckon with under COVID-19. Contributing scholars shine a spotlight (as the pandemic does) on gender, race, class, health, educational, and digital inequalities that were already far-reaching in global childhood; however, there is hope in children's agency and activism and a heightened imperative to work toward true human connection and, ultimately, real social change."

Ingrid E. Castro, *Professor of Sociology, Massachusetts College of Liberal Arts, USA*

COVID-19 and Childhood Inequality

The COVID-19 pandemic and the global response to it have disrupted the daily lives of children in innumerable ways. These impacts have unfolded unevenly, as nation, race, class, sexuality, citizenship status, disability, housing stability, and other dimensions of power have shaped the ways in which children and youth have experienced the pandemic. *COVID-19 and Childhood Inequality* brings together a multidisciplinary group of child and youth scholars and practitioners who highlight the mechanisms and practices through which the COVID-19 pandemic has both further marginalized children and exacerbated childhood disparities.

Featuring an introduction and ten chapters, the volume "unmasks" childhood inequalities through innovative, real-time research on children's pandemic lives and experiences, situating that research within established child and youth literatures. Using multiple methods and theoretical perspectives, the work provides a robust, multidisciplinary, and holistic approach to understanding childhood inequality as it intersects with the COVID-19 pandemic, particularly in the USA. The chapters also ask us to consider pathways toward resilience, offering recommendations and practices for challenging the inequities that have deepened since the entrée of SARS-CoV-2 onto the global stage.

Ultimately, the work provides a timely and vital resource for childhood and youth educators, practitioners, organizers, policymakers, and researchers. An illuminating volume, each chapter brings a much-needed focus on the varied and exponential impacts of COVID-19 on the lives of children and youth.

Nazneen Khan is an associate professor of Sociology at Randolph-Macon College in Ashland, Virginia, USA. She is an active member of the Children and Youth Section of the *American Sociological Association* and currently serves as the section's Treasurer-Secretary. Her research and teaching employs intersectional theory and methodology and focuses on families, childhood, and motherhood at the crossroads of broader racial, economic, and political formations in the USA. Her recent scholarship has been published in *Children & Society*, *Contexts*, *Sociological Focus*, *Critical Research on Religion*, and *Understanding and Dismantling Privilege*.

The COVID-19 Pandemic Series

This series examines the impact of the COVID-19 pandemic on individuals, communities, countries, and the larger global society from a social scientific perspective. It represents a timely and critical advance in knowledge related to what many believe to be the greatest threat to global ways of being in more than a century. It is imperative that academics take their rightful place alongside medical professionals as the world attempts to figure out how to deal with the current global pandemic, and how society might move forward in the future. This series represents a response to that imperative.

Series Editor: J. Michael Ryan

Titles in this Series:

COVID-19
Two Volume Set
Edited by J. Michael Ryan

COVID-19
Volume I: Global Pandemic, Societal Responses, Ideological Solutions
Edited by J. Michael Ryan

COVID-19
Volume II: Social Consequences and Cultural Adaptations
Edited by J. Michael Ryan

COVID-19: Social Inequalities Human Possibilities
J. Michael Ryan and Serena Nanda

Experiences of Health Workers in the COVID-19 Pandemic
In Their Own Words
Edited by Marie Bismark, Karen Willis, Sophie Lewis and Natasha Smallwood

Creative Resilience and COVID-19
Figuring the Everyday in a Pandemic
Edited by Irene Gammel and Jason Wang

COVID-19 and Childhood Inequality
Edited by Nazneen Khan

COVID-19 and Childhood Inequality

Edited by
Nazneen Khan

LONDON AND NEW YORK

First published 2022
by Routledge
4 Park Square, Milton Park, Abingdon, Oxon OX14 4RN

and by Routledge
605 Third Avenue, New York, NY 10158

Routledge is an imprint of the Taylor & Francis Group, an Informa business

© 2022 selection and editorial matter, Nazneen Khan; individual chapters, the contributors

The right of Nazneen Khan to be identified as the author of the editorial material, and of the authors for their individual chapters, has been asserted in accordance with sections 77 and 78 of the Copyright, Designs and Patents Act 1988.

All rights reserved. No part of this book may be reprinted or reproduced or utilised in any form or by any electronic, mechanical, or other means, now known or hereafter invented, including photocopying and recording, or in any information storage or retrieval system, without permission in writing from the publishers.

Trademark notice: Product or corporate names may be trademarks or registered trademarks, and are used only for identification and explanation without intent to infringe.

British Library Cataloguing-in-Publication Data
A catalogue record for this book is available from the British Library

Library of Congress Cataloging-in-Publication Data
A catalog record has been requested for this book

ISBN: 978-1-03-216909-5 (hbk)
ISBN: 978-1-03-216910-1 (pbk)
ISBN: 978-1-00-325093-7 (ebk)

DOI: 10.4324/9781003250937

Typeset in Bembo
by Newgen Publishing UK

Dedicated to my children, Imani and Aksel, and to all the children and youth burdened by oppression—may the systemic barriers to your wildest aspirations and creative potential be dismantled through the struggle for social justice.

In loving remembrance of the children whose lives were lost too soon to COVID-19.

Contents

List of Illustrations   xi
Notes on Contributors   xii
Foreword   xvii
  J. MICHAEL RYAN

Introduction: Unmasking Childhood Inequality   1
NAZNEEN KHAN

PART 1
Unmasking Childhood Inequality   11

1   Pandemic Eugenics: Reproductive Justice and Racial Inequality in Childhood   13
    NAZNEEN KHAN AND AMAYA BOSWELL

2   LGBTQ+ Youth and the COVID-19 Pandemic   35
    JESSICA N. FISH, MEG D. BISHOP, AND V. PAUL POTEAT

3   Turning a Blind Eye: COVID-19 and Homeless Children   45
    YVONNE VISSING

4   The Impact of COVID-19 on Children with Thalassemia and Their Families in India   58
    RACHANA SHARMA

PART 2
Unmasking Institutional Entanglements   73

5   Youth at the Margins: Continuity of Services During the COVID-19 Pandemic   75
    ANDREA N. HUNT AND TAMMY RHODES

6 Consequences of COVID-19 Realities and Misconceptions for Rural PK–12 Students: Implications from Rural Education Research 88
MEAGAN C. ARRASTÍA-CHISHOLM, LEE EDMONDSON GRIMES, AND HEATHER M. KELLEY

7 The Impact of Parental Burnout and Time with Children: Family Stress in a Large Urban City During COVID-19 99
WENDY WAGNER ROBESON AND KIMBERLY D. LUCAS

PART 3
Unmasking Pandemic Agency 117

8 When Six Feet Feels Like Six Miles: Children's Images of Their Lives During the COVID-19 Pandemic 119
SANDI K. NENGA

9 The COVID-19 Pandemic: Childhood Inequalities Unmasked in the Caribbean 133
ALDRIE HENRY-LEE

10 Risk-Taking Among Older Youth at the Outset of the COVID-19 Pandemic in the USA 153
MARIE C. JIPGUEP-AKHTAR, DENAE BRADLEY, AND TIA DICKERSON

Index 172

Illustrations

Figures

I.1	"Masked": Pandemic artwork by Imani Kane (age 14)	4
3.1	Macro and micro factors driving homelessness	46
8.1	The grocery store by Allison (age 9)	123
8.2	In-person and online school by Penelope (age 12)	124
8.3	Masked Guadalupe Bass fish by Ryan (age 12)	128

Tables

4.1	Worries and challenges faced by the families of the patient	64
4.2	Coping mechanisms	68
9.1	Basic socioeconomic indicators for selected Caribbean countries	135
9.2	Legal and policy contexts	138
9.3	Family tensions—causes and effects	140
9.4	Gender inequalities in education	143
9.5	Findings from primary data collected from 55 PE teachers (N=55)	145
9.6	Summary of main findings of this study	147
10.1	Descriptive statistics and reliability scores for study variables	158
10.2	Correlation coefficients for study variables	159
10.3	Hierarchical regression analyses for variables predicting COVID-19 risk behavior	162

Notes on Contributors

Meagan C. Arrastía-Chisholm is an associate professor of Educational Psychology at Valdosta State University, USA. Her professional and research interests include parental separation, rural education, and college counseling. Her work has been published in journals such as the *National Youth-at-Risk Journal, Peabody Journal of Education, Journal of Hispanic Higher Education, Theory & Practice in Rural Education,* and the *Rehabilitation Counseling Bulletin*.

Meg D. Bishop is a doctoral candidate in the Department of Human Development and Family Sciences and a trainee at the Population Research Center at the University of Texas at Austin, USA. Her research examines the role of sexual and gender diverse youth's intersectional identity development for health and thriving and currently explores how the timing of sexual minority identity development has changed across sociohistorical time, and how this timing relates to mental health and substance use.

Amaya Boswell is a recent graduate from the Sociology and Black Studies program at Randolph-Macon College, USA, and hopes to attend a graduate program in investigative journalism. She has extensive community-based experience working with marginalized children both in Ashland and in her hometown near Baltimore, MD.

Denae Bradley is a PhD student in the Department of Sociology and Criminology at Howard University, USA. She is also a Health Policy Research Scholar (HPRS), a national leadership program supported by the Robert-Wood Johnson Foundation. Her research interests include race and ethnicity, incarcerated populations, and health policy and she is currently collaborating on several projects that investigate policing and social determinants of health. She previously worked in community development and education in the Mississippi Delta.

Tia Dickerson is a PhD student in the Department of Sociology and Criminology at Howard University, USA. Her research focuses on the roles of race-neutral social welfare and crime policy in perpetuating generational inequality in Black families. Her current projects examine the relationship between race and perceptions of policing during the COVID-19 pandemic, and the impact of racial unrest and the COVID-19 pandemic on relationship satisfaction of Black couples. She has previously presented work on Black Americans' COVID-19 vaccine hesitancy and reluctance to participate in clinical trials, as well as the roles of race ideology and intermarriage on the declining marriage rates of Black women.

Jessica N. Fish is an assistant professor of Family Health and Wellbeing in the School of Public Health at the University of Maryland, USA, where she is also Deputy Director for Research and Evaluation at the Prevention Research Center. Her work focuses on the social and personal factors that shape the development and health of lesbian, gay, bisexual, transgender, and queer (LGBTQ) people and their families, with a specific focus on LGBTQ youth and young adults. Her work is designed to inform developmentally sensitive policies, programs, and prevention strategies that promote the health of LGBTQ people across the life course.

Lee Edmondson Grimes is an associate professor of Counseling and Program Coordinator for the Counselor Education Programs at Valdosta State University, USA. She publishes and presents frequently on school counseling and her research focuses on rural school counseling, P–12 career development, and interventions for meeting the needs of diverse learners. She has previously worked as a high school teacher and school counselor at elementary, middle, and high levels.

Aldrie Henry-Lee is the University Director of the Sir Arthur Lewis Institute of Social and Economic Studies (SALISES) at the University of the West Indies (UWI). She has researched and published widely on social policy issues in small island developing states (SIDS), public policy, poverty, gender, human rights, and childhood. She has conducted research for the Canadian International Development Agency (CIDA), the Department for International Development (DFID), the Caribbean Development Bank (CDB), Pan American Health Organisation (PAHO), the United Nations Development Programme (UNDP), the United Nations Children's Fund (UNICEF), and the World Bank.

Andrea N. Hunt is an associate professor of Sociology and Director of the Mitchell-West Center for Social Inclusion at the University of North Alabama, USA. Her teaching, research, and community efforts cover a range of interrelated topics including trauma, identity, inequality, and trauma-informed practices. She works regularly with local judges, probation officers, mental health professionals, social workers, youth in juvenile detention, K–12 teachers, and adults in recovery. She is a court-appointed special advocate and is currently pursuing a degree in clinical mental health counseling to better support and advocate for her community.

Marie C. Jipguep-Akhtar is an associate professor of Sociology at Howard University, USA. Her research interests include race, ethnicity, gender, the life course, and "place" disparities in health and the criminal justice system. Her current work focuses on exploring the intersection of gender with social institutions, namely, the health care and criminal justice systems and their impacts on health behaviors and outcomes, particularly during periods of social upheaval. Her research has been published in *Social Psychology Quarterly*, the *Journal of Ethnicity in Substance Abuse*, *Social Forces*, the *Journal of Black Psychology*, and the *Journal of Men's Health*.

Heather M. Kelley is the Head of the Department of Human Services and an associate professor of Educational Psychology in the College of Education and Human Services at Valdosta State University, USA. Her research focuses on teaching and learning in the K–12 education setting. More specifically, her interests include self-efficacy, culturally responsive teaching, and academic achievement in under-performing groups.

Nazneen Khan is an associate professor of Sociology at Randolph-Macon College, USA. She is an active member of the Child and Youth Section of the *American Sociological Association* and currently serves as the section's Treasurer-Secretary. Her research and teaching employs intersectional theory and methodology and focuses on families, childhood, and motherhood at the crossroads of broader racial, economic, and political formations in the USA. Her recent scholarship has been published in *Children & Society*, *Contexts*, *Sociological Focus*, *Critical Research on Religion*, and *Understanding and Dismantling Privilege*.

Kimberly D. Lucas serves as the Interim Executive Director of the MetroLab Network. She is trained as an economic sociologist and her primary interests include early childhood workforce policy, early childhood market dynamics, and the development of civic researchers whose academic work has direct bearing on policy and practice. Questioning who we think of as "expert" and how stakeholders identify "value" are common threads that pervade their work.

Sandi K. Nenga is a professor of Sociology at Southwestern University, USA. Her primary areas of scholarship are the sociology of childhood and youth and the lived experience of social class. She has published articles in *Journal of Contemporary Ethnography, Childhood, Sociological Studies of Children and Youth,* and *Journal of Youth Studies*. With Allison Hurst, she is the co-editor of *Working in Class: Recognizing How Social Class Shapes Our Academic Work* (Rowman & Littlefield, 2016).

V. Paul Poteat is a professor in the Department of Counseling, Development, and Educational Psychology at Boston College, USA. He conducts research on the school-based experiences of sexual and gender minority youth. His research on Gender-Sexuality Alliances (GSAs) has identified individual- and group-level mechanisms by which these school-based extracurricular groups foster empowerment and resilience among youth from diverse sexual orientations and gender identities. His work also examines bias-based harassment using an ecological framework to consider individual and peer factors that influence such behavior.

Tammy Rhodes is the Director of First Year Experience at the University of North Alabama, USA and a doctoral candidate at Trevecca Nazarene University, USA. Her work focuses on retention of academically at-risk students, specializing in first generation minority students. Her higher education research interests include student success initiatives for first- and second-year students in higher education and abolitionist teaching techniques. Her criminal justice research interests include exploration of Black and Indigenous femicide and the lack of media reporting, examining the school to prison pipeline for Black youth, and the impact of trauma on ethnic minorities.

Wendy Wagner Robeson is Senior Research Scientist with the Work, Families, and Children Research Group at the Wellesley Centers for Women. She has extensive experience of research in child development, early childhood care and education, childcare policy, and school readiness. She has served as principal investigator or project director of numerous studies. Since the beginning of the pandemic, she has worked with early childhood education advocates from across Massachusetts to assess the impact of COVID-19.

J. Michael Ryan is an assistant professor of sociology at Nazarbayev University (Kazakhstan). He was previously a researcher for the TRANSRIGHTS Project at The University of Lisbon (Portugal) and has taught courses at The American University in Cairo (Egypt), Facultad Latinoamericana de Ciencias Sociales (FLACSO) (Ecuador), and the University of Maryland (USA). Before returning to academia, he worked as a research methodologist at the National Center for Health Statistics in Washington, D.C. He is the author (with Serena Nanda) of *COVID-19: Social inequalities and human possibilities* (Routledge 2022) and editor of multiple volumes including *COVID-19: Global pandemic, societal responses, ideological solutions* (Routledge 2021), *COVID-19: Social consequences and cultural adaptations* (Routledge 2021), *Trans Lives in a Globalizing World: Rights, identities, and politics* (Routledge 2020), and *Core Concepts in Sociology* (Wiley 2019). He is also the founding editor of Routledge's *The COVID-19 Pandemic* series.

Rachana Sharma is an assistant professor of Sociology at Guru Nanak Dev University (GNDU), India. Her research focuses on social exclusion, economic sociology, and gender. She is the author of the book *Shops and the Malls: A Sociological Exploration of Indian Retail Business* (Kalpaz Publications, 2015). She has also worked as a consultant for Youth Affairs at the Punjab State AIDS Control Society and works with various NGOs to support and empower women and children.

Yvonne Vissing is a professor of Healthcare Studies and founding director of the Center for Childhood & Youth Studies at Salem State University, USA.

She is the USA Child Rights Policy Chair for the International Hope for Children Convention on the Rights of the Child Policy Center. She is also on the Human Rights Council for the Association for the Advancement of Science and the steering committee for Human Rights Educators USA, and was on the board of the National Coalition for the Homeless. She is the author of numerous books on child well-being, including, with Christopher G. Hudson and Diane Nilan, *Changing the Paradigm of Homelessness* (Routledge 2020).

Foreword

When the severe acute respiratory syndrome coronavirus 2 (SARS-CoV-2) virus began to alter the face of the world in early 2020, I set about pulling together a two-volume set of edited volumes to help add a social scientific voice to pandemic understandings. Although I was thrilled to have each of the contributors to those volumes on board, I was especially pleased to have longtime friend from graduate school, and editor of this volume, Nazneen Khan, as a contributor. I was already familiar with Nazneen's work, both from graduate school, as well as from her accomplished professional career, and her contribution to my own volumes brimmed with her usual exemplary scholarship and keen, critical insights.

After the success of those two volumes, I have since become the series editor for Routledge's *The COVID-19 Pandemic Series* and was again delighted, nay honored, to quickly receive a proposal from Nazneen for the book you are now reading. I have enthusiasm for all contributors to my series, but I must confess an extra layer of affection for Nazneen and her scholarship.

Nazneen's established career as a scholar of childhood studies made her the ideal candidate to edit this very important volume. Knowing her personally, I already had no doubts about her abilities, and having known her professionally for more than a decade secured my faith that she was the ideal candidate to lead this ambitious project. That faith was not disappointed. The range, insights, credentials, and accessibility of the work contained in these pages are without comparison at the increasingly important intersection of childhood and COVID-19 studies.

Children's relationship with the pandemic is a topic that has been alternately ignored, downplayed, and, as current trends indicate, overlooked. The contributors to this volume have made no such mistakes and have, as indicated by the speed with which they have produced this scholarship, been thinking about these issues all along. Their foresight is our gain as this volume contains contributions from many of the pioneers of childhood COVID-19 research.

Many of us have children. An unfortunately increasing number of us have children who have, are, or will suffer from the COVID-19 pandemic. And all of us live in a world where our present, and future, generations are at even greater risk if we do not better understand not only the medical, but also the social–scientific relationship between the pandemic and children. Put simply, the pandemic has impacted every human being on the planet in some way or another and children have been no exception. This volume is a leading contribution to not only exploring pandemic impacts on the youngest among us, but also to furthering understandings of what those impacts mean—for us, for them, and for our societies as a whole.

As a dedicated mother of two, Nazneen has overseen what will no doubt become a foundational work in the quickly growing research area of how the pandemic has impacted children. Her accomplished panel of contributors has shown the same dedication, insights, and commitment to humanity that first drew me to Nazneen as a friend and colleague. I am now honored to add "series contributor" to that list of relationships.

J. Michael Ryan

Introduction

Unmasking Childhood Inequality

Nazneen Khan

Unmasked

The entrée of the severe acute respiratory syndrome coronavirus 2 (SARS-CoV-2) virus onto the global stage has disrupted the daily rhythms of childhood in unquantifiable ways. Because the virus causes a potentially deadly disease infamously known as coronavirus disease 2019 (COVID-19), federal and state protective measures have necessitated significant modifications to the customary ways in which educational, medical, and social services are delivered to children and youth in the United States of America (USA). Yet, the impacts of shuttered institutions and modified routines have unfolded unevenly, laying bare and even amplifying the historical and structural inequalities that are woven into the fabric of childhood.

The fact that the COVID-19 pandemic has exposed and intensified the scope of childhood inequality is an understatement. As an institution (Corsaro 2018; Qvortrup 2002) childhood is a permanent but ever-changing and dialectical form that co-constitutes the broader systems of power in which it is embedded. In this vein, this volume highlights the copious ways in which societal responses to COVID-19 are patterned by systems of power and, therefore, reproduce unequal childhoods. "Unequal childhoods" is a phrase that was widely popularized by sociologist Annette Lareau, whose groundbreaking research highlighted how social and economic advantages and disadvantages are transmitted to children through deeply entrenched ideologies and practices that are class-bifurcated (see Lareau 2011). The chapters that comprise this volume extend Lareau's materialist analysis to understand and unmask how nation, race, class, citizenship status, sexuality, disability, and other intersecting dimensions of power shape the ways in which children and youth experience the COVID-19 pandemic.

Consider that in the USA, Black and Hispanic children are more likely to live in families that have experienced three or more economic and/or health-related hardships as a result of COVID-19, twice the rate of their White counterparts (Padilla and Thompson 2021). Black children are more likely than any other group to live in families reporting housing instability during the pandemic, with one in every three Black households with children reporting rent or mortgage deficiencies (Lloyd et al. 2021). When homelessness happens, COVID-19 health precautions have rendered emergency housing even more difficult to access, leaving these children, approximately 1 out of every 18 US children aged five and below (Lloyd, Shaw, and Balding 2021), vulnerable to a host of negative psychological and physiological health risks (Duffield 2020; Vissing 2021, this volume). Additionally, Black and Hispanic children are the vast majority of those who have been hospitalized and have died from COVID-19 complications (Bixler et al. 2020). American-Indian adolescents have the highest rates of COVID-19-related mortality; they are seven times more likely to die from COVID-19 than White adolescents (COVKID 2021). Children with disabilities face life-threatening gaps in care (Sharma 2021, this volume) as medical supplies and prescription drug supply chains are disrupted. Lesbian, gay, bisexual, transgender, and queer (LGBTQ) youth, many of whom are confined to quarantine with unsupportive and non-affirming family members, also face precarious and distinct barriers to well-being (Fish, Bishop, and Poteat 2021, this volume; Valencia 2020).

Sadly, this list of injustices reveals only the surface of much more deeply rooted childhood inequality. Deep below the surface lie the social disparities that antedate COVID-19 and implicate the racialized, gendered, and class biases that were historically integral to the settler colonialist racial projects carried out in the USA as part of broader global formations of imperial power, reaching as far back as the transatlantic slave trade and the displacement of Indigenous peoples (see Mintz 2004). The COVID-19 pandemic has conspicuously revealed that the past is ever-present and that children are global subjects. Largely US-focused, this volume assembles 20 childhood and youth scholars from multiple disciplinary locations whose objective is to unmask the ways in which our responses to SARS-CoV-2 have distributed harm and risk differentially across groups of children. Working from different theoretical frameworks and methodologies, the work charts a robust understanding of unequal childhoods amidst the global pandemic. Chapters both reach downward, grounding their work in the historical and structural roots of inequality, and reach upward to reimagine the future of childhoods in a post-pandemic world.

The Urgent Need for Pandemic Social Research

The optimistic hope that COVID-19 would be a fleeting inconvenience in the modern milieu has been replaced by the dystopian reality that SARS-CoV-2 and its variants pose an ongoing threat whose impacts will reverberate into the unforeseeable future. High rates of vaccine hesitancy in the USA in conjunction with unequal access to vaccinations more globally mean that we will need to learn to co-exist with and adapt to SARS-CoV-2 and its dangerous and more contagious variants. In the USA, the direct effects of COVID-19 and its highly transmissible variants (i.e., B.1.1.7 and Delta) on children and youth are escalating as indicated by the late spring 2021 public health crisis in Michigan and the rise in COVID-19 positive cases among younger populations. In May 2021, the state of Michigan reported a record high of 70 children hospitalized due to severe COVID-19, one as young as two months old, and many of whom are on ventilators and are being diagnosed with COVID-19 pneumonia (NPR 2021). Amidst this wave of youth infections is the heartbreaking story of Chicagoan Dykota Morgan, who died just two days after testing positive for COVID-19. Only 15 years of age, the African-American teen had no known underlying conditions and was well known as an exceptionally talented multi-sport athlete. In the words of her despairing father, "this could be anybody's child" (NBC Chicago 2021). On May 10, 2021 the Pfizer vaccine was approved for use in children as young as 12 (US Food and Drug Administration 2021) but it will be sometime before this younger cohort is fully vaccinated. The unfair reality is that vaccine rollout has been racially biased across most states in the USA (Johnson, Kastanis, and Stafford 2021) and there is no reason to expect this trend to reverse as children and youth are vaccinated. Indeed, Black, Hispanic, and American-Indian parents are far more likely to experience the premature death of a child.

Just as positive cases began to decline in the USA, the COVID-19 delta variant reversed these trends, leaving unvaccinated children who are headed back to in-person schooling in more danger than at any other time during the pandemic. Although more data is needed, the variant is believed to not only make children sicker, but to lead to hospitalization and severe illness more quickly. Many regions across the south are reporting more hospitalized children in August 2021 than they have at any other time during the pandemic. According to the American Academy of Pediatrics (2021), July 2021 alone witnessed a sevenfold increase in COVID-19 cases among children. Indeed, the direct and indirect impacts of the pandemic will be long-lasting. Even as the exigency of the moment wanes, the impact and traumas born out will be forever imprinted on the hearts and minds of children and youth. This became evermore salient to me when I saw that my daughter's sketchbook was sprinkled with pandemic-themed artwork, signaling just how deeply anxious and impacted children and youth have been, and will continue to be, throughout the pandemic (see Figure I.1). As J. Michael Ryan (2021) argued, "the contemporary cohort will be forever marked by the presence of the SARS-CoV-2 virus and the associated COVID-19 pandemic" (xi). For all these reasons, pandemic research is not only timely, it is also urgent.

The research and recommendations presented in this volume contest the misguided view that pandemic research will soon be obsolete. Indeed, the precarious economic, environmental, political, and social context in which the pandemic is unfolding makes this work all the more urgent. Given the severity and longevity of the pandemic, it is imperative that social scientists examine and give witness to this unprecedented public health crisis—both its traumas and the opportunities for revolutionary change that it could engender. When read holistically, the chapters comprise a robust toolkit for child and youth educators, practitioners, and scholars who aim to take seriously and embrace an optimism

Figure I.1 "Masked": Pandemic artwork by Imani Kane (age 14).

for the future of childhood. The chapters also underscore the imperative that any viable future must include the voices of children and youth.

Masked

As COVID-19 cases spiked across the USA, governors across the nation extended mask mandates to include very young children. That young children were asked to also mask demonstrates that their behavior has profound implications and can shape public health and civic life just as much as that of adults. At the same time that we have recognized this, we have misrecognized and even ignored the significance of their perspectives. Perhaps because children have proved much less vulnerable to COVID-19, they have largely been voiceless throughout the pandemic. In this way, masks, now a life-saving wardrobe staple, also offer a powerful metaphor for the ways in which children's voices have been dismissed, ignored, and shuttered throughout the pandemic. Despite the impact of COVID-19 on children and youth, their experiences and perspectives have largely been masked—as if they are not stakeholders in their own lives. Rarely, if ever, have policymakers invited children to the decision-making table despite the powerful ways in which those decisions shape and organize their everyday lives.

This masking of young voices underscores Qvortrup's (2002) conceptualization of children, in which he points out that children constitute a marginalized group in relation to adults. Even in child-focused institutions such as public schools, which have largely reopened in virtual platforms, children are first taught to mute themselves. Regularly admonished for speaking out, their chat features are commonly disabled, prohibiting children from connecting with their peers. Such silencing practices shutter the few modes through which children can use technology to gain control over their daily lives. It should come as no surprise that so many children have become disinterested in virtual school as educational technologies commonly morph from pedagogical tools to policing and surveillance tools. This can be experienced as discouraging as it shifts children from being subjects of learning to objects of the techno-capital apparatus. At the same time, children who lack access to Wi-Fi and remote learning tools have become even more invisible and have dropped out of school altogether; many school districts across the USA are reporting spikes in high school dropout rates (Hollingsworth 2021).

In contrast, this volume impels us to remove the metaphorical mute buttons and masks that silence our children's voices and perspectives. In line with the "new sociology of childhood," which conceptualizes children as interpretive social beings who are also affectual creators of their social environs (Corsaro 2018; Matthews 2007), this volume impels the reader to consider the systemic inequalities that have and continue to be unmasked amidst this public health crisis and calls us to integrate the voices and perspectives of children and youth in respectful ways that support and foster childhood resilience.

A significant and growing body of research highlights the significance of adverse childhood experiences (ACEs) on the future health and well-being of children. However, this volume purports that the pandemic need not only offer lessons in powerlessness. Children are not determined by statistical probabilities—as Muhammad (2021) argues, adversity can empower children to "dream, achieve goals and continue to blaze paths forward" (2). Indeed, their capacity for resilience is astonishing and should impel adults to garner the appropriate supports needed for children and youth to chart pathways of resilience. The same core social institutions that have shuttered, dismissed, and overlooked the voices and perspectives of children and youth during this pandemic can be agents of social justice moving forward. As the reader will see, many of the recommendations put forward in this volume call for the unmasking and unmuting of children's voices and perspectives. In this way, the volume conceptualizes children as both objects and agents of social structure.

Organization of the Volume

This volume works in conjunction with other volumes in the COVID-19 Pandemic Series (Routledge). While it uniquely focuses on childhood, children, and youth, it shares with the other volumes in the series a focus on mapping COVID-19 impacts and inequalities and considers future possibilities. The chapters in this volume are organized into three parts. Chapters in Part 1, "Unmasking Childhood Inequality," explore various dimensions of inequality as they have been reproduced, heightened, concealed, and exposed throughout the pandemic.

In Chapter 1, "Pandemic Eugenics: Reproductive Justice and Racial Inequality in Childhood," Nazneen Khan and Amaya Boswell contextualize, synthesize, and critically examine emergent literature on the ways in which the COVID-19 pandemic has exacerbated and unmasked childhood racial inequality. Using a reproductive justice framework, they highlight racial inequality as impacted by the pandemic in three core childhood institutions—health, economics, and education. They demonstrate that societal responses to SARS-CoV-2 are stratified, thereby operating as mechanisms of eugenicide as they render "undesirable" children and youth socially obsolete and undermine routine reproductive tasks in ways that expose children of color to illness and premature death.

Building on the theme of childhood inequality, Jessica N. Fish, Meg D. Bishop, and V. Paul Poteat focus on LGBTQ+ youth in Chapter 2, entitled "LGBTQ+ Youth and the COVID-19 Pandemic." Although the pandemic's emotional weight has been universally felt, they demonstrate that LGBTQ+ youth face unique stressors due to changes in access to affirming and supportive resources. Their chapter explores three distinct but overlapping contexts relevant to LGBTQ+ youth and COVID-19: schools, families, and the Internet. They discuss how changes in these environments during the COVID-19 pandemic presented unique experiences and opportunities for LGBTQ+ youth and discuss the implications of these experiences.

In Chapter 3, entitled "Turning a Blind Eye: COVID-19 and Homeless Children," Yvonne Vissing highlights the ways in which COVID-19 poses unique challenges to health and well-being for unhoused children. As policy chair for the United Nations Convention on the Rights of the Child and founding director of the Center for Childhood and Youth Studies at Salem State University, Vissing offers a unique scholar-activist perspective on the challenges experienced by homeless children and youth in navigating educational, medical, and social services throughout the pandemic. Vissing's analysis provides a much-needed analysis and unmasking of the human rights violations inherent in the pandemic housing crisis.

In Chapter 4, "The Impact of COVID-19 on Children with Thalassemia and Their Families in India," Rachana Sharma widens lens beyond the USA, focusing on children with disabilities in India. Sharma exposes the unique struggles of children with thalassemia as they navigate continuity of care throughout the pandemic. Sharma notes that the struggles she discusses resonate far and wide as they are shared by children and youth with disabilities and chronic illnesses around the globe. Disruptions and barriers to the continuity of medical, psychological, and educational services for children with disabilities reverberate beyond the child and, as Sharma highlights, can disrupt the dynamics of family life.

Part 2 of the volume, entitled "Unmasking Institutional Entanglements," examines the primary institutions within which children's lives unfold. Familial and educational institutions serve as core interlocutors and arbiters of children's lives and have been impacted by pandemic restrictions and responses. Educational, mental health, medical, and caregiving services have all been forced to halt or completely modify their standard operations. This part of the volume explores how children's lives are interconnected with the broader institutions in which their lives are embedded. As the lives of parents and caregivers are upended, the rhythms and routines of childhood are disrupted.

Spearheading this part is "Youth at the Margins: Continuity of Services During the COVID-19 Pandemic," in which Andrea N. Hunt and Tammy Rhodes explore disruptions to the already-strained mental health services in schools and juvenile detention centers. They illuminate the distinct disadvantages experienced by marginalized youth, especially incarcerated youth, due to the COVID-19 pandemic. After discussing the unique challenges to receiving trauma-informed mental health care, the authors provide recommendations for practitioners and researchers to implement in future practice.

In Chapter 6, "Consequences of COVID-19 Realities and Misconceptions for Rural PK–12 Students: Implications from Rural Education Research," Meagan C. Arrastía-Chisholm, Lee Edmondson Grimes, and Heather M. Kelley examine barriers to educational services that are specific to children living in rural areas of the USA. Children in low-income and poor rural communities experience heightened educational inequalities, and the COVID-19 pandemic both exposes and exacerbates these inequities in profound ways. The authors provide critical insights into these inequities and map solutions for grappling with rural-specific challenges.

In Chapter 7, "The Impact of Parental Burnout and Time with Children: Family Stress in a Large Urban City During COVID-19," Wendy Wagner Robeson and Kimberly D. Lucas consider parent–child entanglements within the family. They bring to light the intimate ways in which a global pandemic can map onto the individual child, parent, and parent–child relationship. Using a qualitative approach, the impacts of parental burnout on children's lives are unmasked through the raw and uncensored lens of parents. Children's externalizing behaviors as revealed by parents suggest that children are seeking to gain control over their lives in these moments of anomie and uncertainty.

The chapters that comprise Part 3, "Unmasking Pandemic Agency," underscore the interpretive nature of childhood and the ways in which children and youth appropriate society. As childhood sociologist William Corsaro explains, "children do not simply imitate or internalize the world around them. They strive to interpret or make sense of their culture and to participate in it" (2018, 23). Indeed, this theoretical assertion is particularly salient in these final chapters as both demonstrate that children appropriate and exert force on social institutions. These chapters are purposefully placed at the end of the volume to circle back to and remind the reader of the creative capacities of children and youth amidst turbulence.

In Chapter 8, "When Six Feet Feels Like Six Miles: Children's Images of Their Lives During the COVID-19 Pandemic," Sandi K. Nenga situates her research in the new sociology of childhood as she frames her innovative study of children's pandemic agency through the theoretical lens of interpretive reproduction. Using participatory drawing and photovoice methods, Nenga centers children's perspectives on COVID-19 in the production of social science. Her analysis of her subjects' voices and drawings reveals not only the creative ways in which children appropriate and reproduce adult perspectives on the pandemic, but also how they wrestle against, redefine, and reshape adult imperatives.

Similarly, Aldrie Henry-Lee's research highlights the voices of children and advocates for acknowledgement of their agency. In Chapter 9, "The COVID-19 Pandemic: Childhood Inequalities Unmasked in the Caribbean," she examines the fallout of COVID-19 on the chain of islands that comprise the Caribbean. Using a mixed-methods approach, Henry-Lee amplifies the voices of children and youth in this region, where experiences of marginalization have been particularly severe. Focusing on the impact of the pandemic on the institutions of family, education, and recreation, the author reminds us that for children and youth in the global south, face masks and hand sanitizer are luxury commodities. She also poignantly underscores the need for policymakers, educators, and parents to include their voices and perspectives as we continue navigating this dangerous pandemic.

Marie C. Jipguep-Akhtar, Denae Bradley, and Tia Dickerson examine pandemic risk-taking behaviors among older youth. This final chapter, entitled "Risk-Taking Among Older Youth at the Outset of the COVID-19 Pandemic in the USA," importantly examines a cohort of youth that tend to be overlooked in the literature due to advanced age, but are still in many ways youthful. As the authors examine the impact of the COVID-19 pandemic on risk-taking behaviors, they reveal that youth risk-taking behaviors can be thought of as strategies through which youth coming-of-age seek to gain control of their lives during societal crises and changes. They find that gendered constructs influence how youth internalize safety measures and that older adolescent boys express greater risk-taking behaviors. This finding is a powerful and alarming indicator that pathways to more empowering forms of youth autonomy are riddled with systemic barriers. Their findings are a lurid wake-up call to our childhood institutions to pay attention, reimagine, and reform. Jipguep-Akhtar, Bradley, and Dickerson's unique focus on late adolescence contributes to the literature by illustrating that the societal impacts of COVID-19 will be carried forward as the pandemic generation comes of age.

As the chapters in this volume highlight, the need for this work is not only timely, but urgent. Although children have demonstrated agency through their appropriation of COVID-19 current events and language, there has also been immense anxiety, trauma, and loss. The need to document this is imperative, but more importantly, we need to highlight pathways to resilience and ways of moving forward *with* our marginalized children and youth so that they can overcome pandemic challenges and chart pathways to success. It is the hope of the contributors of this volume that as mask mandates are lifted, the voices of our children and youth will be acknowledged and included in the conversations that regulate their lives. While it may sound cliché, I hope that institutions will chart and create an imaginative pathway forward that is in service to childhood well-being. We need to demand that children who inhabit the marginal spaces and borderlands of society can, like their privileged counterparts, unmask their dreams and aspirations. To quote sociologist Eve Ewing (2017) in her letter to incarcerated youth, I hope this "rain" will "grow green and wonderful" possibilities for our children and youth.

References

American Academy of Pediatrics. 2021. "Children and COVID-19: State-Level Data Report." Accessed August 15, 2021. www.aap.org/en/pages/2019-novel-coronavirus-covid-19-infections/children-and-covid-19-state-level-data-report/.

Bixler, Danae, Allison D. Miller, Claire P. Mattison, et al. 2020. "SARS-CoV-2-Associated Deaths Among Persons Aged <21 Years—United States, February 12-July 31, 2020." *Morbidity and Mortality Weekly Report* 69: 1324–29. www.cdc.gov/mmwr/volumes/69/wr/mm6937e4.htm?s_cid=mm6937e4_w.

Corsaro, William. 2018. *The Sociology of Childhood*. Thousand Oaks, CA: Pine Forge Press.

COVKID 2021. "COVKID Disparities Data Dashboard." Accessed May 7, 2021. www.covkidproject.org/disparities.

Duffield, Barbara. 2020. "Reimagining Homelessness Assistance for Children and Youth." *Journal of Children and Poverty* 26 (2): 293–313. https://doi.org/10.1080/10796126.2020.1813535.

Ewing, Eve. 2017. *Electric Arches*. Chicago, IL: Haymarket Books.

Fish, Jessica, N., Meg D. Bishop, and V. Paul Poteat. 2021. "LGBTQ+ Youth and the COVID-19 Pandemic." In *COVID-19 and Childhood Inequality*, edited by Nazneen Khan. London and New York: Routledge.

Hollingsworth, Heather. 2021. "US Schools Fight to Keep Students Amid Fear of Dropout Surge." Associated Press, May 11, 2021. https://apnews.com/article/coronavirus-pandemic-health-education-1b0eb720342a1978383c703e5a001a90.

Johnson, Carla, Angeliki Kastanis, and Kat Stafford. 2021. "AP Analysis: Racial Disparity Seen in US Vaccination Drive." Associated Press News, January 30, 2021. https://apnews.com/article/race-and-ethnicity-health-coronavirus-pandemic-hispanics-d0746b028cf56231dbcdeda0fba24314.

Lareau, Annette. 2011. *Unequal Childhoods: Class, Race, and Family Life*, Second Edition. Berkeley, CA: University of California Press.

Lloyd, Chrishana M., Sara Shaw, Marta Alvira-Hammond, Ashley M. Hazelwood, and Alex DeMand. 2021. "Racism and Discrimination Contribute to Housing Instability for Black Families During the Pandemic." *Child Trends*, March 18, 2021. Accessed May 3, 2021. www.childtrends.org/publications/racism-and-discrimination-contribute-to-housing-instability-for-black-families-during-the-pandemic.

Lloyd, Chrishana M., Sara Shaw, and Susan Balding. 2021. "Housing Systems Must Better Support Families with Young Children Experiencing Homelessness." *Child Trends*, May 12, 2021. www.childtrends.org/blog/housing-systems-must-better-support-families-with-young-children-experiencing-homelessness.

Matthews, Sarah. 2007. "A Window on the 'New' Sociology of Childhood." *Sociology Compass* 1 (1): 322–34. https://doi.org/10.1111/j.1751-9020.2007.00001.x.

Mintz, Steven. 2004. *Huck's Raft: A History of American Childhood*. Cambridge, MA: Harvard University Press.

Muhammad, Bahiyyah. 2021. "Letter from the Research Principle Investigator." In *Children of Incarcerated Parents: Pathways to Resilience and Success Research Report*, by Bahiyyah Muhammad, Britany J. Gatewood, and Sydni Turner, p. 2. Prepared for

Thurgood Marshall College Fund, Center for Advancing Opportunity. Washington, DC. www.drmuhammadexperience.com/white-paper-2021.

NBC Chicago. 2021. "Parents Advocate for COVID Vaccine, Vigilance with Health Protocols After Teen's Death." *NBC Chicago,* May 7, 2021. www.nbcchicago.com/news/coronavirus/parents-advocate-for-getting-covid-vaccine-vigilance-with-health-guidelines-after-death-of-15-year-old-daughter/2504766/.

NPR. 2021. "Michigan Experiences Highest Rates of U.S. COVID-19 Cases." *NPR,* April 28, 2021. www.npr.org/2021/04/28/991503908/michigan-experiences-highest-rate-of-new-u-s-covid-19-cases.

Padilla, Christina, and Dana Thomson. 2021. "More Than One in Four Latino and Black Households with Children are Experiencing Three or More Hardships During COVID-19." *Child Trends,* January 13, 2021. www.childtrends.org/publications/more-than-one-in-four-latino-and-black-households-with-children-are-experiencing-three-or-more-hardships-during-covid-19.

Qvortrup, Jens. 2002. "Sociology of Childhood: Conceptual Liberation of Children." In *Childhood and Children's Culture,* edited by Flemming Mouritsen and Jens Qvortrup, pp. 43–78. Esbjerg, Denmark: University Press of Southern Denmark.

Ryan, J. Michael. 2021. *COVID-19: Volume 1: Global Pandemic, Societal Responses, Ideological Solutions.* London: Routledge.

Sharma, Rachana. 2021. "The Impact of COVID-19 on Children with Thalassemia and Their Families in India." In *COVID-19 and Childhood Inequality,* edited by Nazneen Khan. London and New York: Routledge.

US Food and Drug Administration. 2021. "COVID-19 Update: FDA Authorizes Pfizer- BioNTech COVID-19 Vaccine for Emergency Use in Adolescents in Another Important Action in Fight Against Pandemic." Accessed May 14, 2021. www.fda.gov/news-events/press-announcements/coronavirus-covid-19-update-fda-authorizes-pfizer-biontech-covid-19-vaccine-emergency-use.

Valencia, Misha. 2020. "The Challenges of the Pandemic for Queer Youth." *The New York Times,* June 29, 2020. www.nytimes.com/2020/06/29/well/family/LGBTQ-youth-teenagers-pandemic-coronavirus.html.

Vissing, Yvonne. 2021. "Turning a Blind Eye: COVID-19 and Homeless Children." In *COVID-19 and Childhood Inequality,* edited by Nazneen Khan. London and New York: Routledge.

Part 1
Unmasking Childhood Inequality

1 Pandemic Eugenics

Reproductive Justice and Racial Inequality in Childhood

Nazneen Khan and Amaya Boswell

It has been well established by social science research that the impacts of the coronavirus disease 2019 (COVID-19) pandemic have laid bare and exacerbated social inequality (Ryan 2021a and 2021b). In particular, research demonstrates that the pandemic is heightening racial inequalities in child well-being and outcomes across numerous domains, including education, economics and welfare, physical and mental health, and the juvenile justice system (Parolin 2021). This chapter provides a critical synthesis of emergent research on childhood racial inequality in the United States of America (USA), highlighting core patterns of inequality as both revealed and intensified by the impacts of, and societal responses to, COVID-19. Our analysis highlights three domains of inequality: health, economics, and education. We frame our analysis through a reproductive justice (RJ) paradigm, which enables us to situate real-time pandemic patterns of racial inequality in their historical and ideological context and to highlight the ways in which historical patterns of injustice are reformulated in contemporary society. We begin the chapter with a discussion of our conceptual framework; understanding the field of eugenics as practiced in the early 20th century is vital to understanding the patterns of pandemic racial inequality presented in this chapter.

Eugenics versus Reproductive Justice

Eugenics

In 1883, Francis Galton coined the term "eugenics" which aimed at "racial betterment" largely through the selective regulation of marriage and sexual partners as a mechanism for controlling fertility along racial lines (McCann 1994). In the 1920s, the eugenics movement gained social and political influence in the USA. Proponents of eugenics advocated for "race uplift" through measures designed to control reproduction. While positive eugenics aimed to increase the fertility rate among middle and upper status White women, negative eugenics was designed to eliminate the childbearing of women of color and poor women (McCann 1994). Negative eugenics, a crucial and central dimension of these campaigns in the USA, was advanced largely through

DOI: 10.4324/9781003250937-3

state-sanctioned compulsory sterilization programs that targeted Black, Latinx, Indigenous, and other women of color as well as poor White women and women with disabilities and criminal records (Solinger 2013). Not only were these women viewed as "unfit" by social progressives and conservatives alike, but their reproduction was also viewed as antithetical to the vitality of the nation. The formulation of social policies that curbed, controlled, and inevitably sought to contain the fertility rates of those deemed "unfit" (McCann 1994, 103) was furthered by proponents of the field of eugenics and sterilization laws spread throughout the USA as its ideological underpinnings intertwined with nationalist aspirations (Solinger 2013). In the early to mid-twentieth century, nationalist aspirations were also Progressive-era capitalist aspirations that pursued "racial directions," a system that Cedric Robinson ([1983] 2020, 2) defines as racial capitalism. Eugenics served as a core tool to advance racial capitalism as it justified an array of discriminatory practices carried out by industrial capitalists and their state sympathizers including exploitative working conditions and wages, withholding of labor rights and benefits, and exclusions from welfare-oriented reforms (Leonard 2016).

Children of color and other groups of "unfit" children were also excluded from the child-saving efforts of the Progressive Era. The field of eugenics utilized predominant biological definitions of race to hierarchically rank and sort children and energized animosity and disdain toward those groups of children who were low-ranking. This disdain was exemplified in *Tomorrow's Children*, a widely read monograph written by Ellsworth Huntington in collaboration with the American Eugenics Society (1935). In the monograph they purport that children of "poor biological inheritance" are incompetent, spawn social evils, and are the cause of illness. This derogatory view drove new forms of institutionalized discrimination toward groups of children deemed inferior, including withholding of aid and social services, substandard education and medical care, and systemic barriers to parental care including the removal of children from their families, quintessentially exemplified by federally mandated boarding schools for American-Indian children (Ross and Solinger 2017) and early child welfare systems (see Roberts 2002). Systems of state-sanctioned child mistreatment both undermined parents' ability to care for and raise their children in safe and dignified ways and extended eugenics practices beyond the regulation of fertility and into other forms of reproduction including the disruption of core aspects of childrearing.

Along these lines, Ross and Solinger (2017) specify that reproduction encompasses the caretaking practices that enable the well-being and survival of children. These caretaking practices are socially dependent and as such the ability to access the resources needed to adequately care for children is differentially distributed across populations and is shaped by global and national policies and processes (Ginsburg and Rapp 1995). The field of eugenics was impactful as it impelled and produced systemic barriers to caretaking, thereby contributing to the production of differential outcomes along core indices of child well-being, including health, economic well-being, and educational attainment.

Poor economic and social outcomes, an outgrowth of inequality, then became the further justification for coerced sterilization, caretaking obstacles, and other forms of reproductive injustice. In this way, systemic forms of discrimination also served to further advance eugenics sensibilities. This circular process aimed to render undesirable populations obsolete and/or unable to fully participate in societal institutions. In this way, eugenics can be understood as both disrupting the ability of "undesirable" children to survive *and* thrive.

The COVID-19 pandemic response in the USA unambiguously manifests the ways in which reproductive practices and policies are globally and nationally stratified and operate according to the logic of eugenics by impeding the survival and prosperity of disadvantaged groups of children. Stratified reproduction, defined by Colen (1995) as the ways in which "social reproductive tasks are accomplished differentially according to inequalities," is structured by broader systems of power such as race and class. In many ways, societal responses to COVID-19 are shaped by such systems of power and, like the treatment of marginalized children during the Progressive era who were under-prioritized and excluded from social benefits and supports, marginalized children today are often excluded from COVID-19-related benefits, reforms, policies, and practices. These exclusions both advance eugenics, albeit through contemporary logics, and are a violation of RJ.

Reproductive Justice

RJ is an intersectional theoretical and methodological framework that was first mapped out in 1994 by an alliance of Black women, including the well-known scholar-activist Loretta Ross. The framework is guided by three core values: the right to have a child, the right to not have a child, and the right to safe and dignified parenting (Ross and Solinger 2017, 9). The field of eugenics undermines RJ in at least two ways: first, by coercing women to have (positive eugenics) or not have children (negative eugenics) based on ascribed characteristics such as race, class, disability, and nationality, and, second, by undermining safe and dignified parenting (exposing certain groups of children to risk and harm through institutionalized discrimination). This chapter centers COVID-19 as a case study for further investigating the ongoing tensions between eugenics and RJ.

The RJ framework provides vital tools and an analytic lens for exploring the impact of COVID-19 responses and policies on children and on childhood inequality. It enables an exploration of the ways in which institutional responses impact the right to safe and dignified childrearing, a core component of RJ. While our analysis of the literature revealed a wide range of racial inequalities across many social institutions, our core findings gravitated around three childhood institutions: health, economics, and education. In the following section, we analyze our findings with respect to these institutions and highlight two observations. First, the US pandemic response has energized the ideology and practice of eugenics by stratifying children's ability to survive and thrive throughout the pandemic according to racial and class logics. Second, this advancement of eugenics undermines RJ, particularly the third component of RJ which emphasizes the right of caregivers to access the resources needed to protect their children from harm and to ensure optimal child well-being.

Findings: Eugenics, Stratified Reproduction, and the COVID-19 Pandemic

Our analysis of emergent literature at the intersection of COVID-19 and childhood racial inequality revealed an array of intensifying racial disparities impacting the lives of US children. We grouped these inequalities into three key thematic areas around which the literature gravitated—health inequality, economic inequality, and educational inequality. While we discuss these successively in sections for organizational purposes, we recognize the overlapping and interconnected nature of these inequalities (i.e., health disparities impede educational attainment).

Health Inequality

In *Race After Technology*, Ruha Benjamin (2019) writes that,

> In fact the most common euphemism for eugenics was "racial hygiene": ridding the body politic of unwanted populations would be akin to ridding the body of unwanted germs … The ancient Greek etymon *eugeneia* meant "good birth" and this etymological association should remind us how promises of goodness often hide harmful practices.
>
> (67)

Indeed, as COVID-19 responses rollout, ostensibly in service to public health, devalued populations are at higher risk of disease and death and are excluded from many of the "promises of goodness." The most immediate responses to COVID-19 in the USA egregiously highlight the ways in which societal sorting and ranking of children continues to shape their material lives. Latinx and Black children were socially positioned in proximity to COVID-19 as their caregivers continued to work in industries deemed essential. Their parents were framed as courageous heroes, but most often without wage compensation and/or personal protective equipment to match their heightened risk and elevated hero status. Beaman and Taylor (2020) write, "we cannot miss the role of white supremacy and racial capitalism in providing only gestures to these essential workers, and not actual structural and material resources." The disposability of pandemic "heroes," and the lack of care and consideration for their children is reminiscent of early 20th-century practices that aimed to, as Benjamin states, "rid the body politic of unwanted populations." Early COVID-19 responses in many ways hid harmful practices that put children in danger and framed these practices in the terms of altruistic nationalism. In this way, COVID-19 has been opportunistically appropriated to advance neoconservatism, nationalism, and neoliberal ideologies (Ryan 2021c). And while it is true that children and youth are less likely to experience COVID-19-related severe morbidity and mortality, too many children's lives have unnecessarily ended far too early.

The National Center for Health Statistics and the Centers for Disease Control (CDC) are tracking and monitoring cases of COVID-19 among children and teens. As of August 1, 2021, children represented about 14.2% of all US cases of COVID-19, with 4.3 million US children testing positive since the onset of the pandemic (American Academy of Pediatrics 2021). As of late March 2021, 582 COVID-19-related child deaths were reported; 2,702 intensive care hospitalizations and 14,624 cumulative hospitalizations were reported as of February 2021 (COVKID 2021). The delta variant is rapidly pushing these numbers up; in July 2021, child infections increased sevenfold, with Florida hospitals reporting 35 new child admissions per day and many children's hospitals overwhelmed by recent surges (Eunjung Cha 2021). Buried in these numbers are deep-seated racial disparities. The materialization of racial disparities in COVID-19 disease transmission, severe illness, mortality, and access to vaccination among US children has been well documented as have the underlying reasons for these disparities.

The numbers reveal that a child's likelihood of contracting severe acute respiratory syndrome coronavirus 2 (SARS-CoV-2), of being hospitalized due to COVID-19 illness, and even the risk of death, is racialized. Indigenous, Latinx, and Black youth are far more vulnerable to suffer severe COVID-19 illness. According to a CDC analysis of data gathered across 14 states, hospitalization rates are much higher among Black and Hispanic children, who are, respectively, five and eight times more likely to be hospitalized in comparison to White children (Kim et al. 2020). Hispanic and Black children are more likely than their White counterparts to present with an underlying condition, most commonly obesity and chronic lung disease (Kim et al. 2020). Underlying conditions are often present among children who are diagnosed with multisystem inflammatory syndrome (MIS-C), a dangerous condition in which multiple organs and body parts can become inflamed. In a New York City study, obesity and asthma were found as the most common underlying conditions among children diagnosed with MIS-C, with rates of incidence being much higher among and Black and Hispanic children (Lee et al. 2020).

While child mortality rates due to COVID-19 are low relative to adult mortality rates, Indigenous children are particularly more vulnerable; they are 5.8 times more likely to die than are non-Hispanic White children. Black children are 3 times more likely to die, Hispanic children are 2.5 times more likely to die, and Asian and Pacific Islander children are 2.1 times more likely to die than their White counterparts (COVKID 2021). Mortality data analyzing the first 107 child deaths tell us that Hispanic children accounted for 44% of deaths, and Black children were 27% of deaths (COVKID 2020). Altogether, children and youth of color account for 81% of COVID-19-related child deaths in the USA.

These numbers are driven by systemic racial discrimination in what many refer to as "the social determinants of health," including access to nutritious food and food security, safe and uncrowded housing conditions, financial resources shaped by parental wealth and income, neighborhood quality, educational resources, health insurance, and access to culturally appropriate and quality care, and so forth (White, Liburd, and Coronado 2021). RJ includes parental access to all these vital resources (Ross and Solinger 2017)—the lack of which leads to chronic health conditions such as diabetes, obesity, cardiovascular disease, and asthma. When comorbid with COVID-19, these underlying conditions can lead to greater likelihood of intensive care hospitalizations and death (COVKID 2021).

Beyond these pre-existent health disparities, it is vital to acknowledge that other social injustices drive these trends. Societal responses also drive mortality and morbidity rates among Black, Indigenous, and Latinx children and youth because they engineer the social landscape in ways that place children of color in greater proximity to COVID-19. In comparison to White children, Black and Latinx children are less likely to have parents who can work remotely (Brown 2020). Racialized patterns of occupational segregation, in which Black and Latinx workers are concentrated in "essential" industries such as nursing and residential care facilities, waste management, warehousing, grocery stores, and public transit, render their children highly vulnerable to COVID-19 exposure (Brown 2020). Racialized disparities in educational attainment also play a large role as parents without college degrees were far less likely to have access to teleworking in comparison to those with a college degree (US Bureau of Labor Statistics 2021).

Surely, medical personnel were necessary and vital, but multinational corporations continued their operations as well, and received more than $1.5 trillion of taxpayer-funded stimulus to do so (Ryan 2021c). Thus, when nation-states engineer the social landscape such that some parents are given access to the resources needed to ensure their children's survival and success, they are engaging in an important, although perhaps less obvious, form of eugenics. Early pandemic responses to COVID-19 prioritized the needs of racial capitalism, which has always relied upon the labor, bodies, and exploitation of marginalized groups of children and adults.

Incarceration

Particularly marginal and at risk of severe illness are children in institutionalized settings, especially juvenile detention facilities. As COVID-19 spread throughout these facilities, peaking in late 2020, calls for diverting youth from the criminal justice system were widespread. The call was answered, but only for White youth, who experienced a 6% decline in detainment (Gray 2021). Conversely, the population of incarcerated Latinx youth rose by 2% and the population of incarcerated Black youth rose by 14%. Overall, the youth incarceration rate reached a record high in early 2021, largely accounted for by the rise in incarcerated Black youth, who were also being detained for longer periods than their White counterparts (Gray 2021). Many centers canceled in-person visits and home furloughs, canceled support services such as counseling, and placed youth on full lockdown, adding significantly to their fear, anxiety, and uncertainty (NPR 2021). These racial disparities in detainment and pace of release imply that Black and Latinx youth are not worth protecting and saving. Indeed, as of March 31, 2021, the Sentencing Project reported nearly 4,000 cases of COVID-19 among incarcerated youth (Rovner 2021). Similar to previous historical moments, discriminatory practices leave youth of color beyond the scope of life-saving efforts, bearing the residue of eugenics.

Vaccinations

Supporters of eugenics have always attacked public health efforts to improve the health of "unfit" populations (Pernick 1997), including the universalization of life-saving vaccinations. Similarly, pandemic responses have undermined RJ by placing poor, low-income, and children of color in closer proximity to COVID-19 while also ironically positioning them further from access to vaccination (Nguyen et al. 2021). While essential organizations could have prioritized racialized groups most at risk, thereby mitigating disparate health outcomes, people of color in the USA were under-prioritized in vaccine distribution. In Virginia, for example, the rate of vaccination as of March 2021 for White adults was two times greater than that for Black and Latinx adults (Virginia Department of Health 2021), again leaving children in minoritized households at greater risk of exposure. Virginia is not unique—as the delta variant spreads across the USA, Black and Hispanic adults have lower rates of vaccination across most states (Ndugga et al. 2021). In line with the logic of eugenics, "White people received a higher share of vaccinations in comparison to their share of cases in most states reporting data" (Ndugga et al. 2021). Despite stereotypes, these differences are not rooted in racial disparities in vaccine intentions. While some studies have found elevated levels of hesitancy among racial and ethnic minorities (Nguyen et al. 2021), they note that disparities in access play a prominent role in vaccine differentials and that hesitancy toward a medical procedure does not necessarily indicate intention. An NPR/PBS Newshour poll took this factor into account and, according to their 2021 poll, found that 73% of Black people and 70% of White people reported receiving or *intending* to receive the vaccine, despite concerns about its emergency authorization and unknown long-term effects (Summers 2021).

As vaccines continue to roll out, officials have turned their attention to adolescents aged 12 and above, who have lower vaccination rates compared to adults. According to the Kaiser Family Foundation (2021), it is difficult to assess racial disparities in youth vaccination due to a dearth of systematic data on race/ethnicity for younger cohorts. However, they project that vaccination rates are and will be lower for Black and Hispanic youth at these earlier phases of vaccine rollout. Throughout the early 20th-century eugenics movement, numerous efforts were made to design public health interventions in ways that withheld life-preserving technologies from non-Whites (Pernick 1997); placing racialized children and youth in proximity to disease, while failing to prioritize vaccinations in their communities, is nothing short of eugenics.

Economic Inequality

Beyond driving racial disparities in public health efforts, the field of eugenics influenced and pervaded Progressive-era economic policies as well (Leonard 2003). Core to the urban uplift policies of the so-called Progressive period was the view that ridding the industrial working class of the "unfit" (i.e., workers of color, global south workers) was vital to the well-being of the nation-state. Race, incorrectly understood as biological, was identified as the root cause of economic problems; therefore, economic policies designed to support the nation were, by design, engineered to render unfit populations obsolete (Leonard 2003). Similarly, COVID-19-related economic policies and practices are not socially neutral and their impacts render certain groups obsolete through disenfranchisement, exclusion, and lack of consideration for their distinct needs.

Beyond the direct health impacts, COVID-19 responses have exacerbated economic precarity and income inequality, generating particularly severe financial struggles for families headed by parent(s) without college degrees (US Bureau of Labor Statistics 2021). In July 2020 alone, 31.3 million people reported that they could not work due to pandemic-related business closures (US Bureau of Labor Statistics 2021), impeding the ability of parents to access the resources needed to protect their children from food and housing insecurity. In a social system organized by racial capitalism and undergirded by scientific racism, the economic precarity that impedes adequate childrearing differentially impacts children of color.

Latinx and Black children are significantly more likely to live in households reporting job and income loss and reporting inability and difficulty paying household expenses due to COVID-19 (Padilla and Thomson 2021). Job losses in Black and Latinx households are devastating because these families have less access to wealth and earned lower wages prior to the pandemic. A *Child Trends* study found that more than one in four Latino and Black households with children experienced three or more hardships due to COVID-19 (Padilla and Thomson 2021). Hardships were defined as COVID-19-related food insufficiency, poor physical and mental health, job loss, difficulty/inability to pay for housing and household expenses, and lack of or loss of health insurance coverage. The rates of hardship for Latinx and Black households were twice the rate reported in Asian and White households with children. While 43% of White households with children and 45% of Asian households reported no hardships, only 24% of Black and Hispanic households with children reported no hardships (Padilla and Thomson 2021).

Rates of child poverty, one of the greatest barriers to RJ, also increased from 2019 to 2020 (15.7 to 17.5%), although the overall rates obscure that increases in child poverty occurred only for children of color (Chen and Thomson 2021). Prior to the pandemic, the numbers of Black and Hispanic children living in poverty were in decline (although they were still three times more likely to be living in poverty compared to their Asian and White counterparts) (Thomas and Fry 2020). But, the US Census Bureau's Household Pulse Survey, which tracks the economic effects of COVID-19 on US households, revealed major setbacks, with Black and Latinx households reporting disproportionately high rates of job loss (US Census Bureau 2021), causing 1.2 million children to fall into poverty. While poverty rates among White children remained stable from 2019 to 2020 (9.1%), child poverty rates increased for Black children (26.4 to 29.2%) and Latinx children (23 to 27.3%) (Chen and Thomson 2021).

Food Insecurity

Lost employment has translated into widespread food insecurity, in which access to food is uncertain or limited, as households reporting job loss are also more likely to report food insecurity (Chen 2020). Throughout the pandemic, food insecurity among children has intensified, and nearly half of food insecure children live in Black and Hispanic or Latinx households (Morales, Morales, and Beltran 2021). According to the Hispanic Research Center, one in five Latinx and Black households with children were food insufficient in the early months of the pandemic (Chen 2020). Additionally, families of color with job loss were also more likely than White families with job loss to report food insecurity. For example, 30% of Black households and 28% of Hispanic households with children and with job loss also reported food insecurity, in comparison to 20% of White families (Chen 2020). Beyond the mental health impacts of food insecurity including an increase in depressive symptoms, research documents impacts on the general health of children as well as an increased rates of acute and chronic health conditions among children (Thomas, Miller, and Morrissey 2019). Significantly worse general health is an alarming concern given that a strong immune system is vital to combat contagious diseases. In this way, food insecurity compounds and amplifies the negative health impacts of COVID-19.

Stimulus for Some

Similar to the social landscape at the height of eugenics, the cumulative disadvantages of racial capitalism make it very difficult for children of color to survive and thrive. The withholding of support via lack of social interventions, particularly the slow and meager financial support offered to US families under the Trump Administration, demonstrated a lack of care and concern for socially disadvantaged groups of children. Vaccine hesitancy, driven by anti-vax ideologies and conspiracy theories disseminated by former US President, Donald Trump, is now causing severe illness and death among children who are contracting the delta variant of COVID-19.

Three waves of direct stimulus payments sent out to US households (in April 2020, January 2021, and March 2021) were meant to help offset some of these economic hardships. These stimulus payments were paltry in comparison to the emergency funds distributed to for-profit businesses (Ryan 2021c). Again though, systemic racism penalized the most marginalized children, reducing their benefit in substantial ways. The Hispanic Research Center notes that 60% of Hispanic and Black low-income family households had no access or limited access to banks (Guzman and Ryberg 2020). Unable to receive direct deposits, many of these families rely on predatory and expensive financial services to cash their checks, who charge high fees for their services and reduce the cash amount going to children's needs, stealing from families with the least to spare and leaving children without access to their full benefit. Children with one or more non-citizen parents or guardians were ineligible for relief payments (Guzman and Ryberg 2020). Many of these children live in Latinx households that are more likely to be overcrowded, to be economically challenged, and to not have access to private health insurance (Guzman and Ryberg 2020). Not only does this withholding of relief minimize their parents' vital economic contributions, but it is also inhumane as Latinx households have been among those hardest hit by pandemic-related mortality and morbidity in the USA. Children with mixed-status parents, in which one parent is a citizen, were also ineligible for stimulus payments. This practice of exclusion ends up denying 3.7 million children who are US citizens or who are legal immigrants without access to the CARES Act relief payments (Migration Policy Institute 2020).

Punitive welfare systems, in which cash forms of welfare assistance are withheld from certain groups, have long been commonly practiced in the USA and has historical roots in policies influenced by eugenics (Ladd-Taylor 1997). Beyond that children in these families were viewed as undesirable and undeserving of material care, a core eugenics belief undergirding punitive welfare policies was that withholding monetary assistance from undesirable women would curb their birth rates, a belief that continues to shape dominant approaches to family welfare today (Pierson-Balik 2003). It was, and still is, commonly believed that government cash assistance generates dependent, stunted, and "deformed" children (Briggs 2017). Opponents of direct cash stimulus payments echoed these same sentiments.

Parental/Caregiver Loss

Nathan and Isaiah are brothers—Latinx teens living in Texas who lost both parents within two weeks to COVID-19. Their grandmother utilized an online platform to raise nearly $200,000 to support their present and future well-being. When interviewed, the brothers told news reporters that they aspired to be engineers. Despite their loss and grief, their robust family network of support is ensuring their resiliency—their lives will not be determined by COVID-19. Nathan and Isaiah are among over 40,000 children who have lost one or both parents to COVID-19, with Black children being most likely to experience such a loss (Jenco 2021). Many will not have a network of family to assume the economic and emotional functions that are vital to the caregiving role. From March to July 2020 in New York State alone, 4,200 children lost a parent to COVID-19. Black and Hispanic children were more than two times more likely than White children to experience the death of a parent; Asian children also experienced heightened rates of parental death. Twenty-three percent of these children are likely to enter the foster care system and 50% are at risk of falling into poverty (United Hospital Fund 2020). Once entering the child welfare system, they are likely to be re-traumatized and to be more vulnerable to pandemic stressors (Vivrette and Barlett 2020). The mental health toll on children will be deep and long-lasting as the loss of a parent is a leading adverse childhood experience (ACE) and impacts lifelong health and opportunity (Centers for Disease Control 2020).

Untimely parental death is a devastating exemplar of reproductive injustice and impedes a child's access to both material and socio-emotional resources. Inequitable engineering of COVID-19 responses across the USA undergirds unnecessary parental loss and many states are denying children access to the workers compensation that might temporarily stave off the negative consequences of parental income loss. Most states have not rolled out workers compensation coverage for illness and death due to job-related transmission of COVID-19 and there are widespread reports that most workers' compensation claims are being denied for essential employers who are not first responders. This includes those jobs that are essential but more likely to be performed by Black and Latinx workers, including warehouse, public transit, and grocery store workers (DeFusco 2021; Weber 2021). Here again, punitive assistance policies are undergirded by eugenics ideology. As Luna (2020) states regarding women of color's access to RJ, "economics clearly underpins rights" (14). Limiting access to RJ, as Luna further explains, has long been a political and economic strategy linked to the expansion of US capitalist interests. Eugenic ideology has historically been used to advance this expansion by weaving it into policy and legislation (see Luna 2020 for further discussion on reproduction as a political project). This is particularly salient regarding US educational responses to COVID-19.

Educational Inequality

In Fall 2020, one of the authors of this chapter (Amaya) recorded the following experience in her field notes.

> I head back in from my morning walk as I step over children littering the staircases of our apartment hallway, huddled around two electronic devices. As I set up for my online class from the inside of Apartment K it is nearly impossible to ignore their loud voices, a combination of laughter and frustrated exasperations. I open my apartment door, with the purpose of asking the children to lower their voices, as I had a degree to complete. There was absolutely no way I could possibly afford to miss class, even amidst the switch to virtual learning. "Hey sorry but can y'all quiet down?" I ask. "I have class in five minutes and I have to be able to be heard if I turn

my mic on to participate." With little hesitation, one of the young boys, responds with a question of his own. "Can we have your Wi-Fi password? We're supposed to be in class right now, too but we don't have any Wi-Fi and everyone else's is locked. The library is closed right now!"

The children in Amaya's apartment building walkway were Black and Latinx. Her observations contradict stereotypical portrayals of poor Black and Latinx children as academically disinterested and/or unworthy of investment. The children outside Apartment K were eager to participate and even garnered an electronic device to do so, yet still could not participate due to the unequal distribution of vital technological resources. Her story also reflects the ways in which the residue of eugenics ideology continues to shape education.

In *Eugenics and Education in America*, Ann Winfield (2007) maps the close relationship between US public education and the field of eugenics. She traces how early 20th-century eugenics was embraced by progressive policymakers who folded eugenics ideologies into educational institutions and used schools as sites for defining and sorting students according to the logic of scientific racism, with grave implications for contemporary schooling. Educational inequalities are widening in real time as the pandemic unfolds, and the digital divide is merely one example. Deep-seated inequalities, particularly disparities in the quality of schooling experienced by non-white poor schools in comparison to white, non-poor schools (EdBuild 2019) are a vivid reminder that eugenics still undergirds public education—an entanglement exacerbated by educational policies and responses to the pandemic.

Lives versus Learning

Due to the disparate impacts of COVID-19 morbidity and mortality, parents have had to choose between lives and learning. Early in the pandemic, parents of color were more concerned about school reopening and with issues of school compliance with safety and health standards. They also expressed more worry about their children contracting COVID-19. In a July 2020 survey, Black and Hispanic parents were less likely than White parents to agree that schools should reopen in the fall and were more supportive of mask mandates (Gilbert et al. 2020). In Chicago, for example, opinions regarding the return to in-person school were bifurcated along racial lines (Cullotta 2020). Upper-income White mothers led the front lines in arguing that an in-person return was better for their children's emotional health, who they argued were suffering from social isolation and academic backslide. Contrarily, only 15% of schools reopening plans nationwide included policies and practices related to the socio-emotional well-being of students (Fulks et al. 2021), refuting these parents claims. In contrast, poor and low-income families worried about COVID-19-related mortality and severe morbidity, as COVID-19 illness and death devastated minority communities across Chicago. Families of color expressed heightened concern about the ability of schools to safely distance children, and they worried about how the virus would rip through families living in multigenerational and doubled-up households (Cullotta 2020).

Similar debates occurred across the nation and former US President Donald Trump and Secretary of Education Betsy DeVos issued capitalist-driven demands that schools reopen at full capacity or lose federal funding (Braginsky 2020). Urban school districts with high percentages of non-White students overwhelmingly chose lives over learning (largely due to teacher-led coalitions and unions who prioritized the lives of their families, their students, and their students' families). According to the Brookings Institute, students of color were more likely to attend school in online-only districts, with two-thirds of students of color living in a remote-only district (Smith and Reeves 2020). Pre-existent inequities, however, meant that no option could be executed in an ideal way. Private schools and public schools in high-property tax neighborhoods were able to purchase trailers to socially distance children, adequate PPE, plexiglass barriers per each student, and extra busing services to ensure social distancing of children. Lacking in resources, however, best practices in distance learning have been difficult for educators to accomplish as poor students are less likely to have access to high-speed Internet, computers, and parents with job flexibility who can support their learning (Gilbert et al. 2020). In a recent national survey of K–12 teachers' perceptions regarding pandemic online learning, the majority reported that online learning was only "slightly better than skipping school completely," especially for children in high poverty schools for whom teachers reported remote learning was largely ineffective (Dickler 2021).

Additionally, many children access mental health, physical health, and educational support resources through their schools and the shift to online learning has stripped many of those resources from children. While some parents of color report benefits of online learning (reduced risk of COVID-19, fewer students being funneled into the school-to-prison pipeline and fewer reports of race-based discrimination including anti-Asian experiences (Akiba 2020)), the disparities highlight important aspects of childhood inequality in the USA. Perceived benefits of remote learning exist because quality schooling is unevenly distributed. For example, low-income non-white schools are far more likely to be staffed with school resource officers while non-poor white schools are far more likely to be staffed with school psychologists (Ramey 2015), contributing to the practices that have engineered the school-to-confinement pathway for poor and low-income youth in non-white schools.

Academic Achievement Gaps

There are also disadvantages to remote learning. Only 15% of qualifying remote students continued to receive school meals (Fulks et al. 2021) during COVID-19 school closures. Racialized gaps in academic achievement are also emerging. Several studies estimate significant losses in learning throughout both the 2019–20 and 2020–21 academic years (Diliberti and Kaufman 2020; Stanford

University 2020). These losses are both class and race differentiated, with students of color estimated by one study to have fallen behind 3–5 months and White students falling behind by 1–3 months (Dorn et al. 2020). The greatest learning losses are estimated to be in racially segregated schools that serve students of color (Dorn et al. 2020). These estimates align with real-time data collected from K–12 public school teachers who are reporting significant learning losses for students, with the most significant setbacks for three groups of students—Black, Hispanic, and students with disabilities (Dickler 2021). Children and youth are resilient to learning losses, but schools with the largest estimated loss of learning are also those who are less likely to have the resources and support needed to implement recovery plans (Stanford University 2020).

The high school dropout rate steadily declined throughout the first two decades of the 21st century, but school districts are now fearing a surge in dropout rates in response to soaring numbers of failing students, declines in school attendance, and shrinking enrollment (Hollingsworth 2021; McMorris-Santoro 2021). The Boston Globe reported that 40% of Boston high school juniors and seniors are chronically absent (missing 10% or more of their classes) and that rates are highest among Black, Latinx, English-learners, and students with disabilities (Martin 2021). Pre-pandemic dropout rates for Black, Latinx, and American Indian and Alaskan Native youth were higher than that of their White and Asian peers (National Center for Education Statistics 2020), a trend that we are seeing exacerbated by the pandemic.

Many affluent parents have not had to make the difficult choice between their children's lives and their children's learning. The continued operation of private schools across the nation, many of which have reported zero cases of COVID-19, highlights not only race-based disparities in the transmission of COVID-19, but also that parents with financial resources are able to continue schooling-as-usual in many respects. Private school enrollment soared as upper-status parents fled remote schooling at the onset of the pandemic (Farrington 2021). Many private schools were able to utilize outdoor space and access mitigation measures more creatively, an option unavailable to many public schools due to pre-existent inequalities and bureaucratic organizational design. In addition to private schooling, many parents have galvanized their economic resources to continue advancing their children's educational success through private tutoring and other costly support services. These resources reflect the realities of stratified reproduction and exacerbate racialized educational inequities.

While many children have lost things of far greater importance than academic information during the pandemic (Nenga 2021, this volume), widening educational inequalities and achievement gaps and rising dropout rates have implications for children's future well-being. Particularly for older youth, any academic setbacks undermine their ability to thrive in a post-industrial economy that privileges college attainment and academic success. Scholars have noted that learning loss without effective supports can lead to earning losses later in life and a widening socioeconomic gap between the rich and the poor

(Engzell, Frey, and Verhagen 2021). In short, pandemic educational inequalities have profound implications for college attendance, future earnings, and long-term socioeconomic status.

Racism and Peer Interaction in Schools

While children and youth may be less likely to experience severe illness, they are no less likely to experiences of COVID-19-related racial discrimination in both in-person and online school. In a nation already deeply racially divided, racialized COVID-19 rhetoric combined with xenophobic societal attitudes are fueling deeper divisions, with any child of Asian descent being the target of stigma and anti-Asian discrimination (Akiba 2020). "Yellow Peril," a racist phrase in which White settler nationalists claimed Asians to be diseased, unfit, and a danger to the "West," is reiterating itself in the racialization of stigmatizing rhetoric surrounding the emergence of SARS-CoV-2 (Cheng and Conca-Cheng 2020). AAPI, a national coalition formed to examine and address anti-Asian pandemic-related discrimination has been tracking and reporting on Sinophobia throughout the pandemic. Derogatory phrases like "Kung Flu" and "the Chinese virus" were commonly used by former President Donald Trump as well as several Republican politicians and were widely disseminated to the public via social media and other media platforms. A 2020 AAPI analysis documented that Trump used 24 stigmatizing, racialized tweets which were "liked" by nearly 4.3 million Americans (AAPI 2020a).

The use of anti-Chinese hate speech has permeated the lives of Asian-American youth, with many youth reporting verbal harassment at school and online. In the first 18 weeks of the pandemic, youth reported nearly 350 incidents of anti-Asian discrimination (AAPI 2020b). In a study published in *Pediatrics*, half of Chinese-American children (10–18 years old) reported online and in-person discrimination. Many of these children reported feeling that Americans harbored Sinophobia and that media promoted such attitudes (Cheah et al. 2020). In a youth-led study conducted by the Stop AAPI Hate Youth Campaign, interviews with nearly 1,000 Asian-American youth revealed that they felt others blamed them personally for the pandemic (AAPI 2020c). Youth reported being bullied for Chinese dietary customs, for instance, a 17-year-old who reported being called a "dirty f---ing dog-eater" after being told to kill herself (Wang 2020). These attitudes mapped onto the mental health of children, with children and youth who experienced COVID-19 racial discrimination reporting higher levels of anxiety and depressive symptoms (Cheah et al. 2020). Other children and youth of color are not immune and have also experienced a heightening of discrimination since the COVID-19 outbreak, reporting that people have presumed that they have COVID-19 because of their race (Ruiz, Menasce, and Tamir 2020).

In summary, the logic of eugenics lies at the heart of societal failures to invest in quality education for non-White and low-income children. Trump, DeVos, and organized collectives of suburban White parents felt entitled to throw less-protected children of color and the teachers who serve them under the metaphorical school bus, even at the risk of death to their lives and their families' lives. They did this to continue procuring economic and educational advantages for their own children. At the same time, while saving lives, remote learning has intensified educational inequalities that have profound implications for the future of children. In many ways, the pandemic has enabled education to be misused as a mechanism for further sorting of children according to hierarchical rankings—again, a characteristic feature of eugenics that also undermines RJ.

Toward Resilience

Critical race scholars have argued that the racial discrimination of the past has been rearticulated through contemporary practices and ideologies (e.g., Alexander 2012; Bonilla-Silva 2003; Collins 2005). Similarly, this chapter argues that pre-pandemic racial discrimination has been rearticulated through pandemic policies and practices. Hundred years after its rise in the USA, the field of eugenics has been energized through the societal response to COVID-19, which has generated numerous barriers to RJ by excluding children of color from life-saving protections and socioeconomic supports. This chapter has examined these rearticulations of racism in the institutional arenas of health, economics, and education. Through an RJ lens, we have synthesized contemporary research, highlighting examples of the ways in which pandemic responses have disproportionately endangered and even killed Black, Latinx, and Native American children. This revitalization of eugenics has profound implications for childhood institutions, childhood inequality, and children's everyday lives.

Children should not be determined to live lives characterized by trauma and inequality; they can be resilient when given the social and economic resources needed to meet these challenges. The costs of racialized pandemic trauma on children of color can be minimized when appropriate interventions are implemented and when a human rights approach is adopted (Vissing 2021, this volume). A trauma-informed approach to caregiving that accounts for the distinct needs of children of color is urgently needed (Vivrette and Barlett 2020). Beyond this, we urgently need systemic change—a revisioning of the global, racial capitalist order, a creative revolution that dismantles childhood inequality in all its intersectional forms so that when societal crises emerge, all children can adequately access the resources needed to survive *and* thrive.

References

AAPI. 2020a. "The Return of 'Yellow Peril.'" AAPI, October 21, 2020. Accessed March 10, 2021. https://secureservercdn.net/104.238.69.231/a1w.90d.myftpupload.com/wp-content/uploads/2020/10/Stop_AAPI_Hate_2020-Candidates-and-Anti-Asian-Rhetoric_201021.pdf.

AAPI. 2020b. "Stop AAPI Youth Hate Report." Accessed March 10, 2021. https://a1w.90d.myftpupload.com/wp-content/uploads/2020/09/Stop-AAPI-Hate-Report-On-Youth-Incidents-9-17.pdf.

AAPI. 2020c. "They Blamed Me Because I am Asian: Findings from Reported Anti-AAPI Youth Incidents." Asian Pacific Policy and Planning Coalition and the Department of Asian American Studies at San Francisco State University. Accessed March 10, 2021. https://secureservercdn.net/104.238.69.231/a1w.90d.myftpupload.com/wp-content/uploads/2020/09/Stop-AAPI-Hate-Youth-Campaign-Report-9-17.pdf.

Akiba, Daisuke. 2020. "Reopening America's Schools During the COVID-19 Pandemic: Protecting Asian Students from Stigma and Discrimination." *Frontiers in Sociology* 5: 588936. https://doi.org/10.3389/fsoc.2020.588936.

Alexander, Michelle. 2012. *The New Jim Crow: Mass Incarceration in the Age of Colorblindness*. New York: The New Press.

American Academy of Pediatrics. 2021. "Children and COVID-19: State-Level Data Report." Accessed July 9, 2021. https://services.aap.org/en/pages/2019-novel-coronavirus-covid-19-infections/children-and-covid-19-state-level-data-report/.

Beaman, Jean, and Catherine J. Taylor. 2020. "#Courageisbeautiful but PPE Is Better: White Supremacy, Racial Capitalism, and COVID-19." *Contexts*, June 12, 2020. https://contexts.org/blog/courageisbeautiful-but-ppe-is-better-white-supremacy-racial-capitalism-and-covid-19/.

Benjamin, Ruha. 2019. *Race After Technology: Abolitionist Tools for the New Jim Code*. Medford, MA: Polity.

Bonilla-Silva, Eduardo. 2003. *Racism Without Racists: Color-Blind Racism and the Persistence of Racial Inequality in the United States*. Lanham, MD: Rowman & Littlefield Publishers.

Braginsky, Nataliya. 2020. "The Racist Effects of School Reopening During the Pandemic—By a Teacher." *The Washington Post*, July 23, 2020. www.washingtonpost.com/education/2020/07/23/racist-effects-school-reopening-during-pandemic-by-teacher/.

Briggs, Laura. 2017. *How All Politics Became Reproductive Politics: From Welfare Reform to Foreclosure to Trump*. Oakland, CA: University of California Press.

Brown, Steven. 2020. "How COVID-19 Is Affecting Black and Latino Families' Employment and Financial Well-Being." Urban Institute, May 6, 2020. www.urban.org/urban-wire/how-covid-19-affecting-black-and-latino-families-employment-and-financial-well-being.

Centers for Disease Control. 2020. "Adverse Childhood Experiences (ACEs)." Accessed July 8, 2021. www.cdc.gov/violenceprevention/aces/index.html.

Cheah, Charissa S.L., Cixin Wang, Huiguang Ren, Xiaoli Zong, Hyun Su Cho, and Xiaofang Xue. 2020. "COVID-19 Racism and Mental Health in Chinese American Families." *Pediatrics* 146 (5): e2020021816. https://doi.org/10.1542/peds.2020-021816.

Chen, Yiyu. 2020. "During COVID-19, 1 in 5 Latino and Black Households with Children are Food Insufficient." Accessed February 22, 2021. www.hispanicresearchcenter.org/research-resources/during-covid-19-1-in-5-latino-and-black-households-with-children-are-food-insufficient/.

Chen, Yiyu, and Dana Thomson. 2021. "Child Poverty Increased Nationally During COVID, Especially Among Latino and Black Children." *Child Trends*, June 3, 2021. www.childtrends.org/publications/child-poverty-increased-nationally-during-covid-especially-among-latino-and-black-children.

Cheng, Tina L., and Alison M. Conca-Cheng. 2020. "The Pandemics of Racism and COVID-19: Danger and Opportunity." *Pediatrics* 146 (5): e2020024836.

Colen, Shellee. 1995. "'Like a Mother to Them': Stratified Reproduction and West Indian Childcare Workers and Employers in New York." In *Conceiving the New World Order: The Global Politics of Reproduction*, edited by Faye D. Ginsburg and Rayna Rapp, pp. 78–102. Berkeley, CA: University of California Press.

Collins, Patricia Hill. 2005. *Black Sexual Politics: African Americans, Gender, and the New Racism*. New York, NY: Routledge.

COVKID. 2020. "COVID-19 Mortality by Race and Hispanic Ethnicity United States, February 1 to September 12, 2020." Accessed March 5, 2021. www.covkidproject.org/disparities.

COVKID. 2021. "COVKID National Data Dashboard." Accessed March 5, 2021. www.covkidproject.org/.

Cullotta, Karen Ann. 2020. "In the Fight over Reopening Schools Amid the Pandemic, Race and Class Divisions are Stark." *Chicago Tribune*, October 31, 2020. Accessed March 1, 2021. www.chicagotribune.com/coronavirus/ct-covid-19-illinois-schools-opening-pressure-20201031-cwivxnk72bfr7f77jtxwop75ne-story.html.

DeFusco, Jackie. 2021. "'It Feels Like They Don't Care'—Bill Expanding Workers Comp for COVID-19 Leaves Out Large Groups." *ABC News*, February 4, 2021. www.wric.com/news/politics/capitol-connection/it-feels-like-they-dont-care-bill-expanding-workers-comp-for-covid-19-leaves-out-large-groups/.

Dickler, Jessica. 2021. "Virtual School Resulted in 'Significant' Academic Learning Loss, Study Finds." *CNBC*, March 30, 2021. www.cnbc.com/2021/03/30/learning-loss-from-virtual-school-due-to-covid-is-significant-.html.

Diliberti, Melissa Kay, and Julia H. Kaufman. 2020. *Will This School Year Be Another Casualty of the Pandemic? Key Findings from the American Educator Panels Fall 2020 COVID-19 Surveys*. Santa Monica, CA: Rand Corporation. https://doi.org/10.7249/RRA168-4.

Dorn, Emma, Bryan Hancock, Jimmy Sarakatsannis, and Ellen Viruleg. 2020. "COVID-19 and Learning Loss—Disparities Grow and Students Need Help." *McKinsey and Company*, December 8, 2020. Accessed March 3, 2021. www.mckinsey.com/industries/public-and-social-sector/our-insights/covid-19-and-learning-loss-disparities-grow-and-students-need-help.

EdBuild. 2019. "Nonwhite School Districts Get $23 Billion Less than White Districts Despite Serving the Same Number of Students." Accessed July 24, 2021. https://edbuild.org/content/23-billion/full-report.pdf.

Engzell, Per, Arun Frey, and Mark D. Verhagen. 2021. "Learning Loss Due to School Closures During the COVID-19 Pandemic." *PNAS* 118 (17): e2022376118. https://doi.org/10.1073/pnas.2022376118.

Eunjung Cha, Ariana. 2021. "'This is Real': Fear and Hope in an Arkansas Pediatric ICU." *The Washington Post*, August 13, 2021. www.washingtonpost.com/health/2021/08/13/children-hospitalizations-covid-delta/.

Farrington, Robert. 2021. "How COVID-19 Boosted Private School Enrollment Forever." *Forbes*, June 8, 2021. www.forbes.com/sites/robertfarrington/2021/06/08/how-covid-19-boosted-private-school-enrollment-forever/?sh=547dcc0596fc.

Fulks, Emily, Sarah Anderson, Asiya Kazi, Sarah Her, and Alexander Gabriel. 2021. "More Comprehensive State Guidance Can Support the Whole Child During COVID-19." *Child Trends*, January 14, 2021. www.childtrends.org/publications/more-comprehensive-state-guidance-support-whole-child-covid-19.

Gilbert, Leah K., Tara W. Strine, Leigh E. Szucs, Tamara Crawford, Sharyn E. Parks, Danielle Barradas, Rashid Njai, and Jean Y. Ko. 2020. "Racial and Ethnic Differences in Parental Attitudes and Concerns About School Reopening During the COVID-19 Pandemic—United States, July 2020." *Morbidity and Mortality Weekly Report*, 69 (49): 1848–52. http://dx.doi.org/10.15585/mmwr.mm6949a2.

Ginsburg, Faye D., and Rayna Rapp. 1995. "Introduction: Conceiving the New World Order." In *Conceiving the New World Order: The Global Politics of Reproduction*, edited by Faye D. Ginsburg and Rayna Rapp, pp. 1–17. Berkeley, CA: University of California Press.

Gray, Katti. 2021. "COVID-19 Analysis: Record High of Blacks, Low of Whites in Juvenile Facilities." *Juvenile Justice Information Exchange*, April 22, 2021. https://jjie.org/2021/04/22/covid-19-analysis-record-high-of-blacks-low-of-whites-in-juvenile-facilities/.

Guzman, Lina, and Renee Ryberg. 2020. "The Majority of Low-Income Hispanic and Black Households Have Little-to-No Bank Access, Complicating Access to COVID Relief Funds. www.hispanicresearchcenter.org/research-resources/the-majority-of-low-income-hispanic-and-black-households-have-little-to-no-bank-access-complicating-access-to-covid-relief-funds/.

Hollingsworth, Heather. 2021. "US Schools Fight to Keep Students Amid Fear of Dropout Surge." *Associated Press*, May 11, 2021. https://apnews.com/article/coronavirus-pandemic-health-education-1b0eb720342a1978383c703e5a001a90.

Huntington, Ellsworth, and The American Eugenics Society. 1935. *Tomorrow's Children: The Goal of Eugenics*. London: Chapman and Hall.

Jenco, Melissa. 2021. "Estimated 40,000 Children Have Lost a Parent to COVID-19." *American Academy of Pediatrics*, April 5, 2021. www.aappublications.org/news/2021/04/05/children-losing-parents-covid-040521.

Kaiser Family Foundation. 2021. "Disparities in Reaching COVID-19 Vaccination Benchmarks: Projected Vaccination Rates by Race/Ethnicity as of July 4." *Kaiser Family Foundation*, June 14, 2021. www.kff.org/racial-equity-and-health-policy/issue-brief/disparities-in-reaching-covid-19-vaccination-benchmarks-projected-vaccination-rates-by-race-ethnicity-as-of-july-4/.

Kim, Lindsay, Michael Whitaker, Alissa O'Halloran, Anita Kambhampati, Shua J. Chai, Arthur Reingold, Isaac Armistead, et al. 2020. "Hospitalization Rates and Characteristics of Children Aged <18 Years Hospitalized with Laboratory-Confirmed COVID-19-COVID-NET, 14 States, March 1–July 25, 2020." *MMWR*, 69 (32): 1081–8. www.cdc.gov/mmwr/volumes/69/wr/mm6932e3.htm#F2_down.

Ladd-Taylor, Molly. 1997. "Saving Babies and Sterilizing Mothers: Eugenics and Welfare Politics in the Interwar United States." *Social Politics: International Studies in Gender, State & Society* 4 (1): 136–53. https://doi.org/10.1093/sp/4.1.136.

Lee, Ellen H., Kelsey L. Kepler, Anita Geevarughese, et al. 2020. "Race/Ethnicity Among Children with COVID-19-Associated Multi-System Inflammatory Syndrome." *JAMA Network Open*, 3 (11): e2030280. https://doi.org/10.1001/jamanetworkopen.2020.30280.

Leonard, Thomas C. 2003. "'More Merciful and Not Less Effective': Eugenics and American Economics in the Progressive Era." *History of Political Economy*, 35 (4): 687–712.

Leonard, Thomas C. 2016. *Illiberal Reformers: Race, Eugenics, and American Economics in the Progressive Era*. Princeton, NJ: Princeton University Press.

Luna, Zakiya. 2020. *Reproductive Rights as Human Rights: Women of Color and the Right for Reproductive Justice*. New York, NY: New York University Press.

Martin, Naomi. 2021. "40 Percent of Boston High School Juniors and Seniors Are Chronically Absent." *Boston Globe*, February 28, 2021. www.bostonglobe.com/2021/03/01/metro/40-percent-boston-high-school-juniors-seniors-are-chronically-absent-raising-concerns-about-their-futures/.

McCann, Carole R. 1994. *Birth Control Politics in the United States, 1916-1945*. Ithaca, NY: Cornell University Press.

McMorris-Santoro, Evan. 2021. Thousands of Students Have Dropped Out of School Due to COVID-19. These Are the Educators Trying to Track Them Down." *CNN*, March 8, 2021. www.cnn.com/2021/03/06/us/covid-pandemic-high-school-dropout/index.html.

Migration Policy Institute. 2020. "Mixed-Status Families Ineligible for CARES Act Federal Pandemic Stimulus Checks." *Migration Policy Institute*, May 2020. Retrieved February 22, 2021. www.migrationpolicy.org/content/mixed-status-families-ineligible-pandemic-stimulus-checks.

Morales, Danielle Xiaodan, Stephanie Alexandra Morales, and Tyler Fox Beltran. 2021. "Food Insecurity in Households with Children amid the COVID-19 Pandemic: Evidence from the Household Pulse Survey." *Social Currents* 8 (4): 314–25. https://doi.org/10.1177/23294965211011593.

National Center for Education Statistics. 2020. "The Condition of Education 2020 (NCES 2020- 144), Status Dropout Rates by Race/Ethnicity." *US Department of Education, National Center for Education Statistics*. Accessed August 13, 2021. https://nces.ed.gov/fastfacts/display.asp?id=16.

Ndugga, Nambi, Olivia Pham, Latoya Hill, Samantha Artiga, and Noah Parker. 2021. "Latest Data on COVID-19 Vaccinations by Race/Ethnicity." *Kaiser Family Foundation*, July 8, 2021. www.kff.org/coronavirus-covid-19/issue-brief/latest-data-on-covid-19-vaccinations-race-ethnicity/.

Nenga, Sandi K. 2021. "When Six Feet Feels Like Six Miles: Children's Images of Their Lives During the Pandemic." In *COVID-19 and Childhood Inequality*, edited by Nazneen Khan. London and New York: Routledge.

Nguyen, Long H., Amit D. Joshi, David A. Drew, Jordi Merino, Wenjie Ma, Chu-Han Lo, Sohee Kwon, et al. 2021. "Racial and Ethnic Differences in COVID-19 Hesitancy and Uptake." *medRxiv* February 2021. https://doi.org/10.1101/2021.02.25.21252402.

NPR. 2021. "COVID-19 Lockdowns Have Been Hard on Youth Locked Up." *NPR*, March 29, 2021. www.npr.org/2021/03/29/979986304/covid-19-lockdowns-have-been-hard-on-youth-locked-up.

Padilla, Christina M., and Dana Thomson. 2021. "More than One in Four Latino and Black Households Are Experiencing Three or More Hardships During COVID-19." *Child Trends*. Accessed February 22, 2021. www.childtrends.org/publications/more-than-one-in-four-latino-and-black-households-with-children-are-experiencing-three-or-more-hardships-during-covid-19.

Parolin, Zachary. 2021. "What the Pandemic Reveals about Racial Differences in Child Welfare and Child Well-Being: An Introduction to the Special Issue." *Race and Social Problems*, 13 (1): 1–5. https://doi.org/10.1007/s12552-021-09319-2.

Pernick, Martin S. 1997. "Eugenics and Public Health in American History." *American Journal of Public Health* 87 (11): 1767–72. https://doi.org/10.2105/AJPH.87.11.1767.

Pierson-Balik, Denise A. 2003. "Race, Class, and Gender in Punitive Welfare Reform: Social Eugenics and Welfare Policy." *Race, Gender, and Class* 10 (1): 11–30.

Ramey, David. 2015. "The Social Structure of Criminalized and Medicalized School Discipline." *Sociology of Education* 88 (3): 181–201. https://doi.org/10.1177/0038040715587114.

Roberts, Dorothy. 2002. *Shattered Bonds: The Color of Child Welfare*. New York, NY: Basic Civitas Books.

Robinson, Cedric. [1983] 2020. *Black Marxism: The Making of the Black Radical Tradition*, 3rd edition. Chapel Hill, NC: The University of North Carolina Press.

Ross, Loretta J., and Rickie Solinger. 2017. *Reproductive Justice: An Introduction*. Oakland, CA: University of California Press.

Rovner, Josh. 2021. "COVID-19 in Juvenile Facilities." *The Sentencing Project*, May 18, 2021. www.sentencingproject.org/publications/covid-19-in-juvenile-facilities/.

Ruiz, Neil G., Juliana Menasce Horowitz, and Christine Tamir. 2020. Many Black and Asian Americans Say They Have Experienced Discrimination amid the COVID-19 Outbreak. *Pew Research Center*, July 1, 2020. www.pewsocialtrends.org/2020/07/01/many-black-and-asian-americans-say-they-have-experienced-discrimination-amid-the-covid-19-outbreak/.

Ryan, J. Michael, ed. 2021a. *COVID-19: Volume 1: Global Pandemic, Societal Responses, Ideological Solutions*. London: Routledge.

Ryan, J. Michael, ed. 2021b. *COVID-19: Volume 2: Social Consequences and Cultural Adaptations*. London: Routledge.

Ryan, J. Michael. 2021c. "The Blessings of COVID-19 for Neoliberalism, Nationalism, and Neoconservative Ideologies." *COVID-19: Volume I: Global Pandemic, Societal Responses, Ideological Solutions*, edited by J. Michael Ryan, pp. 80–93. London: Routledge.

Solinger, Rickie. 2013. *Reproductive Politics: What Everyone Needs to Know*. New York, NY: Oxford University Press.

Smith, Ember, and Richard V. Reeves. 2020. "Students of Color Most Likely to be Learning Online: Districts Must Work Even Harder on Race Equity." Wednesday, September 2020. www.brookings.edu/blog/how-we-rise/2020/09/23/students-of-color-most-likely-to-be-learning-online-districts-must-work-even-harder-on-race-equity/.

Stanford University. 2020. *Estimates of Learning Loss in the 2019-2020 School Year*. Stanford, CA: Center for Research on Education Outcomes.

Summers, Juana. 2021. "Little Difference in Vaccine Hesitancy Among White and Black Americans, Poll Finds." *National Public Radio*, March 12, 2021. www.npr.org/sections/coronavirus-live-updates/2021/03/12/976172586/little-difference-in-vaccine-hesitancy-among-white-and-black-americans-poll-find.

Thomas, Deja, and Richard Fry. 2020. "Prior to COVID-19, Child Poverty Rates Had Reached Record Low in U.S." *Pew Research Center*, November 30, 2020. www.pewresearch.org/fact-tank/2020/11/30/prior-to-covid-19-child-poverty-rates-had-reached-record-lows-in-u-s/.

Thomas, Margaret M.C., Daniel P. Miller, and Taryn W. Morrissey. 2019. "Food Insecurity and Child Health." *Pediatrics* 144 (4): e20190397. https://doi.org/10.1542/peds.2019-0397.

United Hospital Fund. 2020. "UHF Report Finds 4,200 Children in NYS Have Lost a Parent to COVID-19." *United Hospital Fund*, September 30, 2021. https://uhfnyc.org/news/article/uhf-report-4200-children-nys--lost-parent-covid-19/.

US Bureau of Labor Statistics. 2021. "Supplemental Data Measuring the Effects of the Coronavirus (COVID-19) Pandemic on the Labor Market." Accessed July 22, 2021. www.bls.gov/cps/effects-of-the-coronavirus-covid-19-pandemic.htm.

US Census Bureau. 2021. "Measuring Household Experiences During the Coronavirus Pandemic." Accessed March 10, 2021. www.census.gov/data/experimental-data-products/household-pulse-survey.html.

Virginia Department of Health. 2021. "COVID-19 Vaccine Demographics." Accessed March 10, 2021. www.vdh.virginia.gov/coronavirus/covid-19-vaccine-demographics/.

Vissing, Yvonne. 2021. "Turning a Blind Eye: COVID-19 and Homeless Children." In *COVID-19 and Childhood Inequality*, edited by Nazneen Khan. London: Routledge.

Vivrette, Rebecca, and Jessica Dym Bartlett. 2020. "Trauma-Informed Strategies for Supporting Children and Youth in the Child Welfare System During COVID-19." *Child Trends*, September 30, 2020. www.childtrends.org/publications/trauma-informed-strategies-for-supporting-children-and-youth-in-the-child-welfare-system-during-covid-19.

Wang, Claire. 2020. "'You Have Chinese Virus!': 1 in 4 Asian American Youths Experience Racist Bullying, Report Says." *NBC News*, September 17, 2020. www.nbcnews.com/news/asian-america/25-percent-asian-american-youths-racist-bullying-n1240380.

Weber, Lauren. 2021. "Why So Many Workers' Comp Claims are Being Rejected." *Wall Street Journal*, February 14, 2021. www.wsj.com/articles/why-so-many-covid-19-workers-comp-claims-are-being-rejected-11613316304.

White, Arica, Leandris C. Liburd, and Fatima Coronado. 2021. "Addressing Racial and Ethnic Disparities in COVID-19 Among School-Aged Children: Are We Doing Enough?" *Preventing Chronic Disease* 18:E55. https://doi.org/10.5888/pcd18.210084.

Winfield, Ann Gibson. 2007. *Eugenics and Education in America: Institutionalized Racism and the Implications of History, Ideology, and Memory.* New York, NY: Peter Lang.

2 LGBTQ+ Youth and the COVID-19 Pandemic

Jessica N. Fish, Meg D. Bishop, and V. Paul Poteat

Introduction

In the early months of the coronavirus disease 2019 (COVID-19) pandemic, a flurry of opinions forecasted economic and health risks; few centered the impacts of the pandemic on lesbian, gay, bisexual, transgender, and queer/questioning and others (LGBTQ+) populations, and even fewer focused on the potential effects for LGBTQ+ youth (Salerno et al. 2020). Still, with the enormous swell of published research on COVID-19 in the past year, a limited number of studies empirically investigate how the pandemic and its social consequences have altered the daily experiences of LGBTQ+ youth.

Although the pandemic is a universal experience, LGBTQ+ youth face unique stressors and strains due to changes in access to affirming and supportive resources (Fish et al. 2020; Paceley et al. 2021; Poteat et al. 2020). Prior to the pandemic, LGBTQ+ youth were at a greater risk of poor mental health, substance use, suicide attempts, and homelessness as the results of stigma, victimization, and rejection compared to their heterosexual, cisgender peers (Fish, Baams, and McGuire 2020; Plöderl and Tremblay 2015; Russell and Fish 2016). The psychological, social, and economic consequences of the COVID-19 pandemic have compounded these pre-pandemic stressors and created distinct problems for LGBTQ+ youth during the pandemic (Fish et al. 2020; Salerno et al. 2020; Salerno et al. 2021. These immediate stressors and consequences may lead to prolonged unique challenges in the years to come.

Research on LGBTQ+ youth development and well-being often reflects an ecological perspective focused on environments that are sources of both adversity and support for LGBTQ+ youth, such as schools, families, and communities (Fish 2020; Russell and Fish 2016). However, with the onset of the pandemic and physical distancing requirements, access to these physical environments was restricted and, in some ways, blurred the boundaries between these contexts for LGBTQ+ youth. Therefore, we focus on three distinct but overlapping contexts—two physical and one virtual—relevant to LGBTQ+ youth and COVID-19: schools, families, and the Internet. We discuss how changes in these environments during the COVID-19 pandemic presented unique experiences and opportunities for LGBTQ+ youth.

DOI: 10.4324/9781003250937-4

School

Schools have played a key role in meeting the needs of young people during crises (Ronan and Johnston 2005). For example, during the pandemic, young people and their caregivers looked to schools to provide a degree of structure, familiar routine, and opportunities to maintain social connections (Colao et al. 2020). LGBTQ+ youth have faced unique challenges under these circumstances (Chisholm 2020; Cromar 2020; Wang et al. 2020). Still, schools have remained a vital resource for many of them.

As many schools shifted to remote or hybrid instruction, LGBTQ+ youth used online spaces to learn and solicit social support (Cromar 2020; López 2020). Although virtual spaces and communities have served to connect LGBTQ+ youth and their allies before the pandemic, LGBTQ+ youth have faced harassment and discrimination in these spaces as well (Evans et al. 2017; GLSEN, CiPHR, and CCRC 2013; Ybarra, Mitchell, Palmer, and Reisner 2015). A growing number of schools have adopted anti-bullying policies that extend explicit protection to LGBTQ+ youth, along with procedures to report, review, and respond to such incidents (Kull et al. 2016). Nevertheless, not all existing policies and procedures may consider virtual learning spaces and how LGBTQ+ youth experience discrimination in these contexts. Safe and LGBTQ+-affirming school climates are associated with better well-being and school experiences for LGBTQ+ youth (Day, Ioverno, and Russell 2019; Gower et al. 2018; Kull et al. 2016). It remains unclear how adults and youth may have promoted comparable norms and climates in the context of remote learning during the pandemic.

Outside of formal instruction, schools are a context wherein LGBTQ+ youth access support from trusted adults and peers and build community. Many LGBTQ+ youth feel comfortable disclosing their sexual orientation and/or gender identity to these individuals, but not necessarily to their caregivers (Ryan et al. 2009; Watson, Wheldon, and Russell 2015). Supportive peers also buffer the adverse effects of parental rejection on LGBTQ+ youth mental health (Parra et al. 2018). Encouragingly, 97% of LGBTQ+ youth can identify an LGBTQ+-affirming adult at school, and 61% can identify six or more (Kosciw et al. 2018). At the same time, many of these supportive adults are individuals with whom LGBTQ+ youth interact informally while at school. The shift to remote instruction forced adults and youth to be more deliberate in connecting. Adding to this challenge, both youth and adults have had to contend with serious personal and professional stressors and trauma that have made it difficult to maintain regular communication throughout the pandemic. In other ways, virtual instruction has increased the overlap between school and living contexts that were otherwise compartmentalized for some LGBTQ+ youth, such as navigating their identity development and disclosure to others (Mehus et al. 2017). Consequently, this may have limited youth's discussion of LGBTQ+-related stressors and required adults and peers to take additional precautions to protect the confidentiality of LGBTQ+ youth's sexual orientation and/or gender identity when communicating with them.

Certain school spaces have served as essential resources for LGBTQ+ youth, particularly Gender-Sexuality Alliances (GSAs; Griffin et al. 2004; Poteat et al. 2017). These school-based clubs are now present in 37% of secondary schools across the United States (Centers for Disease Control and Prevention n.d.). They offer an affirming place for LGBTQ+ youth and allies to solicit and provide support, socialize, access LGBTQ+-affirming resources, discuss LGBTQ+ topics, and engage in advocacy and awareness-raising efforts. Unfortunately, the pandemic forced many schools to limit in-person extracurricular activities; this constrained LGBTQ+ youth's access to GSAs and other crucial supports when they may have been most needed. Some GSAs continued to hold virtual meetings during the pandemic. However, they faced challenges in doing so. These challenges included facilitating engaging meetings, retaining members, overcoming technology constraints and "Zoom fatigue" (i.e., cognitive exhaustion from extended virtual engagement), and addressing privacy and confidentiality concerns for some members. Still, these virtual spaces remained an essential outlet for youth to connect and socialize, process ongoing sociopolitical crises, and seek support from peers and adult advisors throughout the pandemic.

Family

Family support and rejection are critical factors influencing LGBTQ+ youth's health and well-being (McGeough and Sterzing 2018; Newcomb et al. 2019). Due to stigma related to holding a marginalized sexual orientation and/or gender identity, LGBTQ+ youth are more likely to report rejection from parents and caregivers than their peers. LGBTQ+ youth are also disproportionately more likely to experience adverse childhood experiences, including physical, emotional, and sexual victimization, than their heterosexual, cisgender counterparts (Schneeberger et al. 2014). Rejection and victimization from family members are associated with health vulnerability among LGBTQ+ youth, including depression, suicidality, substance use, and sexual risk-taking (Bouris et al. 2010; Newcomb et al. 2019; Ryan et al. 2009).

During the COVID-19 pandemic, necessary public health measures (e.g., physical distancing, school closures, remote work) meant that many LGBTQ+ youth were relegated to homes with non-affirming, rejecting, and even hostile family members (Fish et al. 2020; Nelson et al. 2020). Some LGBTQ+ youth felt "re-closeted" while quarantining at home (Fish et al. 2020; Venkatraman 2020). Stay-at-home orders also limited access to supportive peers, adults, and mandated reporters. They forced many LGBTQ+ youth to avoid disclosing, discussing, or expressing their sexual orientation and/or gender identity, leaving youth feeling distressed and unsafe at home (Silliman Cohen and Bosk 2020). In one study (Wray-Lake et al. 2020), sexual minority and non-binary youth reported less support and greater parental conflict during the early months of the COVID-19 relative to their heterosexual and cisgender peers.

While at home, LGBTQ+ youth also discussed how they missed being with other LGBTQ+ people and in spaces where they felt safe to express their

LGBTQ+ identity (Fish et al. 2020; Paceley et al. 2021; Venkatraman 2020). Even when LGBTQ+ youth could maintain connections to affirming peers and adults outside of the home through virtual platforms, many were fearful that parents might overhear or monitor their conversations, particularly those related to sexual orientation and gender identity (Paceley et al. 2021). These fears are well founded given that LGBTQ+ youth are overrepresented in foster care and youth homelessness (Baams, Wilson, and Russell 2019; Morton et al. 2018; Wilson and Kastanis 2015). As a result, many LGBTQ+ youth stopped engaging with LGBTQ+ peers and providers over the phone or Zoom to limit accidental disclosure to family. At the same time, LGBTQ+ youth have increased engagement with text-based platforms to connect with LGBTQ+ peers, communities, and services (Fish et al. 2020). Unfortunately, for some LGBTQ+ youth, this switch led to feeling disconnected and isolated.

Although family rejection and concealment from family may have exacerbated health vulnerabilities for some LGBTQ+ youth during the pandemic, many LGBTQ+ youth are also part of loving and supportive families that may have been important sources of strength and resilience. Prior research has demonstrated that LGBTQ+ youth who perceive their families as more supportive report better mental health and less substance use relative to their less supported peers (Bouris et al. 2010; Olson et al. 2016; Ryan et al. 2009). For LGBTQ+ youth with affirming home lives, spending more time in these contexts may have provided an escape from other spaces that are less affirming, such as school. In one study, some youth described the positive aspects of being home and not having to deal with peer harassment at school (Fish et al. 2020); other youth reflected on the benefits of having time to immerse themselves in their identity exploration away from school and peers. O'Brien, Parra, and Cederbaum (2021) found that some LGBTQ+ youth reported that their family relationships improved through shared activities and time spent together during the pandemic. In one of my ongoing studies (J.N.F.), several LGBTQ+ youth reported watching shows and movies with their parents that featured LGBTQ+ characters during the pandemic, which gave them a venue to discuss LGBTQ+ identity and issues.

(Virtual) Communities and Resources

LGBTQ+ youth have a rich history of utilizing the Internet to access LGBTQ+ support when in-person community resources are scant (Craig and McInory 2014; Craig et al. 2021). More recently, LGBTQ+ youth have relied on Internet-based support to circumvent the stress and isolation caused by the pandemic. Recent studies have demonstrated that access to interactive online communities such as LGBTQ+-affirming chat spaces (e.g., Fish et al., 2020; Salerno et al., 2020) improved LGBTQ+ youth's mental health during the COVID-19 pandemic. One study showed that the perceived strength of youth's parasocial (i.e., one-way) relationships with LGBTQ+ media personalities on platforms such as TikTok and YouTube helped to buffer the links between family support, loneliness, and depression (Woznicki et al. 2021). In their investigation on sexual minority youth's coping strategies during COVID-19, O'Brien, Parra, and Cederbaum (2021) noted that connection with others was the most important form of self-care mentioned by participants; however, some youth were more apt than others to initiate remote connections with peers. Thus, virtual communities and resources have acted as important, but not always accessible, contexts of social support for LGBTQ+ youth through the pandemic.

Unfortunately, few virtual platforms are designed specifically for LGBTQ+ youth to connect outside moments of crisis. The available research on LGBTQ+ youth navigating COVID-19 shows that youth felt alone and wanted a place to be themselves (i.e., LGBTQ+; Fish et al. 2020; Hawke et al. 2021). They also missed the ability to connect to and be in community with LGBTQ+ peers and affirming adults (Fish et al. 2020; Nelson et al. 2020; Paceley et al. 2021). Unsurprisingly, LGBTQ+ youth-support platforms like *Trevor Chat* and *Q Chat Space* have seen a twofold increase in the number of youth engaging with their services since the start of the pandemic (Fish et al. 2020; The Trevor Project 2021). At the same time, general youth-focused technology platforms have observed disproportionately high engagement among LGBTQ+ youth (e.g., Planned Parenthood's Sexual Health Chat Bot Roo; okso.co ask anything text platform; D. Levine, personal communication, August 3, 2021). These observations suggest the need for more interactive and live, chat-based Internet support for LGBTQ+ young people.

Many cities are also home to LGBTQ+-focused community centers that cater to LGBTQ+ young people's unique needs (Fish et al. 2019; Williams, Levine, and Fish 2019). Before the pandemic, these organizations offered a safe and supportive physical space for LGBTQ+ youth to meet one another, build community, and engage with social support programs (e.g., support groups, free therapy, and work programs). At the start of the pandemic, these centers swiftly transitioned their in-person services online; many set up Discord servers and Zoom accounts to coordinate social events (e.g., drop-in, gaming groups) and support services (e.g., teletherapy, identity-based support groups) for youth members.

Although the transition to online services was rapid and stressful, a positive unintended consequence of online services was that many of these centers could serve more LGBTQ+ youth than ever before—particularly youth who experienced barriers to accessing in-person services before the pandemic (e.g., from fear of being "outed"; living too far away; D. Levine, personal communication, April 10, 2021). In my (J.N.F) conversations with staff at several of these centers, many reported that they would keep these online resources active even after returning to in-person services to help facilitate engagement among youth who might not otherwise be able to access services. At the same time, more recent conversations suggested that, as the pandemic progressed, centers noted a substantial drop in online activity and virtual meeting engagement, citing "Zoom fatigue" and the increased possibility for in-person connection. Some discussed how, despite youth's need for connection, many felt the digital space was insufficient to address their desires for more personal and meaningful relationships with others.

Implications and Conclusions

Despite the limited empirical attention to LGBTQ+ youth during the COVID-19 pandemic, the data are unequivocal: LGBTQ+ youth are experiencing the pandemic in unique ways. Notably, the pandemic is interconnected with an extended period of incredible social and political upheaval. Just like the stress of the pandemic may be compounded for LGBTQ+ youth, these stressors and strains may be particularly complex for LGBTQ+ youth of color—Black LGBTQ+ youth, in particular—and those who experience economic instability (Sasse 2020; The Trevor Project 2021). Recognizing the interdependence of these stressors underscores the need for continued research and services that acknowledge and address how intersecting experiences shape the day-to-day lives of LGBTQ+ youth during the pandemic and in its wake.

Schools and community groups may seek to maintain certain online services and resources initially offered during the height of the pandemic. In doing so, it will be imperative to ensure that these services and resources are accessible, carefully overseen, and responsive, offer adequate protections to youth's confidentiality and adhere to any relevant regulations (e.g., Health Insurance Portability and Accountability [HIPAA] compliance), and are regularly updated. In addition, reports from LGBTQ+ youth and adults during the pandemic suggest both benefits and trade-offs to providing services and resources entirely online or within virtual spaces. Thus, groups may wish to consider how some of their online services or resources could complement and enhance in-person services or potentially stand alone. In short, schools and community groups may wish to debrief and identify potential best practices in supporting LGBTQ+ youth in general and in the event of future health and sociopolitical crises.

Ultimately, the COVID-19 pandemic is a stark reminder that we lack adequate resources for marginalized and minoritized youth, including LGBTQ+ youth. As with any crisis, the pandemic has accentuated our shortcomings and has given us a better sense of the challenges and opportunities that lie before us. Moving forward, we must be more fervent in our development and implementation of innovative resources and strategies to support LGBTQ+ youth in our communities.

References

Baams, Laura, Bianca D.M. Wilson, and Stephen T. Russell. 2019. "LGBTQ+ Youth in Unstable Housing and Foster Care." *Pediatrics* 143 (3): e20174211. https://doi.org/10.1542/peds.2017-4211.

Bouris, Alida, Vincent Guilamo-Ramos, Angela Pickard, Chengshi Shiu, Penny S. Loosier, Patricia Dittus, Kari Gloppen, and J. Michael Waldmiller. 2010. "A Systematic Review of Parental Influences on the Health and Well-being of Lesbian, Gay, and Bisexual

Youth: Time for a New Public Health Research and Practice Agenda." *The Journal of Primary Prevention* 31 (5): 273–309. https://doi.org/10.1007/s10935-010-0229-1.

Centers for Disease Control and Prevention. (n.d.). "LGBT Youth Resources." Accessed August 13, 2021. www.cdc.gov/lgbthealth/youth-resources.htm.

Chisholm, N. Jamiyla. 2020. "COVID-19's Impact on the Black LGBTQ+ Community Creates New Traumas." *Color Lines,* May 27, 2020. www.colorlines.com/articles/covid-19s-impact-black-lgbtq-community-creates-new-traumas.

Colao, Annamaria, Prisco Piscitelli, Manuela Pulimeno, Salvatore Colazzo, Alessandro Miani, and Stefania Giannini. 2020. "Rethinking the Role of the School after COVID-19." *The Lancet Public Health* 5 (7): e370. https://doi.org/10.1016/S2468-2667(20)30124-9.

Craig, Shelley L., and Lauren McInroy. 2014. "You Can Form a Part of Yourself Online: The Influence of New Media on Identity Development and Coming Out for LGBTQ+ Youth." *Journal of Gay & Lesbian Mental Health* 18 (1): 95–109.

Craig, Shelley L., Andrew D. Eaton, Lauren McInroy, Vivian W.Y. Leung, and Sreedevi Krishnan. 2021. "Can Social Media Participation Enhance LGBTQ+ Youth Well-Being? Development of the Social Media Benefits Scale." *Social Media + Society* 7 (1): 2056305121988931.

Cromar, Ainslie. 2020. "Queer and Quarantined: Coronavirus Challenges Spark a Resurgence in LGBTQ+ Online Communities." *Boston.com*, April 15, 2020. www.boston.com/news/local-news/2020/04/15/queer-and-quarantined-coronavirus-challenges-spark-a-resurgence-in-lgbtq-online-communities.

Day, Jack K., Salvatore Ioverno, and Stephen T. Russell. 2019. "Safe and Supportive Schools for LGBT Youth: Addressing Educational Inequities through Inclusive Policies and Practices." *Journal of School Psychology* 74: 29–43. https://doi.org/10.1016/j.jsp.2019.05.007.

Evans, Yolanda N., Samantha J. Gridley, Julia Crouch, Alicia Wang, Megan A. Moreno, Kim Ahrens, and David J. Breland. 2017. "Understanding Online Resource Use by Transgender Youth and Caregivers: A Qualitative Study." *Transgender Health* 2 (1): 129–39. https://doi.org/10.1089/trgh.2017.0011.

Fish, Jessica N. 2020. "Future Directions in Understanding and Addressing Mental Health Among LGBTQ Youth." *Journal of Clinical Child & Adolescent Psychology* 49 (6): 1–14. https://doi.org/10.1080/15374416.2020.1815207.

Fish, Jessica N., Laura Baams, and Jenifer K. McGuire. 2020. "Sexual and Gender Minority Mental Health Issues Among Children and Youth." In *The Oxford Handbook of Sexual and Gender Minority Mental Health*, edited by Esther D. Rothblum, pp. 229–44. New York, NY: Oxford University Press.

Fish, Jessica N., Laura B. McInroy, Megan S. Paceley, Natasha D. Williams, Sara Henderson, Deborah S. Levine, and Rachel N. Edsall. 2020. "'I'm Kinda Stuck at Home with Unsupportive Parents Right Now': LGBTQ+ Youths' Experiences with COVID-19 and the Importance of Online Support." *Journal of Adolescent Health* 67 (3): 450–2.

Fish, Jessica N., Raymond L. Moody, Arnold H. Grossman, and Stephen T. Russell. 2019. "LGBTQ+ Youth-Serving Community-Based Organizations: Who Participates and What Difference Does It Make?" *Journal of Youth and Adolescence* 48 (12): 2418–31.

GLSEN, CiPHR, and CCRC. 2013. *Out Online: The Experiences of Lesbian, Gay, Bisexual and Transgender Youth on the Internet*. GLSEN. www.glsen.org/sites/default/files/2020-01/Out_Online_Full_Report_2013.pdf.

Gower, Amy L., Myriam Forster, Kari Gloppen, Abigail Z. Johnson, Marla E. Eisenberg, John E. Connett, and Iris W. Borowsky. 2018. "School Practices to Foster

LGBT-Supportive Climate: Associations with Adolescent Bullying Involvement." *Prevention Science* 19 (6): 813–21. https://doi.org/10.1007/s11121-017-0847-4.

Griffin, Pat, Camille Lee, Jeffrey Waugh, and Chad Beyer. 2004. "Describing Roles that Gay-Straight Alliances Play in Schools." *Journal of Gay & Lesbian Issues in Education* 1 (3): 7–22. https://doi.org/10.1300/J367v01n03_03.

Hawke, Lisa D., Em Hayes, Karleigh Darnay, and Joanna Henderson. 2021. "Mental Health Among Transgender and Gender Diverse Youth: An Exploration of Effects During the COVID-19 Pandemic." *Psychology of Sexual Orientation and Gender Diversity* 8 (2): 180–7. http://dx.doi.org/10.1037/sgd0000467.

Kosciw, Joseph G., Emily A. Greytak, Adrian D. Zongrone, Caitlin M. Clark, and Nhan L. Truong. 2018. *The 2017 National School Climate Survey: The Experiences of Lesbian, Gay, Bisexual, Transgender, and Queer Youth in our Nation's Schools.* GLSEN. www.glsen.org/sites/default/files/2019-10/GLSEN-2017-National-School-Climate-Survey-NSCS-Full-Report.pdf.

Kull, Ryan M., Emily A. Greytak, Joseph G. Kosciw, and Christian Villenas. 2016. "Effectiveness of School District Antibullying Policies in Improving LGBT Youths' School Climate." *Psychology of Sexual Orientation and Gender Diversity* 3 (4): 407–15. https://doi.org/10.1037/sgd0000196.

López, Canela. 2020. "LGBTQ Teens Are Cut Off from Support Networks in Quarantine, So They're Building Community Online Instead." *Insider*, April 28, 2020. www.insider.com/lgbtq-teens-are-building-community-online-while-quarantined-2020-4.

McGeough, Briana L., and Paul R. Sterzing. 2018. "A Systematic Review of Family Victimization Experiences Among Sexual Minority Youth." *The Journal of Primary Prevention* 39 (5): 491–528. https://doi.org/10.1007/s10935-018-0523-x.

Mehus, Christopher J., Ryan J. Watson, Marla E. Eisenberg, Heather L. Corliss, and Carolyn M. Porta. 2017. "Living as an LGBTQ Adolescent and a Parent's Child: Overlapping or Separate Experiences." *Journal of Family Nursing* 23 (2): 175–200.

Morton, Matthew H., Amy Dworsky, Jennifer L. Matjasko, Susanna R. Curry, David Schlueter, Raul Chávez, and Anne F. Farrell. 2018. "Prevalence and Correlates of Youth Homelessness in the United States." *Journal of Adolescent Health* 62 (1): 14–21.

Nelson, Kimberly M., Allegra R. Gordon, Steven A. John, Claire D. Stout, and Katharyn Macapagal. 2020. "'Physical Sex Is Over for Now': Impact of COVID-19 on the Well-being and Sexual Health of Adolescent Sexual Minority Males in the US." *Journal of Adolescent Health* 67 (6): 756–62.

Newcomb, Michael E., Michael C. LaSala, Alida Bouris, Brian Mustanski, Guillermo Prado, Sheree M. Schrager, and David M. Huebner. 2019. "The Influence of Families on LGBTQ Youth Health: A Call to Action for Innovation in Research and Intervention Development. *LGBT Health* 6 (4): 139–45. https://doi.org/10.1089/lgbt.2018.0157.

O'Brien, Rory P., Luis A. Parra, and Julie A. Cederbaum. 2021. "'Trying my Best': Sexual Minority Adolescents' Self-Care During the COVID-19 Pandemic." *Journal of Adolescent Health* 68 (6): 1053–8.

Olson, Kristina R., Lily Durwood, Madeleine DeMeules, and Katie A. McLaughlin. 2016. "Mental Health of Transgender Children Who Are Supported in Their Identities." *Pediatrics* 137 (3): e20153223. https://doi.org/10.1542/peds.2015-3223.

Paceley, Megan S., Sloan Okrey-Anderson, Jessica N. Fish, Lauren McInroy, and Malcolm Lin. 2021. "Beyond a Shared Experience: Queer and Trans Youth Navigating COVID-19." *Qualitative Social Work* 20 (1–2): 97–104.

Parra, Luis A., Timothy S. Bell, Michael Benibgui, Jonathan L. Helm, and Paul D. Hastings. 2018. "The Buffering Effect of Peer Support on the Links Between Family Rejection and Psychosocial Adjustment in LGB Emerging Adults." *Journal of Social and Personal Relationships* 35 (6): 854–71.

Plöderl, Martin, and Pierre Tremblay. 2015. "Mental Health of Sexual Minorities. A Systematic Review." *International Review of Psychiatry* 27 (5): 367–85. https://doi.org/10.3109/09540261.2015.1083949.

Poteat, V. Paul, Robert A. Marx, Jerel P. Calzo, Russell B. Toomey, Caitlyn Ryan, Caitlyn M. Clark, and Selin Gülgöz. 2020. "Addressing Inequities in Education: Considerations for LGBTQ+ Children and Youth in the Era of COVID-19." *SRCD Statement of the Evidence*. Accessed May 12, 2021. www.srcd.org/research/addressing-inequities-education-considerations-lgbtq-children-and-youth-era-covid-19.

Poteat, V. Paul, Hirokazu Yoshikawa, Jarel Calzo, Stephen T. Russell, and Stacey Horn. 2017. "Gay-Straight Alliances as Settings for Youth Inclusion and Development: Future Conceptual and Methodological Directions for Research on These and Other Student Groups in Schools." *Educational Researcher* 46 (9): 508–16. https://doi.org/10.3102/0013189X17738760.

Ronan, Kevin, and David Johnston. 2005. *Promoting Community Resilience in Disasters: The Role for Schools, Youth, and Families*. New York, NY: Springer and Business Media.

Russell, Stephen T., and Jessica N. Fish. 2016. "Mental Health in Lesbian, Gay, Bisexual, and Transgender (LGBT) Youth." *Annual Review of Clinical Psychology* 12: 465–487. https://doi.org/10.1146/annurev-clinpsy-021815-093153.

Ryan, Caitlyn, David Huebner, Rafael Diaz, and Jorge Sanchez. 2009. "Family Rejection as a Predictor of Negative Health Outcomes in White and Latino Lesbian, Gay, and Bisexual Young Adults." *Pediatrics* 123 (1): 346–52. https://doi.org/10.1542/peds.2007-3524.

Salerno, John P., Jackson Devadas, M Pease, Bryanna Nketia, and Jessica N. Fish. 2020. "Sexual and Gender Minority Stress Amid the COVID-19 Pandemic: Implications for LGBTQ+ Young Persons' Mental Health and Well-being." *Public Health Reports* 135 (6): 721–7.

Salerno, John P., Cho-Hee Shrader, Angel B. Algarin, Ji-Young Lee, and Jessica N. Fish. 2021. "Changes in Alcohol Use Since the Onset of COVID-19 are Associated with Psychological Distress Among Sexual and Gender Minority University Students in the U.S." *Drug and Alcohol Dependence* 221: 108594. https://doi.org/10.1016/j.drugalcdep.2021.108594

Sasse, Ryan. 2020. "The Case for Intersectionality: Supporting LGBTQ Amidst COVID-19." *UNICEF,* June 25, 2021. www.unicefusa.org/stories/case-intersectionality-supporting-lgbtq-youth-amidst-covid-19/37418.

Schneeberger, Andres R., Michael Dietl, Kristina H. Muenzenmaier, Christian G. Huber, and Undine E. Lang. 2014. "Stressful Childhood Experiences and Health Outcomes in Sexual Minority Populations: A Systematic Review." *Social Psychiatry and Psychiatric Epidemiology* 49 (9): 1427–45.

Silliman Cohen, Rachel I., and Emily Adlin Bosk. 2020. "Vulnerable Youth and the COVID-19 Pandemic." *Pediatrics* 146 (1): e20201306.

The Trevor Project. 2021. "Implications of COVID-19 for LGBTQ Youth Mental Health and Suicide Prevention." *The Trevor Project,* April 3, 2020. www.thetrevorproject.org/2020/04/03/implications-of-covid-19-for-lgbtq-youth-mental-health-and-suicide-prevention/.

Venkatraman, Sakshi. 2020. "For LGBTQ Youth, Home Might Not be a Safe Place to Self-Isolate." *NBC News*, July 18, 2021. www.nbcnews.com/feature/nbc-out/lgbtq-youth-home-might-not-be-safe-place-self-isolate-n1181721.

Wang, Yuanyuan, Bailin Pan, Ye Liu, Amanda Wilson, Jianjun Ou, and Runsen Chen. 2020. "Health Care and Mental Health Challenges for Transgender Individuals During the COVID-19 Pandemic." *The Lancet Diabetes & Endocrinology* 8 (7): 564–5. https://doi.org/10.1016/S2213-8587(20)30182-0.

Watson, Ryan J., Christopher W. Wheldon, and Stephen T. Russell. 2015. "How Does Sexual Identity Disclosure Impact School Experiences?" *Journal of LGBT Youth* 12 (4): 385–96. https://doi.org/10.1080/19361653.2015.1077764.

Williams, Natasha D., Deborah S. Levine, and Jessica N. Fish. 2019. *2019 Needs Assessment: LGBTQ+ Youth Centers and Programs*. Fort Lauderdale, FL: CenterLink. www.lgbtcenters.org/Assets/Images/PageContent/Full/2019-needs-assessment-LGBTQ+-youth-centers-and-programs.pdf.

Wilson, Bianca D.M., and Angeliki A. Kastanis. 2015. "Sexual and Gender Minority Disproportionality and Disparities in Child Welfare: A Population-Based Study." *Children and Youth Services Review* 58: 11–17.

Woznicki, Nathaniel, Andrew Arriaga, Norian A. Caporale-Berkowitz, and Mike C. Parent. 2021. "Parasocial Relationships and Depression Among LGBQ Emerging Adults Living with Their Parents During COVID-19: The Potential for Online Support." *Psychology of Sexual Orientation and Gender Diversity* 8 (2): 228–37. https://doi.org/10.1037/sgd0000458.

Wray-Lake, Laura, Sara Wilf, Jin Yao Kwan, and Benjamin Oosterhoff. 2020. "Adolescence During a Pandemic: Examining US Adolescents' Time Use and Family and Peer Relationships During COVID-19." *PsyArXiv* October 1, 2020. https://doi.org/10.31234/osf.io/7vab6.

Ybarra, Michele L., Kimberly J. Mitchell, Neal A. Palmer, and Sari L. Reisner. 2015. "Online Social Support as a Buffer Against Online and Offline Peer and Sexual Victimization Among U.S. LGBT and non-LGBT Youth." *Child Abuse & Neglect* 39: 123–36. https://doi.org/10.1016/j.chiabu.2014.08.006.

3 Turning a Blind Eye

COVID-19 and Homeless Children

Yvonne Vissing

Homeless children are often out of sight, thus they are also out mind (Vissing 1997). The lives of homeless children are very challenging in general, and the coronavirus disease 2019 (COVID-19) pandemic has made their situation even worse. Their special situation of homelessness makes their exposure, prevention, treatment, and recovery to the virus exponentially more challenging than for housed children.

Homelessness

Homelessness is a process, not just an outcome. It stems from a combination of both macro, structural, and institutional factors and micro-level dynamics. In rare situations (i.e., fire, war, or environmental catastrophes) does homelessness occur over night; it typically occurs over a period of time as resources and supports are eliminated. A graphic representation of the complex, multi-faceted factors leading to homelessness is shown in Figure 3.1. Macro-level institutional factors include healthcare, economic resources, housing, social services, and political policies that impact families. Micro-level factors include getting sick, not having enough to eat, and parents who lose their jobs and can't afford to purchase goods and services that are necessary for survival. This complex systems approach to understanding homelessness means that there are a variety of intervention points that could reduce the likelihood of severe housing distress. Addressing any of the multiplicity of contributing factors could help prevent homelessness.

Housing, from a public health perspective, is a protective factor. Homelessness is a public health risk factor. The reality of getting COVID-19 and recovering successfully from it are markedly different for children who have homes compared with those who do not. Having a home of one's own decreases the spread of disease and puts into place the resources and supports necessary for preventing illness or more quickly recovering from it (Vissing 2021).

Like the COVID-19 pandemic, the nation's current homelessness epidemic is a preventable public health problem (Desjarlais-deKlerk 2021; Vissing, Hudson, and Nilan 2020). The amount of homelessness and housing distress has increased since January 2020 when COVID-19 first made its arrival in the United States

DOI: 10.4324/9781003250937-5

46 Yvonne Vissing

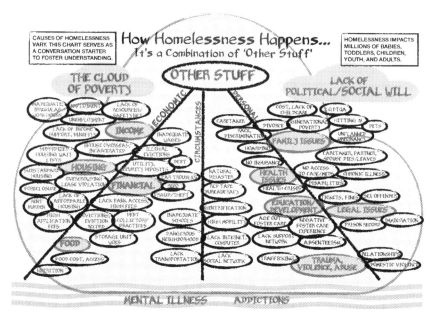

Figure 3.1 Macro and micro factors driving homelessness.

(Cornelissen and Hermann 2020; Greene and McCargo 2020). The housing crisis has disproportionately impacted Black and Latino families. Homelessness has increased by 45% due to COVID-19, with projections of 800,000 homeless people according to a Columbia University economist (Community Solutions 2020). If COVID-19 can't get under control soon, these numbers reflecting the severity of suffering will surely increase (Boston Globe 2018).

COVID-19 and Children

Around the world, most COVID-19 prevention and treatment plans have focused on elderly adults. There has not been an age, class, or race equitable approach to preventing the virus, or vaccinating people, in the United States (Stanley-Becker and Sun 2020). A policy brief for the United Nations Sustainable Development Group (2020) states that while children are not the face of this pandemic, they risk being among its biggest victims. They predict that the pandemic is having a profound effect on the lifelong well-being of all children, but that the harmful effects of this pandemic will not be distributed equally. The negative impacts of the pandemic are expected to be most damaging for the poorest children, whether found in poor nations, poor neighborhoods, or those who are already in disadvantaged or vulnerable situations.

As noted by many researchers, within the United States poverty is as significant as found in least-developed, formerly called third-world, countries (Abt 2017; Huffington 2011; McGirt and Jenkins 2020). The United States has not had a national policy for children and their families, and they certainly haven't had a comprehensive strategy to prevent homeless children and adults from contracting COVID-19 (Patrick 2020). The nation's approach to dealing with the chaos and catastrophe associated with COVID-19 has been haphazard at best. Families have fallen into financial destitution, schooling has been disrupted, health expenses have skyrocketed, juggling work and family obligations have been extraordinarily stressful for everyone, mental illness and distress have increased, family violence has risen, and people have gotten sick or died, with most of this being preventable if there had been a comprehensive, transparent national plan (Garfield and Chibadambaram 2020; Nicola et al. 2020; Stracqualursi 2021).

Many theories exist that justify the lack of attention to children in general, and homeless children in particular, as being at high risk when it comes to COVID-19 (Wu 2020). The major assumption has been that children don't get the virus or suffer much if they do, but as time has gone by and more data has been collected, we now know that children do get the virus. While many, perhaps up to 80%, may be asymptomatic, some have died and others developed a condition called multisystem inflammatory syndrome in children (MIS-C), which inflames different parts of the body, such as the heart, lungs, kidneys, brain, skin, eyes, or gastrointestinal organs (Centers for Disease Control 2021). The health conditions experienced by children while their bodies and minds are developing lay the foundation for later health. Longitudinal data from COVID-19 exposure in children is not yet available. However, concerns by the pediatric community over negative long-term impacts are significant (American Academy of Pediatrics 2020; Capatides 2020; Chotiner 2020; Cormier 2020; Fernandes 2020; Gavi 2020; Kim 2020; Leigh 2020; McCarthy 2020; Milstone 2020; Parshley 2020; Peck 2020; Preston 2020; Saplakoglu 2020).

COVID-19 and Homelessness

Both COVID-19 and homelessness are tough enough when they exist on their own, but in combination it can make both worse. The Center on Budget and Policy Priorities (2021) acknowledges that the health and economic impact of the pandemic have been widespread, but are most prevalent among Black, Latino, Indigenous, immigrant, and single-parent households. Institutionalized discrimination toward these groups has become even more oppressive during the pandemic when jobs have been cut or downsized and family members have become ill. Structural racism in education, employment, housing, and healthcare has exacerbated the negative impacts of COVID-19. While in some communities, people in homeless shelters may have some degree of prioritization when it comes to getting the vaccine, adults who are without housing and not in shelters are not included. These include people who are doubled-up, couch-surfing, living in vehicles, motels, and nontraditional places. This makes them, and their children, even more vulnerable to the disease. Poverty, hunger, and housing distress leading to homelessness leave families having no discretionary funds or supports to call upon during times of need. All this makes bad situations even worse.

When family money gets tight, cutting food, healthcare, and housing costs are logical steps. There are many different types of homeless and housing distress that children may face, from doubling-up with family, friends, or acquaintances, couch-surfing, staying in a campground, car, shelter, or when all else fails, people may be found living on the street. Children living in detainment centers, jails, institutions, or some types of residential facilities could be considered homeless because while they have a roof over their head, they have little or no control over their living environment. Congregate living includes communal sleeping areas, shared bathrooms, and multiple people using the kitchen to cook or clean food and dishes. Living in close proximity with strangers makes it hard to physically distance; having no control over who is coming and going, or who those who are around you have been in contact with increases chances of virus contamination.

If you don't have a home of your own, recovery from illness is difficult and may take longer. Having your own space means that you have a refrigerator where you can keep food, a stove where you can cook it, and a bathroom that can be kept sanitized. When homeless children and families don't have a place where they can sleep, eat warm soup, get a cool drink, shower, toilet, rest, and recover, the chances of the illness exacerbating the condition and morphing into new health problems increase (Vissing 1997).

The government did put a moratorium on evictions for a short time, but it is a short-term fix that won't alleviate the financial distress that families face (O'Connell 2021). Besides, the moratorium depends on what state one lives and whether there could be relief such as not turning off one's utilities; some states are more "sympathetic" than others. Courts don't want to process eviction complaints right now, and there is a huge backlog of cases that will come due to be heard once the grace period expires. There are things that could be done to alleviate people's housing distress (Ellen et al. 2020), but this would require long-term investment into making accessible, affordable, and sustainable housing available.

COVID-19 impacts homeless children's health in major ways. These include increased chances of exposure to the virus; reduced lifestyle supports that could curb the spread or longevity of illness; limited access to vaccination, identification, treatment, and recovery; and fewer mental health, educational, and social services. In the trajectory of disease, homelessness complicates routine steps. When people aren't sure about whether they or their children have the virus, they have been discouraged from seeking care due to a skyrocketing COVID-19 demand that is exhausting the resources of medical facilities. Identifying when children may be sick enough to need professional care is often difficult. Children routinely get a fever, a runny nose or cough, or don't feel well.

Figuring out when a child has a self-limiting disorder or when it could be life-threatening may be hard. A child's illness can decline rapidly and put the child at grave risk without appropriate intervention. If parents are overwhelmed trying to figure out how to put a roof over their head and get enough to eat, they may not identify when a condition could be life-threatening.

Finding where to get a doctor, medical care, or a vaccine is hard if you don't have a physical address where you can get mail. If you don't have a telephone or cellular phone, it is very difficult to make a call for an appointment or receive information from providers as payphones are now nonexistent. Internet access requires an electronic device and wireless Internet access. Libraries have traditionally been a place where homeless people could go to use computers and access information, but libraries may be closed or may have very limited hours due to fear of COVID-19.

If you can find a provider, homeless people may find it difficult to get an appointment. Then there is the issue of getting to the appointment. Transporting a sick child to an appointment can be very challenging, especially if parents rely upon public transportation. They may not have discretionary income to pay for a taxi or put gas into a car if they have one, which may leave them walking long distances with a sick child. Taking a symptomatic, or even asymptomatic, child into the public arena could expose other vulnerable people to the virus.

Then there is the issue of how to pay for care received at the appointment. If people have health insurance, they may have their costs covered, but there may be co-pays, prescriptions, or medical supplies that parents can't afford. Consumers are paying more of their health plan premiums and experiencing higher out-of-pocket cost-sharing for all types of healthcare services. Government estimates of healthcare spending do not include the significant discretionary consumers on several products and services (Thomas 2014). One in every four Americans skips healthcare services because they cannot afford them (Leonhardt 2020), and for homeless families the rate is undoubtedly higher because of their lack of discretionary funds.

Adding to these challenges are numerous layers of secondary-level problems, ranging from lost support from teachers, school nurses, and peers due to school closures; overcrowded and confined living conditions; stress around job or money issues; and increased anxiety, aggravation, and depression, all contributing to increased possibilities of interpersonal or domestic violence. Education is a lifeline for homeless children, but challenges of learning remotely if they don't have computers, Wi-Fi, or a quiet place to study impair children's chances of success. There is thus a domino adverse impact of COVID-19 on homeless children.

Symbolic Meaning of our National Response

Rhetoric espouses that all children are special, as a nation we care about them and feel they are entitled to have their needs met. It is common to believe that because welfare programs exist, homeless children and families can obtain needed services and resources. However, this is not necessarily true. While some may like to think that homeless children get the food, healthcare, shelter, education, and supports that they need in order to live a good life, this is typically a fantasy held by those who do have adequate resources (Lesley 2020; Nilan 2020; Vissing, Hudson, and Nilan 2020). Symbolic interactionists note that people in positions of power have the ability to define situations the way they want them to be seen (Becker 1963). In the case of homeless children, while government officials or the public may think that they are adequately cared for, homeless children's reality is much different from those of housed children. As First Lady Melania Trump's coat read when she went to visit homeless children who were separated from their families at the US–Mexico border, "I really don't care, do you?" (BBC 2018).

Cultural theorist and sociologist Harriet Martineau (1837) observed long ago that there is a big difference between ideal and real culture. Ideal culture refers to the way we want to believe things should be; real culture refers to the way things actually are. When we think children's needs are being addressed by someone else, it takes the responsibility off our shoulders to do anything for them. Because we are not thinking about them, homeless children fall through the cracks. When we blame homeless people for their poverty and lack of housing, we turn a blind eye to the fact that they may be victims of things over which they have no control. Struggling parents do the best they can but are juggling many obstacles as they try to make ends meet with insufficient resources. While the public may think that destitute parents and their children receive adequate aid from the government or other "helpers," usually they don't.

But unless we have first-hand knowledge of this fact, it may go unrecognized. In any experience there are insiders and outsiders, and depending upon our position we may regard things much differently from others. As sociologist Howard Becker (1967) notes, our reactions depend on "whose side we are on." Our views are often somewhat akin to those of Marie Antoinette, who when asked what to do for people who were so poor that they had no bread to eat allegedly responded with "let them eat cake" (History 2018). While we may say we care about homeless children and are doing all we can to protect them from COVID-19, is that actually true? In public vernacular, Jane Austen is often quoted as saying "It isn't what we say or think that defines us, but what we do" (Austin and James-Cavan 2001). For homeless children during the pandemic, we could be doing much better for them.

Perhaps it is because in the stratification of children, some children are regarded to be worth more than others (Zelizer 1981). Poor and homeless children are simply not treated as if they were as valuable as children of elite parents (Menon 2020). While rich people may rake in millions of dollars from corporate welfare, welfare to the poor is doled out in a stingy manner as those holding the purse-strings demean them for daring to fall on hard times (Daley 2017; Lauter 2016). The cost of not investing in all children and allowing children to flounder in poverty is nothing short of a national tragedy (Madrick

2020). Disinvesting in poor and homeless children because they are viewed as dispensable, while investing in upper and upper-middle class children because they are viewed as priceless, is a shameful yet common response (Cohen 2015; Khan and Boswell 2021, this volume). This response indicates that homeless children aren't very important and that they are more expendable than other children, especially housed children in employed two-parent families. Therefore, are homeless children regarded as more justifiably dispensable than more well-to-do children? That may not be what is polite to say, but it could be argued that this is the case from observing our national policy decisions regarding their treatment.

A Child Rights Approach to Helping Homeless Children During the Pandemic

Prior to the pandemic children's needs were not met, and their conditions have declined since the pandemic became an international and long-term reality. The United States is the only member country of the United Nations not to ratify the Convention on the Rights of the Child (CRC). The CRC is the most endorsed human rights treaty in the world, and it is notable that the United States has failed to join the international community to stand up for children's human rights. The United Nations Office of the High Commissioner for Human Rights has developed specific guidelines and statements to protect children during COVID-19. These are important protections that child and youth practitioners should be made aware of (Office of the High Commissioner United Nations Human Rights 2020a and 2020b).

A human rights approach could help prevent children from becoming homeless in the first place. It could also provide housing distressed children greater protection from being exposed to the virus and, in cases where COVID-19 is transmitted, more rapid recovery. The treaty articles are designed to protect children from illnesses and to provide them with the provisions they need to recover. Article 2 of the CRC addresses their right to be free from discrimination based on their parents' status. Just because their parents were poor, lost their job, or were sick themselves and unable to care for the child, children as a special group should not be penalized or forced to suffer because of their parents' status. Article 3 states that the primary consideration of organizational and provider decisions should be the best interests of children. As a group, children are not being tested for COVID-19. Some schools have not put into place the safeguards necessary to ensure their safety. It would be in the child's best interest to assume that they could be exposed to the virus, they could get it, they could get sick from it, and they could suffer from serious morbidity or even mortality from it. These latter assumptions would direct the way we treat children in a very different direction than we do now. Article 6 of the CRC alleges that states must ensure child survival and their maximum development, which a best-interest approach would ensure. Detained and separated children are entitled to special protection and assistance provided by the state according to Article 21, and Article 22 requires that child refugees and asylum seekers receive special protections (United Nations Refugee Agency 2017). Article 24 of the CRC affirms that children have the right to the highest standards of health prevention, treatment, and recovery. Article 27 states that States Parties recognize the right of every child to a standard of living adequate for the child's physical, mental, spiritual, moral, and social development, and Article 19 states that the state must protect children from physical abuse, mental abuse, neglect, and maltreatment.

Article 27 also holds the view that parents or persons responsible for children have the primary responsibility to secure, within their abilities and financial capacities, the conditions of living necessary for child development; therefore, assisting parents to care for children is part of the treaty. States Parties, in accordance with national conditions and within their means, shall take appropriate measures to assist parents and others responsible for the child to implement this right and shall, in case of need, provide material assistance and support programs, particularly regarding nutrition, clothing, and housing. Article 28 protects children's rights to education, and Article 32 is designed to protect children from economic exploitation.

The CRC can be a powerful tool that assists homeless and housing distressed children if communities will implement its articles. It is designed to help children everywhere. Given the extremely vulnerable status of homeless children and the fact that many may not have adults to advocate for them, it is essential that we as rights-respecting, humane communities of care consider how to protect and assist them.

Conclusion

Access to stable housing is a public health protection for children. Homes help keep children safe and healthy. Economic and housing security influences their health status. Poverty, hunger, and housing distress interfere with the prevention, identification, treatment, and recovery of illness in children. Homelessness makes their exposure to diseases like COVID-19 more inevitable, and potentially more deadly. It is more difficult to prevent housing distressed children's exposure the virus. There is a co-morbidity between poverty, housing distress, and illness that is well substantiated in the homelessness literature (Almendrala 2018; Bassuk Center 2018a and 2018b; Dickrell 2016; Patterson 2014).

Macro and micro policies and interventions could improve the overall condition for children, so they don't have to become homeless in the first place. They could also ensure safety procedures to minimize the risk of COVID-19 transmission for those that are in housing distress. COVID-19 has resulted in the closing of many businesses, leading to high unemployment and loss of income for those who still have their jobs. This results in more evictions, bankruptcies, loss of homes, and increase of homelessness. More children are going hungry. Many families have lost their health insurance or cannot afford to pay for necessary medications and resources when they are sick. The nation's economic recovery will be slow in most markets, making the negative impacts of COVID-19 long-lasting (Chotiner 2020; Morgan Stanley 2020; Peck 2020; Vissing 2020).

In order to address the health needs of homeless and housing distressed children during this pandemic, communities must come together to design comprehensive COVID-19 prevention and intervention programs. Considering the CRC mandate to always put the best interests of the child in the forefront, communities are encouraged to make resources available, accessible, and affordable to this vulnerable group of young people. This may require creating community partnerships or redesigning institutions and services so that children's best interests are a priority in every community, service, and funding decision.

In conclusion, this chapter has explored how children in housing-distressed living situations are especially vulnerable to catching COVID-19 and receiving adequate treatment. It concludes that while there is a global severe acute respiratory syndrome coronavirus 2 (SARS-CoV-2) pandemic, there is also a pandemic of insensitivity of the impact of poverty and dislocation on children. If children received the care standards as outlined in the UN CRC, the epidemic of the virus would not attack them as heavily, and if it did there would be adequate resources to assist in their identification, treatment, and recovery.

References

Abt, Parker. 2017. "There Is a Third World in America that No One Notices." *Washington Post*, November 22, 2017. www.washingtonpost.com/opinions/theres-a-third-world-america-that-no-one-notices/2017/11/21/640c4c1a-c499-11e7-aae0-cb18a8c29c65_story.html.

Almendrala, Anna. 2018. "Hospitals Are Releasing Homeless Patients Back to the Streets. There's a Better Way." *Huffington Post*, April 24, 2018. www.huffpost.com/entry/homeless-patients-hospitals-recuperative-care_n_5ad91023e4b03c426dacc350.

American Academy of Pediatrics. 2020. "Guidance Related to Childcare During COVID-19." Accessed July 7, 2021. https://services.aap.org/en/pages/2019-novel-coronavirus-covid-19-infections/clinical-guidance/guidance-related-to-childcare-during-covid-19/.

Austen, Jane, and Kathleen James-Cavan. 2001. *Sense and Sensibility*. Ontario: Broadview Press.

Bassuk Center. 2018a. "Family Homelessness." Accessed July 7, 2021. www.bassukcenter.org/.

Bassuk Center. 2018b. "The Bassuk Center on Homeless and Vulnerable Children and Youth." Accessed July 7, 2021. www.bassukcenter.org/.

BBC. 2018. "Melania Trump Says Her Coat Sent a Message." *BBC*, October 14, 2018. www.bbc.com/news/world-us-canada-45853364.

Becker, Howard. 1963. *Outsiders: Studies in the Sociology of Deviance*. London: Free Press of Glencoe.

Becker, Howard. 1967. "Whose Side Are We On?" *Social Problems* 14 (3): 239–47. https://doi.org/10.1525/sp.1967.14.3.03a00010.

Boston Globe. 2018. "US Data Vastly Underestimate Number of Homeless Kids, Families." *Boston Globe*, December 21, 2018. www.bostonglobe.com/opinion/letters/2018/12/21/data-vastly-underestimate-number-homeless-kids-families/asfFt5J0uC8A3j7SHhREbI/story.html.

Capatides, Christina. 2020. "Pediatrician Says 80% of Kids Likely Have the Coronavirus but They Are so Asymptomatic You'd Never Know." *CBS*, April 14, 2020. www.cbsnews.com/news/coronavirus-children-pediatrician-80-percent-asymptomatic/.

Center on Budget and Policy Priorities. 2021. "Tracking the COVID-19 Recession's Effect on Food, Housing and Employment Hardships." Accessed June 14, 2021. www.cbpp.org/research/poverty-and-inequality/tracking-the-covid-19-recessions-effects-on-food-housing-and.

Centers for Disease Control. 2021. "Multisystem Inflammatory Syndrome in Children Associated with COVID." Accessed June 14, 2021. www.cdc.gov/coronavirus/2019-ncov/daily-life-coping/children/mis-c.html.

Chotiner, Isaac. 2020. "The Coronavirus Crisis Will Lead to Catastrophic Hunger." *The New Yorker*, May 12, 2020. www.newyorker.com/news/q-and-a/the-coronavirus-crisis-will-lead-to-catastrophic-hunger.

Cohen, Patricia. 2015. "Aid to the Needy Often Excludes the Poorest in America." *New York Times*, February 16, 2015. www.nytimes.com/2015/02/17/business/economy/aid-to-needy-often-excludes-the-poorest-in-america.html.

Community Solutions. 2020. "Analysis on Unemployment Projects a 40–45% Increase in Homelessness." Accessed May 11, 2020. https://community.solutions/analysis-on-unemployment-projects-40-45-increase-in-homelessness-this-year/.

Cormier, Zoe. 2020. "How COVID-19 Can Damage the Brain." *BBC*, June 22, 2020. www.bbc.com/future/article/20200622-the-long-term-effects-of-covid-19-infection.

Cornelissen, Sharon, and Alexander Hermann. 2020. "A Triple Pandemic: The Economic Impacts of COVID-19 Disproportionately Affect Black and Hispanic Households." *Joint Center for Housing Studies of Harvard University*, July 7, 2020. www.jchs.harvard.edu/blog/a-triple-pandemic-the-economic-impacts-of-covid-19-disproportionately-affect-black-and-hispanic-households.

Daley, Beth. 2017. "3 Myths About the Poor." *The Conversation*, December 13, 2017. https://theconversation.com/3-myths-about-the-poor-that-republicans-are-using-to-support-slashing-us-safety-net-89048.

Desjarlais-deKlerk, Kristen. 2021. "Housing As Health Care: Mitigations of Homelessness During a Pandemic." In *COVID-19 Volume II: Social Consequences and Cultural Adaptations*, edited by J. Michael Ryan, pp. 72–84. London: Routledge.

Dickrell, Stephanie. 2016. "Child Homelessness Can Have Long-Term Consequences." *SC Times*, June 4, 2016. www.sctimes.com/story/news/local/homelesskids/2016/06/04/child-homelessness-can-have-long-term-consequences/84902750/.

Ellen, Ingrid, Erin Graves, Katherine O'Regan, and Jenny Schuetz. 2020. "Strategies for Increasing Affordable Housing Amid the COVID-19 Economic Crisis." *Brookings*, June 8, 2020. www.brookings.edu/research/strategies-for-increasing-affordable-housing-amid-the-covid-19-economic-crisis/.

Fernandes, Michelle. 2020. "Why Children Aren't Immune to COVID-19." *BBC*, March 31, 2020. www.bbc.com/future/article/20200330-coronavirus-are-children-immune-to-covid-19.

Garfield, Rachel, and Priya Chidambaram. 2020. "Children's Health and Wellbeing During the COVID Pandemic." *Kaiser Family Foundation*, September 24, 2020. www.kff.org/coronavirus-covid-19/issue-brief/childrens-health-and-well-being-during-the-coronavirus-pandemic/.

Gavi. 2020. "Long Term Health Effects of COVID-19." *Gavi*, June 19, 2020. www.gavi.org/vaccineswork/long-term-health-effects-covid-19.

Greene, Solomon, and Alanna McCargo. 2020. "New Data Suggest COVID-19 Is Widening Housing Disparities by Race and Income." *Urban Institute*, May 29, 2020. www.urban.org/urban-wire/new-data-suggest-covid-19-widening-housing-disparities-race-and-income.

History. 2018. "Did Marie Antoinette Really Say Let Them Eat Cake?" August 31, 2018. www.history.com/news/did-marie-antoinette-really-say-let-them-eat-cake.

Huffington, Arianna. 2011. *Third World America*. New York, NY: Crown.

Khan, Nazneen, and Amaya Boswell. 2021. "Pandemic Eugenics: Stratified Reproduction and the COVID-19 Pandemic." In *COVID-19 and Childhood Inequality*, edited by Nazneen Khan. London: Routledge.

Kim, Kwang Sik. 2020. "MIS-C and COVID19: Rare Inflammatory Syndrome in Kids and Teens." *Johns Hopkins Medicine*, 2020. www.hopkinsmedicine.org/health/conditions-and-diseases/coronavirus/misc-and-covid19-rare-inflammatory-syndrome-in-kids-and-teens.

Lauter, David. 2016. "How Do Americans View Poverty?" *Los Angeles Times*, August 14, 2016. www.latimes.com/projects/la-na-pol-poverty-poll/.

Leigh, Suzanne. 2020. "1 in 3 Young Adults May Face Severe COVID-19." *University of California San Francisco*, July 12, 2020. www.ucsf.edu/news/2020/07/418081/1-3-young-adults-may-face-severe-covid-19-ucsf-study-shows.

Leonhardt, Megan. 2020. "1 in 4 Americans are Skipping Medical Care Because of the Cost." *CNBC*, March 12, 2020. www.cnbc.com/2020/03/11/nearly-1-in-4-americans-are-skipping-medical-care-because-of-the-cost.html.

Lesley, Bruce. 2020. "Invisibilizing Homeless Children." *First Focus*, January 29, 2020. https://firstfocus.org/blog/invisibilizing-homeless-children.

Madrick, Jeff. 2020. *Invisible Americans: The Tragic Cost of Child Poverty*. New York, NY: Knopf.

Martineau, Harriet. 1837. *Society in America*. New York, NY: Saunders and Otley.

McCarthy, Claire. 2020. "New Warning of Coronavirus Symptoms in Children." *Harvard Health*, May 14, 2020. www.health.harvard.edu/blog/new-warning-on-coronavirus-symptoms-in-children-what-parents-need-to-know-2020051419826.

McGirt, Ellen, and Arlic Jenkins. 2020. "America Is a Third World Country Now." *Fortune*, September 30, 2020. https://fortune.com/2020/09/30/america-is-a-third-world-country-now/.

Menon, Rajan. 2020. "US Politics Is Failing Children." *Boston Review*, September 21, 2020. http://bostonreview.net/class-inequality-law-justice/rajan-menon-us-politics-failing-children.

Milstone, Aaron. 2020. "Coronavirus in Babies and Children." *Johns Hopkins Health*, 2020. www.hopkinsmedicine.org/health/conditions-and-diseases/coronavirus/coronavirus-in-babies-and-children.

Morgan Stanley. 2020. "Coronavirus: Economic Risk and Recovery." *Morgan Stanley*, October 26, 2020. www.morganstanley.com/Themes/coronavirus-global-economy-markets.

Nicola, Maria, Zaid Alsafi, Catrin Sohrabi, Ahmed Kerwan, Ahmed Al-Jabir, Christos Iosifidis, Maliha Agha, and Riaz Agha. 2020. "The Socio-Economic Implications of the Coronavirus Pandemic (COVID-19): A Review." *International Journal of Surgery* 78: 185–93. https://doi.org/10.1016/j.ijsu.2020.04.018.

Nilan, Diane. 2020. *Dismazed and Driven: My Look at Family Homelessness in America*. Naperville, IL: Hear Us, Inc.

O'Connell, Amy. 2021. "Emergency Bans on Evictions and Other Tenant Protections Related to the Coronavirus." *NOLO*, February 4, 2021. www.nolo.com/legal-encyclopedia/emergency-bans-on-evictions-and-other-tenant-protections-related-to-coronavirus.html.

Office of the High Commissioner United Nations Human Rights. 2020a. "CRC and COVID-19 Statement." Accessed June 14, 2021. www.ohchr.org/en/hrbodies/crc/pages/crcindex.aspx.

Office of the High Commissioner United Nations Human Rights. 2020b. "UN Human Rights Treaty Bodies Call for Human Rights Approach in Fighting COVID-19." Accessed June 14, 2021. www.ohchr.org/EN/NewsEvents/Pages/DisplayNews.aspx?NewsID=25742&LangID=E.

Parshley, Lois. 2020. "The Emerging Long-Term Complications of COVID-19." *Vox*, June 12, 2020. www.vox.com/2020/5/8/21251899/coronavirus-long-term-effects-symptoms.

Patrick, Stephan. 2020. "The Lack of a National Policy Agenda for Children During COVID-19 and Beyond Causes Great Harm." *Stat News*, August 31, 2020. www.statnews.com/2020/08/31/lack-national-policy-agenda-children-covid-19-harm/.

Patterson, Michelle. 2014. "Setting the Stage for Chronic Health Problems: Cumulative Childhood Adversity Among Homeless Adults with Mental Illness in Vancouver, British Columbia." *BMC Public Health* 14: 350.

Peck, Emily. 2020. "An Unprecedented 14 Million Children Are Going Hungry Due to COVID-19." *Huffington Post*, July 10, 2020. www.huffpost.com/entry/14-million-children-going-hungry-coronavirus_n_5f07777cc5b6480493cd5e87.

Preston, Caroline. 2020. "How Will Social Isolation Affect Our Kids?" *KQED*, April 14, 2020. www.kqed.org/mindshift/55729/how-will-social-isolation-during-covid-19-affect-our-kids.

Saplakoglu, Yasmine. 2020. "COVID-19 Looks Different in Children." *Live Science*, May 13, 2020. www.livescience.com/children-coronavirus-infections.html.

Stanley-Becker, Issac, and Lena Sun. 2020. "COVID-19 Is Devastating Communities of Color." *Washington Post*, December 18, 2020. www.washingtonpost.com/health/2020/12/18/covid-vaccine-racial-equity/.

Stracqualursi, Veronica. 2021. "Fauci Says Lack of Candor from Trump Administration Likely Cost Lives." *CNN*, January 22, 2021. www.cnn.com/2021/01/22/politics/fauci-biden-covid-approach-cnntv/index.html.

Thomas, Sarah. 2014. "Dig Deep: Impacts and Implications of Rising Out-of-Pocket Health Care Costs." Accessed July 7, 2021. www2.deloitte.com/us/en/pages/life-sciences-and-health-care/articles/hidden-costs-of-health-care.html.

United Nations Refugee Agency. 2017. *A Guide to International Refugee Protection and Building State Asylum Systems*. Inter-Parliamentary Union and UNHCR. Accessed July 20, 2021. www.unhcr.org/3d4aba564.pdf.

United Nations Sustainable Development Group. 2020. "Policy Brief: Impact of COVID-19 on Children." Accessed June 14, 2021. https://unsdg.un.org/resources/policy-brief-impact-covid-19-children.

Vissing, Yvonne. 1997. *Out of Sight, Out of Mind: Homeless Children and Families in Small Town America*. Lexington: University of Kentucky Press.

Vissing, Yvonne. 2020. "Housing Distressed Children and the Coronavirus." *Medium*, June 17, 2020. https://medium.com/@yvissing/covid-children-and-housing-distress-98aaa2be8500.

Vissing, Yvonne. 2021. "The Pandemic and Housing-Distressed Children." *Rainbows in Our Windows: Childhood in the Time of Corona,* edited by Ruby Turok-Squire. London: Palgrave.

Vissing, Yvonne, Christopher Hudson, and Diane Nilan. 2020. *Changing the Paradigm of Homelessness.* New York, NY: Routledge.

Vissing, Yvonne, and Diane Nilan. 2020. "Homeless Children and COVID-19." *Contexts,* 2020. https://contexts.org/blog/inequality-during-the-coronavirus-pandemic/#nilan.

Wu, Katherine. 2020. "The Coronavirus Spares Most Kids: These Theories May Help Explain Why." *National Geographic,* March 25, 2020. www.nationalgeographic.com/science/2020/03/coronavirus-spares-most-kids-these-theories-may-help-explain-why/#close.

Zelizer, Vivian. 1981. *Pricing the Priceless Child: The Changing Social Value of Children.* New York, NY: Basic Books.

4 The Impact of COVID-19 on Children with Thalassemia and Their Families in India

Rachana Sharma

Introduction

The experiences of past pandemics show us that people with disabilities (PWDs) and their families suffer greatly during public health crises as access to critical medical supplies becomes a challenge and resources diminish (Campbell et al. 2009). Also, higher levels of social isolation and loneliness are widespread in response to physical distancing measures, resulting in increases in health problems such as heart disease and dementia (O' Sullivan and Bourgin 2010). Priestley and Hemingway (2007) argue that during crisis situations the discriminatory attitudes toward PWDs are heightened and can be particularly severe for individuals with specific kinds of disabilities.

Children in particular are more susceptible during infectious disease outbreaks. The literature on children during pandemics informs us that disruptions to children's routines have detrimental consequences (Fischer, Elliot, and Bertrand 2018). Beyond the immediate consequences, the social disruptions caused by unforeseen events present several risks to children's overall health, well-being, and protection. Drawing from examples of the latest outbreaks of infectious disease outbreaks (the 2016–17 cholera outbreak in Yemen and the 2014–16 ebolavirus disease (EVD) epidemic in West Africa), Fischer, Elliot, and Bertrand (2018) observed distinct challenges to traditional child protection responses. Within this broad literature on children and pandemics very little literature exists on children with disabilities. However, existent studies pertaining to how pandemics impact children with disabilities and their families do inform us that children with multiple disabilities are especially emotionally vulnerable during pandemics, particularly when coupled with quarantine isolation and lack of stimulating activities. The practice of social distancing during pandemics can be lethal in practice for PWDs, especially children, due to their dependence on others to meet their numerous physiological, social, emotional, and medical needs (D'Souza 2020).

Disability discourse informs us that disability is not an individual phenomenon but is more of a unique familial phenomenon and the experiences of disability and disablism are shared. As PWDs most often live as a part of their families and depend on a carer (Johns Hopkins University 2020), it is not just

DOI: 10.4324/9781003250937-6

children but the caregivers and the families of children with disabilities who go through similar copious challenges during societal crises. Therefore, it is important for us to understand the impacts of the coronavirus disease 2019 (COVID-19) pandemic on children with disabilities and their families.

In early 2020, severe acute respiratory syndrome coronavirus 2 (SARS-CoV-2) spread globally, affecting various aspects of human life. The biggest challenge brought by this virus has been the difficulties in treating COVID-19-affected patients and the compounded death toll, which spurred fear and panic among the public and governments all over the world. Initially, the majority of countries responded to this unforeseen public health crisis with containment measures to stop viral spread by coercing people to abide by lockdowns. Although, as the media reports, India performed fairly well in the first wave of COVID-19 management, in the second wave, India struggled with handling the COVID-19 spike. Handling this public health crisis has been a challenging task for regions that have been hit hard with the reality of limited existing health infrastructure, health personnel, and apposite planning (Jayachandran 2020). However, high-risk groups, specifically, and the concerns of PWDs in India have not been adequately given scholarly consideration. In the initial stages of pandemic management policies, PWDs were left behind. It was only through the efforts of disability rights activists that governments were persuaded to take pre-emptive, proactive, and effective measures to meet the economic, medical, social, psychological, and emotional needs of the differently abled. This chapter, therefore, intends to look into the challenges faced by children and youth with a blood disorder called thalassemia during the COVID-19 pandemic.

Thalassemics and SARS-CoV-2: A National and State Analysis

Thalassemia poses a serious public health threat globally. Under the Indian RPWD Act (2016) thalassemia is now considered a disability. As per the 2011 Census, nearly 26.8 million of approximately 1.39 billion people in India have a disability. India is known as the thalassemia capital of the world. Although, in the absence of National Registries of patients, the exact numbers are not known (Colah, Italia, and Gorakshakar 2017) yet, these estimates point out that there are nearly 42 million carriers of the β-thalassemia trait in India. Every year in India, more than 10,000 children are born with thalassemia, which accounts for approximately 10% of the total world incidence of thalassemia-affected children, and one in eight of thalassemia carriers lives in India. The prevalence of thalassemia ranges between 0.6% and 15% across South India. Among certain communities such as the Sindhis, Punjabis, Gujaratis, Bengalis, Mahars, Kolis, Saraswats, Lohanas, and Gaurs, the prevalence rates are higher. In West Bengal and North Eastern states, Hb E (a variant of hemoglobin) significantly contributes to the disease burden (Thiyagarajan et al. 2019).

In Punjab, the estimated record of patients suffering from thalassemia major collected by Mathew and Sobti (2018) is around 4,700 and this is a great undercount. They further asserted that in Punjab the magnitude of the problem is poorly defined and there is a paucity of clinical research with respect to the incidence, prevalence, morbidity, and mortality related to thalassemia. Mathew and Sobti (2018) further identified a partial registry of more than 1,890 thalassemia patients supported by various non-governmental organizations (NGOs) and government hospitals in a few districts of Punjab, including Ludhiana, Amritsar, Jalandhar, Patiala, and Faridkot where the majority of children are treated. Likewise in Punjab, Amritsar treats more than 170 children with thalassemia at government hospitals. Jalandhar has more than 80 children registered for blood transfusion. Chandigarh meets the requirement of nearly 350 patients who are registered with the Thalassemia Charitable Trust, PGIMER (Chitlangia 2020). As many as 270 thalassemia patients are enrolled with Dayanand Medical College and Hospital Ludhiana (Chitlangia 2020).

There are similar numbers of patients that come from Faridkot, Ferozepur, Muktsar Sahib, Moga, and Bathinda districts to visit the GMC hospital, Faridkot for treatment. Overall, the highest number of people with thalassemia are found in Patiala district of Punjab wherein they are registered by Thalassemic Children Welfare Association at the Paediatrics Department of Rajendra Hospital, Patiala (Singh et al. 2019). After Patiala district comes Chandigarh, and then Amritsar, followed by Ludhiana and Jalandhar from high to low registered patients. The pervasiveness of thalassemia in the global north has significantly decreased due to prenatal diagnostic testing and massive awareness campaigns. However, it has not been the same in the southern regions of the world. Perhaps the prevalence of thalassemics has increased in South Asian countries due to lack of awareness among the people, medical practitioners, particularly gynecologists, and due to inter-family marriage culture among certain groups (Saeed and Piracha 2016). Hossain et al. (2020) found that 67% of college students have not heard of "thalassemia" disease. Furthermore, 40% were reluctant to donate blood for thalassemia patients due to misconceptions and stigmatization.

Thalassemia is a life-long, genetic blood disorder, a life-threatening disease with no complete treatment (except bone marrow transplantation, which is beyond the economic reach of the majority, risky to life, and uncertain). Other than this, the majority of people with thalassemia are totally dependent on foreign blood that is usually administered to them every two to five weeks for their survival. In India, the requirement of blood units for their treatment is huge. Thalassemia is a complex disease not only because it involves complex treatment but also because it is associated with physiological complications like heart failure, hypogonadism, hypothyroidism, diabetes, and deformity of facial appearance. Furthermore, the social stigmatism can severely affect children's physical competence, their scholastic performance, self-esteem, social relationships, economic and psychological well-being, and the overall quality of life of the patients and their family (Ankush et al. 2019). Because in India there is still a huge unawareness among people regarding this life-threatening disease, there is a need to understand the social facets of disability and disablism during public health crises so that such patients are well taken care of in future medical management programs.

In order to understand the situation of thalassemics in India, and particularly in Punjab, during the ongoing pandemic, local and national reports and journal articles were rigorously analyzed. The clinical impact of SARS-CoV-2 particularly in thalassemia (transfusion and non-transfusion dependent) patients is neither known to date nor well defined (Marhaeni et al. 2020) and likewise goes with the non-clinical impacts. Through secondary sources of data I found that in the wake of COVID-19, the procurement of donor blood and socioeconomic support has been a critical challenge faced by children with thalassemia, not only in India but also globally.

Secondary sources point out that this pandemic followed by the lockdowns had a distressing impact on the lives of children and adolescents suffering from transfusion-dependent thalassemia. The foremost challenge that the thalassemia community encountered during this public health crisis was regarding the procurement of blood and medical supplies for treatment (Dhaliwal 2020; Pavate 2020). Media reports on shortage of blood supply were reported in various parts of the world, such as China and Iran, during the lockdown period (Waheed et al. 2020). During normal circumstances, access to blood remains a persistent challenge as the majority of blood donations come to blood banks through regular camps held in educational institutions and religious congregations, and the number of blood donors are still low compared to the global north. Sorowar, Raheem, and Siddiqee (2020) found that in Kolkata (India), over 80% of blood supply in 108 blood banks comes from blood donation camps. The COVID-19 pandemic exacerbated the circumstances as social life was ceased as a policy move to restrict the spread of the virus. With hardly any blood donation camps held anywhere in the country and community, and with NGOs postponing their blood donation programs due to the national lockdown imposed in the beginning of March 2020, very few donors volunteered for blood donations due to the fear of getting infected with SARS-CoV-2.

As hospitals were converted into COVID-19 treatment centers, fear mounted more among blood donors, leading to depletion of blood units and a critical shortage of volunteers. Likewise, due to closure of public transport it was difficult, and in some cases even impossible, at times for both blood donors and recipients to reach out to each other for help. It is important to note here that as blood transfusion treatment for thalassemics is confined to a few hospitals in urban areas in India it has been a tough time for those coming from smaller cities, towns, and villages (Chitlangia 2020). Furthermore, as a rapid testing facility was made available for priority sections, the patients worried about being silent carriers of the virus.

In the case of India, Maharashtra, West Bengal, Uttar Pradesh, Punjab, and many other states of the country pushed concerns of the aggrieved thalassemic community. As a result, in April 2020 the Union Health Minister of India, Harsh Vardhan, directed states to act mindfully toward those suffering from thalassemia and ensure that their medical needs were met. Through community mobilization and social media awareness, relaxations and arrangements ranging from mobile hospital vans, door-to-door collection of blood, blood banks, procurement of blood by NGOs, and organization of small-scale camps were made by families of children with thalassemia. Despite such efforts, a significant portion of patients were put into a life-threatening condition caused by the acute shortage of blood supply.

Similarly, the financial cost of transfusion-dependent patients is usually very high. As the majority of thalassemia patients come from vulnerable backgrounds, their economic, emotional, and psychological needs have been under-assessed. Although the Indian government took several preemptive, proactive, and effective measures to meet the economic as well as medical needs of thalassemics, there is a need to understand these other dimensions of health impacted by disability and disablism.

Methodology

The broad objective of this research is to create awareness regarding the struggles of adolescents and children with thalassemia in developing countries. By placing this study in the context of the ongoing pandemic, this chapter intends to draw the attention of policymakers for designing inclusive public health preparedness strategies for future unforeseen health crises. The major objectives of this research are (a) to explore the challenges children with disabilities and their families are facing during COVID-19, (b) to examine the management and coping strategies of children with thalassemia and their families during the lockdown, and (c) to examine how COVID-19 changes access to and inclusiveness of care.

Methods

This qualitative study was conducted between April and December 2020, enrolling a total of 30 parents (the parent who takes their child for treatment) of children suffering from beta-thalassemia from the state of Punjab (India). Punjab has 22 districts. The respondents were selected through convenience and random sampling. Interviews were conducted through both offline (14 participants) as well as online and telephonic modes (16 participants). Several thalassemic societies from Punjab were approached online and their members were contacted through the snowball method. In-person (from hospitals treating people with thalassemics) as well as telephonic interviews (as the respondents feared social contact) were conducted using a detailed interview guide. Also, online questionnaires were distributed to respondents through various social media platforms related to various thalassemic societies and NGOs. Familiarity with the topic allowed the researcher to bring out the concerns of the target community in a detailed manner. Online interviews also helped in ensuring randomness and spread, which helped in getting an overall extent of the problem.

The questionnaire consisted of 33 questions and was divided into three parts. The first part explored the background of the respondents, their treatment details, and their perceptions about the pandemic. The second section of the questionnaire focused on respondents' problems and concerns during the pandemic and how it affected their children, and the third section focused on coping strategies and parental opinions on the COVID-19 management plan. The questionnaire and schedule consisted of both open- and closed-ended questions; sufficient options were also given to the respondents for expressing their opinions in case of closed-ended questions. Primary as well secondary sources were consulted for this study. The author gathered COVID-19 data from various public health sources, such as reports, articles, and media coverage to further contextualize the data.

For this chapter the term "chronic illness" is defined as a long-term or permanent event in the life of an individual. In the initial literature on chronic illness, shame and social stigma felt by ill persons and their caregivers were the main focus; however, recent studies place more emphasis on the patient's experiences (Kehoe 2009). According to Bury (1982 and 2001), illness narratives are important to study because they inform as to how people with illness perceive their lives, and the changes or disruption caused by illness. In this context, the narratives portrayed in this chapter explain how the present situation of the COVID-19 pandemic has brought in changes and additional challenges in the lives of people living with the chronic disease, beta-thalassemia. The chapter therefore aims to sensitize the scientific and social community toward thalassemia and the hardships caused by it, especially during the public health crisis so as to diminish their social exclusion and invisibility of the needs of the differently abled in future pandemic management programs.

Subjects

The socioeconomic profile of the respondents indicates that the average age of the respondents is 39 years. Twenty-four (80%) respondents in this study were women—mothers of children with thalassemia who were actively engaged primary caregivers in the treatment of their children. Twenty-three (77%) respondents were in a union/married, five (17%) were separated and divorced, and two (7%) were widowers/widowed. Nineteen (63%) respondents lived with joint families, eight (27%) lived in nuclear family households, and three (10%) lived in extended family households. Twenty-two (73%) were non-working while the other eight (27%) were working. Average monthly family income of the respondents was INR 26,400 (about 355 USD). Sixteen (53%) respondents had two children, nine (30%) had more than two children, and five (17%) had only one child. Out of the total, 22 (73%) had one thalassemic child and eight (27%) had two children with thalassemia. The average age of the respondents' children who were under treatment was 14.75 years. Sixteen (53%) respondents came from villages, while seven (23%) were from nearby towns, and the same number of respondents hailed from the city where their treating center/hospital was located. Twenty-one (70%) respondents used public transport to reach the hospital, while nine (30%) used their own vehicle prior to lockdown. With regard to period of treatment, 16 (53%) respondents stated that they visited the hospital every 15–20 days, and 14 (47%) stated that they visited the hospital once a month for their child's blood transfusion. Twenty-three (77%) of the children were registered for treatment in civil or government hospitals and the remaining seven (23%) respondents stated that their child's treatment was received in private hospitals.

Challenges Faced by Children with Thalassemia and Their Families

Parental perspectives revealed that children with thalassemia and their families faced social and medical challenges. Interviews addressed how parents and children were impacted by the ongoing pandemic, and parents were asked questions including those regarding the impact on treatment and overall child and family well-being. For children and youth with thalassemia and their families, the pandemic and consequent lockdown brought diverse challenges, including sourcing essential supplies, accessing medical assistance, exercising social distancing for safety, travelling safely, managing finances, and maintaining general well-being.

Twenty-two (73%) of the respondents did not possess any information about the COVID-19 pandemic until a national lockdown and curfew was imposed and were not mentally prepared for the lockdown. Followed by the lockdown, immediate parental and child concerns related to blood procurement (97% of respondents), getting infected with the virus (93%), threat to life of the child (77%), accessing the hospital (83%), getting medicines (83%), and management of finances (67%) (see Table 4.1).

For instance, a 42-year-old mother of a 16-year-old stated the following.

> The burden of managing blood and more importantly getting it on time is the main worry and source of stress for us. My child and I feel quite heavy

Table 4.1 Worries and challenges faced by the families of the patient

Challenges	Total* (%)
Managing blood	29 (97)
Safety/infection risk	28 (93)
Procurement of medicine, equipment, and management of health check-up	25 (83)
Access to hospital and medical consultation	25 (83)
Threat to life of ward	23 (77)
Management of finance	20 (67)

★ Multiple responses.

at heart thinking about the safety and management of treatment all the time, it is very taxing and emotionally and physically draining. We have left everything to God, I hope we survive through this.

As the physical distancing became a norm during the lockdown, social distancing naturally followed, which impacted children with thalassemia in different ways. As the myths and home-tried treatments circulated, fear of acquiring COVID-19 through physical proximity and touch occupied the minds of the masses, and families faced difficulty in procuring blood for their children.

The dearth of blood forced 16 (53.3%) children out of the 30 families to declare their disability/thalassemic status to their relatives, wider networks, and also publicly on social media so as to arrange blood donors. Disability in India is associated with stigma and much shame; nearly 13 (43%) respondents felt that this would affect their and their child's social status post-pandemic. One mother shared the following:

> My child is 6 years old, and we have never told our relatives or anyone about the disability status of our child till now. However, because of the current situation and the need to find blood donors, we had to reveal the disability to our relatives and friends to seek help. Obviously, disability carries a stigma and shame in our society as disabled and their families are looked down upon. I feel this would change the way people see my child, after all this ends. There was no other choice.

Another father (48 years old) who lost his first child to thalassemia complications and had a second child under treatment for thalassemia recalled the following:

> I am feeling it is the same situation as it was some ten–fifteen years back; we used to beg before people to donate blood as blood donations were rare at that time and hardly any people knew about thalassemia. Now also, due to lockdown and fear of COVID-19, no one is willing to come to the hospital for blood donations. We understand their concern, they understand ours but it does not help. I spend most of my time these days making calls and requests to friends and relatives and people to come forward for blood donations.

Blood transfusion is vital for thalassemic patients lest they start developing symptoms of weakness in the body and other complications. Hence, for chronically ill thalassemic patients, time-bound therapies have to be taken care of, which could mean regular visits (ranging from every 15 to 30 days) to the hospital for transfusion, monthly medical check-ups, prescribed medicines, and associated medical routines.

As COVID-19 cases spiked in Punjab many of the hospitals were transformed into treatment centers for COVID-19 patients, aggravating the worries of the parents. This created panic not only among the patients and their families but also among blood donors due to the fear of risk of safety and exposure to the virus, as revealed by nearly all of the respondents. Additionally, 25 respondents faced problems in procurement of medicines and in getting their medical consultations, as doctors became unavailable. Although some doctors continued attending to their patients telephonically, they could not meet the requirements of children with thalassemia. Twenty parents stated that they could not get tests conducted on time due to the fear of getting the virus. Some delayed it on their own volition due to the financial crunch caused by the slowdown in businesses, salary cuts, and pandemic-related unemployment.

Nearly 25 families faced barriers to hospital appointments and consultations with doctors. Managing visits to the hospital was still relatively easy for the families living within the city as they could move without passes/permits. However, for those coming from rural areas or nearby towns, reaching the hospital was initially quite inconvenient. As community support and volunteering became widespread and restrictions were relaxed, less discomfort was felt by the respondents during their visits. Generally speaking, the studies indicate that troubles faced by PWDs in rural India are far greater than those faced by urbanites. The major source of strain and inconvenience was to obtain movement passes due to complicated procedures. Even when families possessed the required movement passes, seven (37%) families reported that the accessibility came with great difficulties. Explaining this discomfort, a mother (38 years old) of a 5-year-old child stated:

> For me, traveling from my village to the hospital is no easy task these days, I have not been able to manage a pass/permit, public transport is not available; hence I come with great difficulty after seeking help from some or the other person. In case the police stop we bring our disability certificate and proofs along.

Twenty-three parents felt at risk and felt that their child was under higher risk of death.

A mother (aged 31 years) of a 3-year-old with thalassemia stated the following:

> I do not know where to take my child for a transfusion. I tried to inquire about transfusion facilities in nearby private hospitals as well, but to my disappointment, COVID-19 patients are admitted there, too. I am feeling quite scared thinking of the safety of my child.

As per the directive issued by the National Blood Transfusion Council (NTBC) there is no clinical data as of now to suggest that individuals are at risk of contracting COVID-19 through the blood donation process (Marhaeni 2020). However, patients coming to the hospital for their regular transfusions are always at risk of contracting COVID-19 through other patients or medical attendants who might be asymptomatic carriers of the virus. Additionally, out of the total respondents only four (13%) stated that along with other problems, the pandemic caused additional stress and conflict within their family and in one case it also led to abandonment of the child by the family.

Likewise, for children the pandemic situation has been quite stressful. Reports on the general impact of COVID-19 on children indicate that with schools closed and online education becoming a new normal without real social interaction and any social exposure, children faced great difficulties staying in confined spaces, which often led to frustration, restlessness, and aggressive behaviors (UNESCO 2020). This situation was found to be more intense for children with disabilities. The caregivers of children with thalassemia were asked to share how their children's overall well-being was impacted by the pandemic. Other than academic (100% of the respondents agreed) the respondents also pointed out emotional as well as psychological impacts.

Out of 30, 16 (53%) respondents stated that the pandemic impacted the mental well-being of their children. Of the 16 respondents, 12 (34%) stated that their children felt quite lonely, 11 (31%) stated that their child had problems concentrating in their studies, nine (26%) stated that their child looks more worried than before, and three (9%) stated that their child experienced poor mental health. Furthermore, parents of the children were also asked about their own mental well-being during the pandemic. Twenty-five (30.4%) parents felt a high level of stress, 20 (24%) parents felt anxiety, 19 (23%) parents felt irritability, nine (11%) felt fearfulness, and nine (11%) felt anger as a consequence of COVID-19. Therefore, health-related anxiety, depression, low mood, fear, irritability, anger, nervousness, emotional exhaustion, frustration, boredom, numbness, and insomnia were some of the psycho-emotive states felt by the respondents as well as the children. Additionally, the majority of the parents (19; 63%) strongly agreed and eight (27%) moderately agreed to the question "Do you think COVID-19 has impacted children with thalassemia?"

Overall, it can be said from the above-stated findings that there are unique stresses and challenges that children and their families went through during the COVID-19 crisis, which impacted their physical health, mental/emotional health, and overall well-being. Many of the families hailed from lower socioeconomic backgrounds so the pandemic brought massive economic and subsequently psychological stress. Although on March 17, 2020, the Government of India released a three-month advance pension to PWDs (Balaji 2020), children with thalassemia were left behind from such support, which caused more distress to patients and their families.

Coping and Management

Coping strategies and building behaviors play an imperative role in the life of an individual for maintaining one's overall well-being in sudden and strenuous situations. For families having specially abled, such building behaviors and strategies are essential since they impact the psychosocial health and overall well-being of the child. In this part of the chapter, I analyze the coping strategies adopted by children with thalassemia and their families to tackle this

Table 4.2 Coping mechanisms

Strategies	Total* (%)
Prayers/spirituality/fate	29 (15)
Seeking help from community	26 (13)
Adding recreation to life	27 (14)
More optimism	26 (13)
Humor	24 (12)
Cooperation	22 (11)
More family and social integration	16 (8)
Sought financial help from relatives	12 (6)
Home sample collection facility	11 (5.6)

* Multiple responses.

unpleasant scenario. Respondents were asked several questions pertaining to coping behavior and strategies they and their children adopted to tackle the unprecedented changes caused in their life due to the pandemic (see Table 4.2).

Out of 193 responses, 29 (15%) caregivers stated prayers/spirituality/fate as the most important destressors. A mother of an eight-year-old stated:

> I am constantly worried about my child getting infected with the virus. It disturbs me severely. I cry at night thinking about her survival, but now I have decided to put it all in the hand of gods, I pray more than before.

Additionally, 26 (13%) families were able to manage blood donations through volunteers, friends, and their family. Twenty-seven (14%) caregivers expressed the use of coping behaviors such as physical recreation, 26 (13%) stated optimism, and 24 (12%) stated humor related to the virus and pandemic management policy as another building behavior to cut pandemic-related stress out of life. Similarly, 22 (11%) stated cooperation, 16 (8%) stated family and social integration (through social media audio-video applications and patient families planning for transfusion together) helped them to recoup a sense of normalcy in their as well as their child's life. As the pandemic also brought additional financial strain to each family in general, some of the patient families (12; 6%) were able to manage the financial aspects of medical needs by drawing upon their extended family networks. Likewise, out of the total, 11 (5.6%) utilized a "home sample collection" facility from private laboratories to get the routine tests for their children, whereas the remaining families often delayed their children's medical testing requirements.

As children stayed confined to their homes during the pandemic, they coped with their daily affairs and illness-related needs in various ways. Twenty-eight (31%) parents stated that educating children on myths and prevention by practicing sanitization, wearing masks, etc., helped the children in coping with their treatments safely. Also, 27 (30%) stated "being careful" and 22 (24%)

stated that they increased their children's screen time (social media) to deflect their children's worries about the pandemic. Talking to other peer-patients and friends on phones was another way by which children managed staying safe and engaged during the pandemic, as stated by 14 (15%) respondents.

In the end, it can be said that children with thalassemia and their families experienced diverse hardships during the COVID-19 pandemic, with little institutional support especially during early phases of the pandemic. The experiences and impacts of the pandemic were felt squarely by the children and their families. During this tough time, coping with disability and disablism has been quite strenuous; however, through positive building behavior, social cohesion, and with the support of health professionals and the government, patients and families managed to cope and seek relief.

Discussion

Inequitable response to COVID-19 has made lives of differently abled children and their families difficult, and has heightened their vulnerability and marginality from society. Concerns of children/ adolescents with thalassemia have been invisible, overlooked, and uncushioned in the current pandemic health management policy. For children diagnosed with thalassemia and their families, the pandemic and the consequent lockdown brought in diverse challenges impacting the general well-being of the children and their families. The challenges ranged from procurement of blood for transfusion, sourcing of essential supplies, access to medical assistance, irregularity in the treatment, hinderance to travel, management of finances and failure to harness the community support. As the pandemic has still not subsided and the problems the thalassemics faced in the previous phase are likely to flash in again, restrictive measures are being re-adopted by the Government of India as the COVID-19 continues to affect different people in different ways . Also, it is feared that the problems related to blood supply management are likely to be severe if blood donations are not received prior to the people opting for vaccination drive (across age groups) as after getting vaccinated people cannot donate blood for a minimum of 60 days. It is therefore important for the stakeholders to consider these loopholes in the new pandemic preparedness strategy so that the issues of transfusion-dependent children/adolescents are prioritized and their concerns are not ignored as they were in the first wave of pandemic. There is a need to make health services sensitive to the needs of children with disabilities.

In this regard it is important to put forth that as the second wave of the pandemic brings us back to similar situations, the ongoing pandemic management programs should prioritize the needs of the wider community of persons living with disabilities. As the ongoing wave is taking the toll on young lives, the governments need to design adequate safety nets for these derelict sections of the society who face greater risk of exclusion, lack of access to crucial services and poverty until the pandemic abates.

Acknowledgments

The author is thankful to all the respondents for taking part in the study and providing their personal information.

References

Ankush, Ankush, Amit Dias, M.P. Silveira, Yash Talwadker, and Joachim Piedade Souza. 2019. "Quality of Life in Children with Thalassemia Major Following Up at a Tertiary Care Center in India (GOTQoL)." *International Journal of Contemporary Paediatrics* 6 (1): 168–75. http://dx.doi.org/10.18203/2349-3291.ijcp20185203.

Balaji, Roshani. 2020. "How Coronavirus Crisis Has Made It Difficult for People with Disability to Cope with Daily Tasks." Accessed April 15, 2020. https://yourstory.com/socialstory/2020/04/coronavirus-lockdown-people-with-disability-challenges.

Bury, Michael. 1982. "Chronic Illness as Biographical Disruption." *Sociology of Health and Illness* 4 (2): 167–82. https://doi.org/10.1111/1467-9566.ep11339939.

Bury, Michael. 2001. "Illness Narratives: Fact or Fiction?" *Sociology of Health and Illness* 23 (3): 263–85. https://doi.org/10.1111/1467-9566.00252.

Campbell, Vincent A., Jamylle A. Gilyard, Lisa Sinclair, Tom Sternberg, and June I. Kailes. 2009. "Preparing for and Responding to Pandemic Influenza: Implications for People with Disabilities." *American Journal of Public Health* 99 (2): 294–300. http://doi.org/10.2105/AJPH.2009.162677.

Chitlangia, Risha. 2020. "Covid Crisis: Thalassemia Patients Struggle to Find Hospital Beds, Blood for Transfusion." *Hindustan Times,* June 15, 2020. www.hindustantimes.com/delhi-news/covid-crisis-thalassemia-patients-struggle-to-find-hospital-beds-blood-for-transfusion/story-04oPG2iwwzxSp7FOHJfQ7H.html.

Colah, Roshan, Khushnooma Italia, and Ajit Gorakshakar. 2017. "Burden of Thalassemia in India: The Road Map for Control." *Paediatric Haematology Oncology Journal* 2 (4): 79–84.

Dhaliwal, Tanbir. 2020. "PGI, Another Herculean Task: Soliciting Blood Donors." *Hindustan Times,* April 12, 2020. www.hindustantimes.com/chandigarh/for-pgi-another-herculean-task-soliciting-blood-donors/story-mgN4gAoqrNNfbyBbn8vpvL.html.

D'Souza, Avalanne. 2020. "How to Support Children with Learning Disabilities Amid the COVID-19 Pandemic." *The Indian Express,* June 23, 2020. https://indianexpress.com/article/lifestyle/life-style/how-to-support-children-special-needs-6470363/.

Fischer, Hanna-Tina, Leilani Elliot, and Sara Lim Bertrand. 2018. "Guidance Note: Protection of Children During Infectious Disease Outbreaks." *The Alliance for Child Protection in Humanitarian Action.* Accessed July 22, 2021. https://resourcecentre.savethechildren.net/node/13328/pdf/protection_of_children_during_infectious_disease_outbreak_guidance_note.pdf.

Hossain, Mohammad Sorowar, Mahbub Hasan, Enayetur Raheem, Muhammad Sougatul Islam, Abdullah Al Mosabbir, Mary Petrou, Paul Telfir, and Mahbubel Siddiqee. 2020. "Lack of Knowledge and Misperceptions About Thalassaemia Among College Students in Bangladesh: A Cross-Sectional Baseline Study." *Orphanet Journal of Rare Disease* 15 (54). https://ojrd.biomedcentral.com/articles/10.1186/s13023-020-1323-y#citeas.

Jayachandran, Jesna. 2020. "The Media Coverage of Drugs and Alcohol in Punjab During COVID-19 Pandemic." *Asian Politics and Policy* 12 (3): 469–76.

Johns Hopkins University. 2020. "COVID-19 Poses Unique Challenges for People with Disabilities." *Johns Hopkins University*, April 23, 2020. https://hub.jhu.edu/2020/04/23/how-covid-19-affects-people-with-disabilities/.

Kehoe, Claire. 2009. "The Sociology of Chronic Illness: An Experiential Account of the Benefits of a Sociological Perspective to Students of Medicine." *Socheolas: Limerick Student Journal of Sociology* 1 (1): 46–54.

Marhaeni, Wulandewi, Andreas Budi Wijaya, Khairiyadi, Munawaroh, and Hendriyono. 2020. "Coagulation Abnormalities Due to COVID-19 in a Child with Thalassemia." *The Indian Journal of Paediatrics* 88 (4): 1–2. https://doi.org/10.1007/s12098-020-03600-9.

Mathew, Amrith, and Praveen C. Sobti. 2018. "The Burden of Thalassemia in Punjab: A Roadmap Forward." *Paediatric Haematology Oncology* 2 (4): 85–7.

O'Sullivan, Tracey, and Maxime Bourgoin. 2010. "Vulnerability in an Influenza Pandemic: Looking Beyond Medical Risk." *ResearchGate* (October 2010). www.researchgate.net/publication/282817477_Vulnerability_in_an_Influenza_Pandemic_Looking_Beyond_Medical_Risk.

Pavate, Veeresh. 2020. "Thalassemia: With the 'Red' in the Bag Amid COVID-19 Reflections." *Journal of Patient Experience- Special Interest COVID-19* 7 (4): 439–41.

Priestley, Mark, and Laura Hemingway. 2007. "Disability and Disaster Recovery: A Tale of Two Cities?" *Journal of Social Work in Disability & Rehabilitation* 5 (3–4): 23–42.

Saeed, Umar, and Zahra Zahid Piracha. 2016. "Thalassemia: Impact of Consanguineous Marriages on Most Prevalent Monogenic Disorders of Humans." *Asian Pacific Journal of Tropical Disease* 6 (10): 837–40.

Singh, Gurmeet, Yash Mitra, Kamaldeep Kaur, and Kanchan Bhardwaj. 2019. "Knowledge, Attitude and Practices of Parents of Thalassemic Children in District Patiala, Punjab, India." *Public Health Review: International Journal of Public Health Research* 6 (1): 25–34.

Sorowar, Hossain M., Enayetur Raheem, and Mahbubul H. Siddiqee. 2020. "The Forgotten People with Thalassemia in the Time of COVID-19: South Asian Perspective." *Orphanet Journal of Rare Diseases* 15 (September): 265.

Thiyagarajan, Rulmani, Sudip Bhattacharya, Neha Sharma, Abhay Srivastava, and Deepak Kumar Dhar. 2019. "Need for a Universal Thalassemia Screening Programme in India? A Public Health Perspective." *Journal of Family Medicine and Primary Care* 8 (5): 1528–32.

UNESCO. 2020. "Life in the Times of COVID-19: A Guide for Parents of Disabled Children." www.niepmd.tn.nic.in/documents/parents_guide_covid_19_080520.pdf.

Waheed, Usman, Akhlaq Wazeer, Noore Saba, and Zahida Qasim. 2020. "COVID-19 Pandemic: Implications on Blood Transfusion Needs of Thalassemia Major Patients." *Global Journal of Transfusion Medicine* 5 (3): 235–36. https://doi.org/10.4103/GJTM.GJTM_82_20.

Part 2

Unmasking Institutional Entanglements

5 Youth at the Margins
Continuity of Services During the COVID-19 Pandemic

Andrea N. Hunt and Tammy Rhodes

Data from the National Survey of Children's Health highlights that 16.5% of youth in the sample (aged 0–17 years) were diagnosed with a mental health disorder but nearly half of those children were not receiving needed treatment or counseling from a mental health professional (Whitney and Peterson 2019). For youth, access to treatment is more complicated than for adults because youth may have limited access to intensive mental health treatment in school-based settings, and depending on their age, they may not be able to access community-based services independently. Further data from the Kaiser Family Foundation found that more than one in ten adolescents had anxiety and/or depression prior to the pandemic (Panchal et al. 2021). These data along with the public attention on suicide rates among youth illustrate the extent of the mental health crisis prior to coronavirus disease 2019 (COVID-19). With the pandemic, mental health and youth services professionals are projecting a more severe mental health crisis, with increases in depressive episodes and anxiety among youth resulting from isolation and familial job loss, substance use, and domestic violence (Courtney et al. 2020; Hine et al. 2020; Ornell et al. 2020; World Health Organization 2020).

The COVID-19 pandemic created an increased need for youth services in a system that was already ineffective for many vulnerable, minoritized, and marginalized youth and families. For many youth, school closures disrupted their school-based mental health services and limited their exposure to mandatory reporters (Cohen and Bosk 2020). The National Survey of Drug Use and Health found that 16% of adolescents received mental health services in a specialty mental health setting (e.g., inpatient care or private practice) and another 14.2% of adolescents received some type of mental health services from a school setting in 2018 (SAMHSA 2019). The Substance Abuse and Mental Health Services Administration and Centers for Medicare and Medicaid Services (2019) were already aware that many youth received services in schools from school counselors, social workers, or community-based partners that provide in-school treatment and issued a *Joint Informational Bulletin* in 2019 (pre-COVID-19) to provide guidance to states and school systems that were already overwhelmed with the needs of youth on addressing mental health and substance use issues in schools (McCance-Katz and Lynch 2019). For other youth who received

DOI: 10.4324/9781003250937-8

services from community-based programs associated with juvenile probation, those services were also halted or moved online. While suspending some of the in-person requirements of juvenile probation was in line with public health recommendations (McBride 2020), there were unintended consequences related to the continuity of care during COVID-19. Many community-based programs and agencies were ill-equipped to offer virtual services and had little experience with tele-mental health models (Posick et al. 2020).

Many youth—either those receiving school-based mental health services or youth on probation ordered to community-based programs—were left with limited support networks during the largest collective crisis of their lifetime. This research provides a synthesis and critical examination of the literature on the delivery of trauma-informed services during COVID-19. Trauma-informed care recognizes the range of traumas that youth experience, including the trauma associated with a global pandemic that exacerbated racial and economic issues for families that were already experiencing marginalization. COVID-19 led to further disparities in income, employment, housing, health access, and education. This research provides recommendations at the institutional, organizational, and interactional levels for practitioners working with youth that address the continuity of services during COVID-19.

Trauma-Informed Care and Youth Services

Substance Abuse and Mental Health Services Administration (2014) defines trauma as "an event, series of events, or set of circumstances that is experienced by an individual as physically or emotionally harmful or threatening and that has lasting adverse effects on the individual's functioning and physical, social, emotional, or spiritual well-being." Felitti et al.'s (1998) research was seminal in understanding the relationship between childhood trauma and later life experiences, and the body of research on adverse childhood experiences (ACEs) all stemmed from this. Bryant-Davis (2005) focused on multiculturalism and how trauma operates at the interpersonal (e.g., physical or sexual violence) and societal levels (e.g., racism and homophobia). More recently, Imad (2020) extended the literature on trauma to educational settings and suggests that educators and service providers need to consider how trauma shapes youth experiences in the classroom and their overall well-being.

Trauma-informed care includes transparency through connection and communication, collaboration, youth empowerment, and an intersectional lens. These approaches are critical for understanding the continuity of care for youth services during COVID-19. Youth and families experienced significant disruptions in their daily lives because of the pandemic and likely experienced an increased need for services while service providers also struggled with the same disruptions. Youth lost many of the activities that provide structure to their daily lives (e.g., school, extracurriculars, social interactions, and support systems) and over time these losses can lead to feelings of isolation and hopelessness and worsen symptoms that were already present. Many youth whose homes were unstable prior to the pandemic lost the external resources that provided stable and safe environments away from their homes (Courtney et al. 2020).

Research also suggests that COVID-19 led to increased parental stress related to higher levels of anxiety among their children, strain associated with parental/caregiver job loss, financial disruptions, and even deaths associated with COVID-19 (Chaturvedi, Kumar Vishwakarma, and Singh 2020; Lee et al. 2021). Parents with higher stress and symptoms of depression were less likely to be prepared for remote learning (Lee et al. 2021) and may not have the skills, capacity, or time to provide an ongoing stable and stimulating environment that is conducive to learning. The lockdown of schools and move to remote learning also highlighted disparities between families. Some rural, marginalized, and minoritized families lacked access to technology and had insufficient and minimal Internet access. COVID-19 increased the time spent in online classes and self-study, changed the mediums used for learning, and affected sleeping habits and daily fitness routines (Chaturvedi, Kumar Vishwakarma, and Singh 2020). This in turn can add to the cumulative effect of disadvantage and have larger implications for youth development.

Courtney et al. (2020) also found that an increase in anxiety happens when there is a shift away from meeting higher-order needs, such as self-actualization, as evidenced in Maslow's (1943) hierarchy of needs to meeting basic physiological and safety needs (e.g., food, shelter, and health) that feel threatened during a global pandemic. Henderson (2020) suggests that some youth from marginalized and minoritized communities may have had to contribute financially to the household or even become the primary income earner if a parent/caregiver lost their job. While unemployment increased for youth during COVID-19, Black and Hispanic girls had higher labor force participation rates than other youth (Bauer, Lu, and Moss 2020). Youth may have also had to assist with caregiving for aging or sick family members and/or younger siblings if adults in the household were considered essential workers and picked up multiple shifts or felt pressured to work more than before to keep their jobs in a tenuous labor market. Little data is available on youth caregivers. However, a recent study by the National Alliance for Caregiving and AARP (2020) found that prior to COVID-19 7% of caregivers for adults reported that a child helped provide care. This means that at least 3.4 million children under the age of 18 in the United States (US) were assisting with caregiving for an adult in 2019, which was more common among Hispanic, Black/African-American, and Asian-American families.

Youth and families that were homeless or in transitional or temporary housing experienced even greater effects from COVID-19 (see Vissing 2021, this volume). In addition to structural racism, homophobia, transphobia, and sexism that often lead to disparate rates of homelessness and to its negative outcomes, homeless youth and families still had to consider COVID-19-related safety measures while having a decreased ability to meet their basic needs and increased rates of emotional distress (Auerswald, Adams, and Lightfoot 2020). While emergency housing may have been an option, it was limited in many areas and kinship-based care comes with some additional risks, such as living with older family members who were at high risk of contracting COVID-19 or living in overcrowded housing. Many of the families (e.g., Black and Native American) that have an increased likelihood of housing insecurity also saw increased rates of COVID-19 and earlier mortality among its victims. It is also important to mention that during all of this youth were witnessing and processing police brutality and racial violence in person and on social media that can lead to trauma. The combined effect of COVID-19 and racial violence can increase feelings of despair, social isolation, and hyper-vigilance. Now more than ever, trauma-informed practices have taken center stage in addressing the continuity of mental health services and community-based probation services for youth during the COVID-19 pandemic.

Access to Mental Health Services

Pandemics such as COVID-19 have population level mental health effects that impact both youth and families (Endale, St. Jean, and Birman 2020). Mental health services, especially those for youth, have long been underfunded. COVID-19 exacerbated this and brought increased attention to the barriers in accessing existing services in some areas and the lack of services in other areas. Rightfully so, the primary concern during the first wave of COVID-19 was on physical health. However, this had larger implications for many inpatient mental health services in hospital settings where beds were needed for COVID-19 patients and outpatient mental health services that were also temporarily halted because of concerns for physical safety.

Courtney et al. (2020, 688) suggest that "as a result of the COVID-19 pandemic, disaster psychiatry is becoming a core component of work for mental health professionals around the world." In addition, many practitioners have had to learn how to use telemental health (also referred to as telehealth, telebehavioral health, telepsychology, and virtual care) for the first time and counseling programs are now incorporating this modality more into their training than before. As Hunt (2020) points out, telemental health quickly became the solution to providing treatment in both inpatient and outpatient settings during the COVID-19 pandemic although different forms of telehealth have been used since the 1950s in mental health settings. Along with telemental health, there has been an increase in mental health apps focused on mindfulness, guided relaxation, and meditation.

While telemental health seems like an obvious choice for service delivery during the pandemic, there are additional considerations in the implementation of new therapeutic modalities that include the availability of technology, technological proficiency, access to stable Internet, concerns around privacy and confidentiality, and policy changes (Endale, St. Jean, and Birman 2020; Hunt 2020). In response to some of these concerns, the US Department of Health and Human Services allowed a limited waiver for the Health Insurance Portability and Accountability Act (HIPAA) rules. This means that tools that had not been

HIPAA compliant (e.g., Facetime) were now available to practitioners to use for screenings, evaluations, and treatment (Golberstein, Wen, and Miller 2020). With the challenges in mind, many providers transitioned to telemental health using a range of technologies (e.g., phones and computers) for flexible delivery as a way to disseminate accessible information to families and to continue outreach, case management, and psychosocial support. Telemental health is also an effective tool in trauma-focused cognitive-behavioral therapy similar to in-person treatment (Endale, St. Jean, and Birman 2020; Langarizadeh et al. 2017).

Jeffrey, Marlotte, and Hajal (2020) note that telemental health appointments give the provider a unique opportunity by seeing the client in their own homes. Early intervention services and some agencies affiliated with the Department of Human Resources (DHR) (i.e., those that are court-mandated) have a history of providing in-home services; however, this is often not the case with mental health professionals who provide treatment in office or school-based settings. COVID-19 and the use of telemental health have created opportunities out of necessity for parents/caregivers and providers to have conversations about the resources that they have access to in their home. With this information, providers can develop suitable activities and psychoeducation with limited materials that promote family–youth engagement, give parents/caregivers information on having conversations with their children about the pandemic and processing associated emotions such as stress, and suggest methods for creating or maintaining routines during a time of uncertainty (Endale, St. Jean, and Birman 2020; Jeffrey, Marlotte, and Hajal 2020). Endale, St. Jean, and Birman (2020) describe additional ways to provide services through telemental health, such as creating videos of providers guiding youth and/or parents/caregivers through activities, having group video calls for youth of similar ages and language to encourage social connectedness, and reading books to youth with positive mental health or COVID-19-related themes. Creative solutions such as these consider how structural barriers, basic needs of youth and families, and financial hardship impact continual engagement in the therapeutic process.

Vest Ettekal and Agans (2020) bring attention to the reduction and disruption in out-of-school time (OST) programs during COVID-19 other than direct mental health services that are essential ecological assets to youth development, mental health, and overall well-being. OST programs create opportunities for meaning and self-actualization, and include activities (e.g., social, sport, and skill-building) that encourage cognition, emotional regulation, teamwork, and goal setting. Some of these activities (e.g., sports) can be challenging to adapt to the virtual environment while others may be a little easier to accommodate. For example, 4H programs across the nation shifted many of their indoor and outdoor activities online and had to consider whether youth would have access to the materials or equipment needed to engage at home. Another consideration is how much assistance from adults may be needed and whether parents/caregivers are available (physically, mentally, or emotionally) to provide guidance in these activities. If parents/caregivers are available, they may need some direction themselves in how to lead or facilitate some of these activities. This level of connection with program providers and parents/caregivers benefits the success of direct (e.g., counseling) and indirect (e.g., social, sports, and skill-building activities) mental health services and empowers them to engage in developmentally appropriate, child-centered play despite income and resources (Jeffrey, Marlotte, and Hajal 2020). Another way to address youth and family needs is to engage youth in research and evaluation (i.e., needs-based assessments) (Vest Ettekal and Agans 2020) that can model collaboration, critical-thinking, personal agency, and prosocial development.

Youth Probation Services

On any given day, there are more than 48,000 youth confined in facilities in the US away from their homes (Sawyer 2019). With concerns growing around the spread of COVID-19, the National Governors Association issued a memo on March 30, 2020 addressing the negative impact of COVID-19 in the juvenile justice system (McBride 2020). The memo urged states to release youth to their communities to minimize the risk of mass infection rates while in confinement (McBride 2020; Rovner 2021). Judges and practitioners had to consider which youth in their care could safely be supervised at home or in a community-based setting (Rowe 2020). This was especially pertinent for youth who were confined for committing status offenses or revocations (Rovner 2021; Rowe 2020). However, data suggest that the racial and ethnic disparities in detainment persisted despite the call for release, with Black and Latinx youth remaining overrepresented in the juvenile justice system during COVID-19 (Annie E. Casey Foundation 2021).

The move toward diversion programs and other less restrictive environments had been happening for a while, but COVID-19 created an impetus for other alternatives besides confinement. For those youth who were released, families were strained by the effects of COVID-19 (e.g., sickness, death, mental health, and unemployment) and may not have had sufficient community-based support while their children remained on probation. Another factor to consider is the foster care-to-prison pipeline with some youth not having access to stable housing once released. Further, Goulette, Evans, and King (2016) explained that 2.9 million juveniles are raised by custodial grandparents in the absence of biological parents. With the elderly representing a high-risk group for COVID-19, the question becomes who is supervising or providing the necessary and required reports back to social workers or case managers when and if these juveniles are released to grandparents or older family members. Not only is there a lack of direct supervision but some may leave juvenile facilities only to become caregivers for siblings, while others may need a transitional living program in the absence of suitable family supports. Because of these factors, Leon, Rodas, and Greer (2020) describe youth in detention "at the intersection of invisibility and vulnerability given the impact of the virus on older populations and the unwavering dismissal of incarcerated kids."

León, Rodas, and Greer (2020) found that for those disproportionately Black and Latinx youth in confinement, COVID-19 had a huge impact on how they chose to spend their free time because of the increased restrictions and decreased funding. Their research highlights the issues with lack of communication about COVID-19 protocols and increased isolation. Isolation is detrimental to the mental health and neurological development of youth, particularly those with a history of trauma, which characterizes 80% of juveniles in the justice system (Dierkhising et al. 2013). In addition, the memo sent by the National Governors Association on March 30, 2020 included no guidance on leisure programming for youth in confinement.

Many juvenile detention centers lost financial funds and programming was removed because of required isolation within institutions. Administration believed that funding programs for incarcerated juveniles were no longer needed, when in fact it was needed more than ever. This has left youth in juvenile detention centers with a lack of interaction, removal of familial visiting times, and restrictions on services from outsider providers. The resulting social isolation has caused critical issues that case management from counseling, social workers, and other social service employees will address to ensure that the mental health of incarcerated juveniles is stabilized, and the services and resources of released juveniles are located and being utilized (Buchanan et al. 2020).

Recommendations

Barriers to youth services existed prior to COVID-19, with many youth advocates, practitioners, and activists lobbying for additional funding and working tirelessly to increase access to mental health and community-based support services. The COVID-19 pandemic amplified the issues around access. There are several different potential recommendations for the continuity of services during and after COVID-19 that can address the ongoing need for youth support services. The following recommendations serve as a guideline for practitioners, advocates, and researchers on the institutional, organizational, and interactional levels of change that are needed. It is important to note that youth should not have to continue to deal with adversity and hardship that is often normalized as an individual issue when systemic change is not only possible, but also vital for the well-being of youth. These recommendations support the need for youth voices and perspectives to be amplified to effect real change as we continue to applaud their resilience.

Identify and Remedy the Gaps in Mental Health Access and Delivery

Lobbying for changes in mental health access and delivery first begins by conducting needs assessments with youth, families, and service providers (Vest Ettekal and Agans 2020). León, Rodas, and Greer (2020) suggest using a social justice youth development approach which means asking youth to provide feedback on the systems (e.g., mental health, criminal justice, education) that they are embedded within and how they navigate policies, practices, and services. This can also lead to crucial information in advocating for change while promoting critical consciousness and expanding social awareness among youth. Youth voices are crucial to identifying and remedying the gaps in mental health access and delivery because their lived experiences should be centered in decision-making processes. Otherwise, adults (often well-intentioned) are making decisions about systems that do not directly affect them.

Hine et al. (2020) recommend additional ways of identifying and addressing the gaps in mental health access and delivery. Funds from the Coronavirus Aid, Relief, and Economic Security Act (CARES Act) can be used to purchase Wi-Fi-enabled devices and hotspots, and expand the broadband infrastructure especially in rural areas so that youth and families can access digital learning and telemental health services. Policy and legislation need to be reviewed with an intersectional lens to determine how institutional level decisions such as cuts to mental health funding create additional barriers to access by gender, social class, race/ethnicity, sexual orientation, and disability.

Divert Youth out of the Juvenile Justice System

The Office of Juvenile Justice and Delinquency Prevention (OJJDP) provides guidance on youth programming in the *Model Programs Guide (MPG)* I-Guide (Development Services Group, Inc. 2017) which is focused on diversion. While some youth commit serious offenses and may need to be in a more secure setting, most youth in the juvenile justice system are there for relatively minor offenses and have significant mental health issues that can be better met in community-based settings. Diversion programs were developed as an alternative to confinement for youth who committed minor offenses and would provide them with more appropriate services to address any current issues and to prevent future delinquency. Rowe (2020) argues for more creative ways to maintain youth in their homes and neighborhoods by identifying and building on the inherent strengths in those neighborhoods which would include leveraging local relationships with kinship networks, community members, and local service providers.

Expand Case Management in School-Based Settings

School administrators across the nation were already dealing with increased mental health issues including anxiety, depression, and suicidal ideation among youth prior to COVID-19. Because of this, many states were in the process of creating positions for mental health coordinators and school social workers. COVID-19 further highlighted the need for mental health services and schools will need to be prepared when they fully reopen for the trauma that youth experienced related to COVID-19. Schools should fund qualified allied health staff to provide direct care, expand case management for wraparound services, and ensure funding models acknowledge the complexity in providing services in rural communities (Hine et al. 2020).

Provide Ongoing Training to Medical Providers who have Access to Youth

Courtney et al. (2020) note that child mortality can increase during a global pandemic and not necessarily from COVID-19, but from not accessing services for other health conditions. This may require outreach, mobile clinics, and a different delivery modality among medical providers such as using telehealth. With telehealth, medical providers will need to be aware of the difficulty ensuring confidently for their youth patients. Cohen and Bosk (2020) suggest that medical providers have an important role in identifying the disparate impacts of COVID-19 (beyond health) and referring youth to appropriate services. Medical providers need ongoing training on ACEs and how COVID-19 intensified trauma among youth and families. Further, they need to be aware of community-based services and the growing number of online supports. Medical providers can work in tandem with child welfare agencies, advocacy groups, and mental health professionals to raise awareness and address needed changes in mental health access and community-based services.

Address the Impact of COVID-19 on Service Providers

Mental health and community-based service providers experience compassion fatigue and vicarious trauma which can affect job performance, interpersonal relationships, and the physical and mental health of counselors. Service providers may be struggling with work–life balance, remote learning for their children, caregiving for sick family members, and COVID-19-related deaths. Posick et al. (2020) suggest that agencies need to consider how the transition to remote work is affecting employees. This includes addressing access to equipment and supplies; additional training in telemental health delivery; policy changes such as increasing flextime; assessing how each employee is coping with the transition and assisting with self-care practices; and modeling the commitment to mental health by creating an environment with open communication (Hunt 2020; Posick et al. 2020).

Develop Communication Strategies

Endale, St. Jean, and Birman (2020) identify the rapid identification and dissemination of accessible and accurate information as key for service providers during the COVID-19 pandemic. This allows for active outreach for community-based programs but in a different way and can connect youth and families to mental health services, food pantries, and rent relief programs. Staff members need to provide materials in various languages for non-English-speaking youth and families and distribute them in appropriate ways. This may include front porch or front stoop socially distanced visits, text messages, video check-ins, and using the WhatsApp. WhatsApp is a free, cross-platform centralized messaging and voice-over-IP service owned by Facebook, Inc. Users can send text and voice messages, make voice and video calls, and share documents. The voice calling feature lets users call contacts with international numbers for free and it uses an Internet connection rather than a mobile plan which is why this is such an attractive method of communication for so many immigrant and refugee families (Endale, St. Jean, and Birman 2020).

Conclusion

The COVID-19 pandemic exacerbated the mental health crisis in the US, especially among youth. Many youth receive school-based mental health services and/or community-based supports. COVID-19 disrupted the access to these crucial services for youth while providers figured out ways to address continuity. This research provides a synthesis and critical examination of the literature on the delivery of trauma-informed services for youth during COVID-19. Recommendations at the institutional, organizational, and interactional levels are discussed that address identifying and remedying the gaps in mental health access and delivery, diverting youth out of the juvenile justice system, expanding case management in school-based settings, providing ongoing training to medical providers who have access to youth, addressing the impact of COVID-19 on service providers, and developing clear communication strategies. One thing that COVID-19 has taught all of us is that global pandemics can happen in our lifetime and that we are often unprepared for the trauma associated with it. We now have an opportunity to learn from youth, families, and service providers not only about the barriers they experienced but also about the ingenuity to ensure a continuity of care that enhances the strengths, resources, and resilience of our youth so that they can thrive in the face of trauma (Bryant-Davis 2005).

References

Annie E. Casey Foundation. 2021. "Juvenile Justice Is Smaller, but More Unequal, After First Year of COVID-19." Accessed May 12, 2021. www.aecf.org/blog/juvenile-justice-is-smaller-but-more-unequal-after-first-year-of-covid-19/.

Auerswald, Colette L., Sherilyn Adams, and Marguerita Lightfoot. 2020. "The Urgent and Growing Needs of Youths Experiencing Homelessness During the COVID-19 Pandemic." *Journal of Adolescent Health* 67: 461–2.

Bauer, Lauren, Stephanie Lu, and Emily Moss. 2020. "Teen Disengagement Is on the Rise." *Brookings*, October 1, 2020. www.brookings.edu/blog/up-front/2020/10/01/teen-disengagement-is-on-the-rise/.

Bryant-Davis, Thema. 2005. *Thriving in the Wake of Trauma: A Multicultural Guide.* New York, NY: Rowman and Littlefield Publishers, Inc.

Buchanan, Molly, Erin D. Castro, Mackenzie Kushner, and Marvin D. Krohn. 2020. "It's F**ing Chaos: COVID-19's Impact on Juvenile Delinquency and Juvenile Justice."

American Journal of Criminal Justice 45 (1): 578–600. https://doi.org/10.1007/s12103 020-09549-x.

Chaturvedi, Kunal, Dinesh Kumar Vishwakarma, and Nidhi Singh. 2021. "COVID-19 and Its Impact on Education, Social Life and Mental Health of Students: A Survey." *Children and Youth Services Review* 121. https://doi.org/10.1016/j.childyo uth.2020.105866.

Cohen, Rachel I. Silliman, and Emily Adlin Bosk. 2020. "Vulnerable Youth and the COVID-19 Pandemic." *Pediatrics* 146 (1): e20201306. https://doi.org/10.1542/peds.2020-1306.

Courtney, Darren, Priya Watson, Marco Battaglia, Benoit H. Mulsant, and Peter Szatmari. 2020. "COVID-19 Impacts on Child and Youth Anxiety and Depression: Challenges and Opportunities." *The Canadian Journal of Psychiatry* 65 (10): 688–91.

Development Services Group, Inc. 2017. *MPG I-Guides: Diversion Programs*. Washington, D.C.: Office of Juvenile Justice and Delinquency Prevention. www.ojjdp.gov/mpg-iguides/topics/diversion-programs/.

Dierkhising, Carly B., Susan J. Ko, Briana Woods-Jaeger, Ernestine C. Briggs, Robert Lee, and Robert S. Pynoos. 2013. "Trauma Histories among Justice-Involved Youth: Findings from the National Child Traumatic Stress Network." *European Journal of Psychotraumatology* 4 (1): 20274. https://doi.org/10.3402/ejpt.v4i0.20274.

Endale, Tarik, Nicole St. Jean, and Dina Birman. 2020. "University of Miami, Coral Gables COVID-19 and Refugee and Immigrant Youth: A Community-Based Mental Health Perspective." *Psychological Trauma: Theory, Research, Practice, and Policy* 12 (S1): S225–7. http://dx.doi.org/10.1037/tra0000875.

Felitti, Vincent J., Robert F. Anda, Dale Nordenberg, David F. Williamson, Alison M. Spitz, Valerie Edwards, Mary P. Koss, and James S. Sparks. 1998. "Relationship of Childhood Abuse and Household Dysfunction to Many of the Leading Causes of Death in Adults." *American Journal of Preventative Medicine* 14 (4): 245–58. http://dx.doi.org/10.1016/S0749-3797(98)00017-8.

Golberstein, Ezra, Hefei Wen, and Benjamin F. Miller. 2020. "Coronavirus Disease 2019 (COVID-19) and Mental Health for Children and Adolescents." *JAMA Pediatrics* 174 (9): 819–20. https://doi.org/10.1001/jamapediatrics.2020.1456.

Goulette, Natalie W., Sara Z. Evans, and Dione King. 2016. "Exploring the Behavior of Juveniles and Young Adults Raised by Custodial Grandmothers." *Children and Youth Services Review* 70 (1): 349–56. https://doi.org/10.1016/j.childyouth.2016.10.004.

Henderson, Joy. 2020. "Hiding and Being Found: How Inequity Found Its Spotlight During COVID-19 and What It Means for the Future." *Child & Youth Services* 41 (3): 256–8. https://doi.org/10.1080/0145935X.2020.1834964.

Hine, Rochelle, Andrea Reupert, Phillip Tchernegovski, Jade Sheen, and Darryl Maybery. 2020. "COVID-19 and Vulnerable Families Living in Rural Locations: Building a System for Recovery." *Child & Youth Services* 41 (3): 261–5. https://doi.org/10.1080/0145935X.2020.1834995.

Hunt, Andrea N. 2020. "Access to Mental Health Care During and After COVID-19." In *Social Problems in the Age of COVID-19, Volume 1: US Perspectives*, edited by Glenn W. Muschert, Kristen M. Budd, Michelle Christian, David C. Lane, and Jason A. Smith, pp. 113–21. Bristol, United Kingdom: Policy Press.

Imad, Mays. 2020. "Leveraging the Neuroscience of Now." *Inside Higher Ed*, June 3, 2020. www.insidehighered.com/advice/2020/06/03/seven-recommendations-helping-students-thrive-times-trauma.

Jeffrey, Jessica, Lauren Marlotte, and Nastassia J. Hajal. 2020. "Providing Telebehavioral Health to Youth and Families During COVID-19: Lessons from the Field." *Psychological Trauma: Theory, Research, Practice, and Policy* 12 (S1): S272–3. http://dx.doi.org/10.1037/tra0000817.

Langarizadeh, Mostafa, Mohsen S. Tabatabaei, Kamran Tavakol, Majid Naghipour, Alireza Rostami, and Fatemeh Moghbeli. 2017. "Telemental Health Care, an Effective Alternative to Conventional Mental Care: A Systematic Review." *Acta Informatica Medica* 25 (4): 240–6. https://doi.org/10.5455/aim.2017.25.240-246.

Lee, Shawna J., Kaitlin P. Ward, Olivia D. Chang, and Kasey M. Downing. 2021. "Parenting Activities and the Transition to Home-Based Education During the COVID-19 Pandemic." *Children and Youth Services Review* 122. https://doi.org/10.1016/j.childyouth.2020.105585.

León, Maria, Kevin Rodas, and Mora Greer. 2020. "Leisure Behind Bars: The Realities of COVID-19 for Youth Connected to the Justice System." *Leisure Sciences* 43: 218–24. https://doi.org/10.1080/01490400.2020.1774005.

Maslow, Abraham H. 1943. "A Theory of Human Motivation." *Psychological Review* 50: 370–96.

McBride, Bill. 2020. "Memorandum: COVID-19 Responses in the Juvenile Justice System." *National Governors Association*, March 30, 2020. www.nga.org/wp-content/uploads/2020/04/Memorandum_COVID-19-Responses-in-the-Juvenile-Justice-System.pdf.

McCance-Katz, Elinore, and Calder Lynch. 2019. "Joint Information Bulletin: Guidance to States and School Systems on Addressing Mental Health and Substance Use Issues in Schools." *Substance Abuse and Mental Health Services Administration and the Centers for Medicare and Medicaid Services*, July 1, 2019. www.medicaid.gov/sites/default/files/Federal-Policy-Guidance/Downloads/cib20190701.pdf.

National Alliance for Caregiving and AARP. 2020. *Caregiving in the U.S.* Accessed May 13, 2021. www.caregiving.org/wp-content/uploads/2021/01/full-report-caregiving-in-the-united-states-01-21.pdf.

Ornell, Felipe, Jaqueline B. Schuch, Anne O. Sordi, and Felix Henrique Paim Kessler. 2020. "'Pandemic Fear' and COVID-19: Mental Health Burden and Strategies." *Brazilian Journal of Psychiatry* 42 (3): 232–5. https://doi.org/10.1590/1516-4446-2020-0008.

Panchal, Nirmita, Rabah Kamal, Cynthia Cox, and Rachel Garfield. 2021. "The Implications of COVID-19 for Mental Health and Substance Use." Accessed May 12, 2021. www.kff.org/coronavirus-covid-19/issue-brief/the-implications-of-covid-19-for-mental-health-and-substance-use/.

Posick, Chad, April A. Schueths, Cary Christian, Jonathan A. Grubb, and Suzanne E. Christian. 2020. "Child Victim Services in the Time of COVID-19: New Challenges and Innovative Solutions." *American Journal of Criminal Justice* 45: 680–9. https://doi.org/10.1007/s12103-020-09543-3.

Rovner, Josh. 2021. "COVID-19 in Juvenile Facilities." The Sentencing Project. Accessed April 3, 2021. www.sentencingproject.org/publications/covid-19-in-juvenile-facilities/.

Rowe, William. 2020. "COVID-19 and Youth in Detention." *Child & Youth Services* 41 (3): 310–12. https://doi.org/10.1080/0145935X.2020.1835184.

Sawyer, Wendy. 2019. "Youth Confinement: The Whole Pie 2019." Prison Policy Initiative. Accessed April 3, 2021. www.prisonpolicy.org/reports/youth2019.html.

Substance Abuse and Mental Health Services Administration. 2014. *SAMHSA's Concept of Trauma and Guidance for a Trauma-Informed Approach.* HHS Publication No. (SMA)

14–4884. Substance Abuse and Mental Health Services Administration. https://ncsacw.samhsa.gov/userfiles/files/SAMHSA_Trauma.pdf.

Substance Abuse and Mental Health Services Administration. 2019. *Key Substance Use and Mental Health Indicators in the United States: Results from the 2018 National Survey on Drug Use and Health* (HHS Publication No. PEP19-5068, NSDUH Series H-54). Rockville, MD: Center for Behavioral Health Statistics and Quality, Substance Abuse and Mental Health Services Administration. www.samhsa.gov/data/.

Substance Abuse and Mental Health Services Administration and Centers for Medicare and Medicaid Services. 2019. *Guidance to States and School Systems on Addressing Mental Health and Substance Use Issues in Schools.* Accessed April 4, 2021. www.medicaid.gov/sites/default/files/Federal-Policy-Guidance/Downloads/cib20190701.pdf.

Vest Ettekal, Andrea, and Jennifer P. Agans. 2020. "Positive Youth Development through Leisure: Confronting the COVID-19 Pandemic." *Journal of Youth Development* 15 (2). https://doi.org/10.5195/jyd.2020.962.

Vissing, Yvonne. 2021. "Turning a Blind Eye: COVID-19 and Homeless Children." In *COVID-19 and Childhood Inequality*, edited by Nazneen Khan. London: Routledge.

Whitney, Daniel G. and Mark D. Peterson. 2019. "US National and State-Level Prevalence of Mental Health Disorders and Disparities of Mental Health Care Use in Children." *JAMA Pediatrics* 173 (4): 389–91.

World Health Organization. 2020. "Mental Health and Psychosocial Considerations During the COVID-19 Outbreak." Accessed April 3, 2021. www.who.int/docs/default-source/coronaviruse/mental-health-considerations.pdf?sfvrsn=6d3578af_8.

6 Consequences of COVID-19 Realities and Misconceptions for Rural PK–12 Students
Implications from Rural Education Research

Meagan C. Arrastía-Chisholm, Lee Edmondson Grimes, and Heather M. Kelley

Coronavirus disease 2019 (COVID-19), the disease caused by severe acute respiratory syndrome coronavirus 2 (SARS-CoV-2), has devastated the rural United States of America (USA) in terms of positive cases, deaths, and economic impact, with more than 28.35% of the rural population directly affected by the virus (Mueller et al. 2020, 2). While much of the literature and public discourse has focused on urban and suburban schools, this chapter focuses on rural education. In this chapter, we review rural education research with special attention to the challenges that first faced schools in responding to COVID-19. In addition, we explore the barriers (e.g., resources, infrastructure, misconceptions, etc.) to serving children that rural schools are continuing to overcome as the pandemic continues in the USA. For ongoing and future research, we offer education researchers and practitioners suggestions for further capturing the consequences of the pandemic on the student experience, as well as recommendations for schools on how to serve their students in the case of a future pandemic or crisis. With this information synthesized, it is our hope that children and youth living in rural areas will be better served by their educational institutions.

Many students in rural areas continue to feel the digital divide where a lack of access to technology and a reliable internet connection hinders their ability to learn virtually using videoconferencing. In fact, the upload and download speeds available in some rural areas are not sufficient for video streaming at all (Lai and Widemar 2020, 459). Without a public space to conduct virtual learning as an alternative, these students are not receiving the same quality of education and often do not have access to the same resources as their peers from more sufficiently funded, high-property tax suburban districts (Jensen 2020, 79). Likewise, the proportion of the population who fall into the category of the working poor is high in rural areas with 16.1% compared to 12.6% in non-rural areas (USDA 2020). In general, it is difficult for struggling low-income parents, who may work long hours to make ends meet, to stay home with children to

DOI: 10.4324/9781003250937-9

supervise, ensure basic needs are met, and help facilitate virtual learning activities (Simpson 2020, 41). The tense situation has forced many rural schools to remain open despite upward trends in COVID-19 cases (Parolin and Lee 2021, 525)

Meanwhile, existing achievement gaps grow even larger between rural students in resource-poor areas and urban/suburban students in resource-rich areas (Jensen 2020) where students can participate in quasi-schools their parents construct using their connections and social capital (Richmond et al. 2020, 503). Rural schools have responded to students' basic needs by setting up feeding programs (Dunn et al. 2020). However, such programs are often located in central locations which tend to be very far from students in the most rural areas. Without public transportation, families and their children are unable to reach these resources (Turner 2020), as well as others set up by the community (e.g., public Wi-Fi at public library parking lots). To meet students' needs, rural schools rely on faculty and staff, including school counselors. However, rural schools are less likely to even have a school counselor on staff as compared to urban schools, with almost 75% of rural schools having higher ratios than the recommended 250 students to every school counselor (Gagnon and Mattingly 2016, 3). Now with school counselors being pulled into even more auxiliary responsibilities during the pandemic (e.g., coordinating feeding programs), students are being underserved.

To make mental health services available, school counselors have embraced the technology (despite the issues with technology and lack of privacy for students at home) and have offered one-on-one and small group services. However, burnout and compassion fatigue are pervasive among rural teachers and school counselors and mental health professionals. These educators are tasked with balancing face-to-face and virtual instruction/counseling, which affects their ability to connect with students and families many of whom are grieving loved ones lost to the virus. Future research should capture the efficacy of the services offered to rural students in the face of these challenges.

Rural Challenges for Students

Even before the COVID-19 pandemic, students in rural areas of the USA experienced circumstances that challenged educational success. A major challenge in rural areas is the lack of high-speed internet. As Eisenberg, Pruitt, and Shoemaker (2021) argue, "The COVID-19 era has made more acute something rural communities were already familiar with: high speed internet is the gateway to everything. Education, work, health care, information access, and even social life depend directly on broadband." In a White House Press Brief, the Biden administration addressed the problem stating that 30 million Americans live in an area with minimal to no broadband infrastructure with a particular lack of access in rural areas (The White House 2021). While the lack of high-speed internet affects the lives of both children and adults in a multitude of ways, the digital divide is nowhere more apparent than in schools.

Urban and suburban schools, where communities have access to both high-speed internet and greater financial resources, have long been able to offer services not available in the rural setting.

Oakland (2020) explains that the COVID-19 pandemic increased this discrepancy pointing out glaring differences in the way schools teach and assign work leading to "life-altering impacts" on rural students (435). When children and adolescents do not own a device, often due to poverty, or do not have access to reliable high-speed internet, they are unable to access even the basics of lessons that teachers offer virtually. One group particularly affected by the differences surrounding educational offerings during the COVID-19 pandemic comprises students receiving special education services (Jameson et al. 2020, 181). For example, deaf students require interpreters and captioning of materials. Gathering these resources and making them available at a distance take time. Other student accommodations can require physical manipulation of materials, like demonstrating math problems with blocks during assessments or guiding a student's hand while learning to write. In fact, in one study 87% of rural students with neurodevelopmental disorders were not receiving enough direct remote instruction in lieu of services provided pre-pandemic (McFayden et al. 2021, 72).

Jameson et al. (2020) explained that factors associated with remote instruction sometimes lead to confusion about how services could be offered which when clarified were still difficult to navigate due to the lack of appropriate technology resources in rural schools (184). The authors went on to add that the effects of the pandemic have been devastating but even more so on individuals with disabilities in rural and remote communities (189). Moreover, a survey conducted by the US Department of Education showed that rural schools were more likely to offer full-time, in-person classes than were their urban and suburban counterparts (Kamenetz 2021). This fact leads to the question, "were rural schools forced to make the decision to offer in-person classes because of a lack of resources including broadband, and did this increase the danger for students, teachers, and families for contracting the virus?" Rural inhabitants, especially children and adolescents, experience inequitable life circumstances due to the lack of resources available there, particularly in schools. A broad social issue associated with this notion comes from a conversation about increasing accessibility to (i.e., assessments and treatment) via telehealth visits with providers and counselors. Dornauer and Bryce (2020) refer to the ability to access broadband as a fundamental right and compare the need for high-speed internet in rural areas to the need for electricity in rural areas in the 1930s. This need must be met.

Economic and Academic Impact on Students

The economic impact of the COVID-19 pandemic surpasses that of the Great Recession of 2007 to 2009 and the economic toll is felt internationally (Weber et al. 2020). Even before the pandemic, rural communities struggled economically with few jobs, higher percentages of working poor households, inferior hospital access, and increased vulnerability to economic downfalls (Mueller et al. 2021, 4–5). Mueller et al. (2021) summarized a survey conducted in the rural regions of the Western United States during the summer of 2020 (1). The results found higher rates of unemployment, negative views of the local economy, unemployment insurance use, and mental health problems in the rural regions compared to national and urban (5). According to the US Bureau of Labor Statistics, an estimated 34% of Americans can telework but these jobs require higher educational degrees that are less common in rural regions (Weber et al. 2020). The higher levels of working poverty made it essential for rural regions to serve students in the fall 2020 semester with face-to-face schooling.

A national survey of 477 school districts in August 2020 showed the varying plans for schools in different geographic regions. A notable finding of this survey was that 65% of rural schools were going back to face-to-face classes compared to only 24.1% of suburban schools and 9.2% of urban schools (Gross, Opalka, and Gundapaneni 2020, 3). A previous July 2020 survey of the same school districts showed some evidence of increased academic gaps between rural schools and other regional schools (Gross and Opalka 2020). During the initial lockdown months before summer 2020, about half of the rural districts expected some sort of progress monitoring for all or some students. During this time, less than half of the districts performed attendance or check-ins, and about one-fourth of the districts expected teachers to provide instructions to students (5). The amount of learning loss during the months of March through May of 2020 is monumental and quite a task to predict.

Two notable studies were conducted by Northwest Evaluation Association (NWEA) and the Annenberg Institute for Education Reform at Brown University. Using past data on learning loss during the summer months, NWEA estimated that students came back to school in the fall of 2020 with only 70% of learning gain in reading and 50% of learning gain in mathematics relative to a typical school year (Kuhfeld and Tarasawa 2020, 2). Similarly, the Annenberg Institute used summer learning loss and past literature to predict 63–68% of learning gain in reading and 37–50% learning gain in mathematics (Kuhfeld et al. 2020, 2). These numbers are highly concerning but they do not account for areas of concern that cause academic gaps in rural regions including higher levels of poverty, the increase in trauma during the COVID-19 pandemic, and the high turnover rate of teachers (Pincus et al. 2021, 243; Tran, Smith, and Fox 2018, 4). The rate at which students in rural school districts are lagging without proper parental and school support despite returning to in-person schooling has not been measured, but the future impact may be detrimental in rural areas. Children have lost so much more than learning during this pandemic. For example, risk of domestic violence has increased in rural areas during the pandemic (Hansen and Lory 2020, 732). In addition to losing family members and other community members, students missed out on the social gatherings, sporting events, and positive experiences in a safe place that schools provide (see

Nenga 2021, this volume). Although it is important to acknowledge and address learning loss, learning loss is one of many losses and traumas experienced by children and youth in rural areas.

Educator Innovations for Students

The American School Counselor Association (2019) defines the role of school counselors as one through which services are provided to PK–12 students in the academic, career, and socio-emotional domains (4). According to American School Counselor Association (2019), school counselor responsibilities range in part from using counseling theories (105), to understanding educational and legal systems (105), to conducting lessons based on American School Counselor Association (ASCA) Standards (106), to demonstrating multicultural understanding (107), to school leadership (107), to using data and identifying achievement gaps (112), all in collaboration with other school personnel, administrators, and parents/guardians (111). In short, the role of school counselors when positioned to use their skills appropriately is multifaceted and a powerful force to bring about positive student outcomes. Several factors impact the role of the school counselor in relation to the COVID-19 pandemic and their role in the rural setting. Scholarship is in the early stages of focusing on how school counselors can address the trauma that many children and adolescents faced during the chaos of the pandemic.

Pincus et al. (2020) posit that school counselors are trained in "the areas of human growth and development, group counseling, and counseling theories and techniques; therefore, they have the capability to effectively offer and conduct short-term mental health services to students in need" (251). ASCA and state organizations such as the Georgia School Counselor Association offer their members ideas and suggestions for interventions to address students virtually and as they return to in-school instruction. In an interview, Jill Cook, the Director of ASCA, explains that when ASCA offered school counselors webinars on helping students in the COVID-19 pandemic, 13,000 members registered and crashed the servers and noted that rural school counselors searched for help and support (Morton 2020). With the pandemic changing virtually every aspect of life, school counselors now find themselves also making phone calls to check on attendance, offering virtual lunch bunches, and offering students with socio-emotional struggles counseling sessions via platforms such as Zoom (Meyers 2020).

In rural areas though, the lack of an adequate number of school counselors suggests that these services would be difficult or impossible to offer. In rural schools, 14% of schools do not have a school counselor and many employ less experienced counselors than do urban schools (Quintero and Gu 2019). ASCA recommends a counselor to student ratio of 1 to 250, but in most schools the numbers are 1 to 482; however, in rural Arizona, the ratio is 1 to 924 (Edelman 2017). According to a study discussed by Shelton and Owens (2021), students in rural schools had significantly lower access to mental health services overall

(74). With fewer school counselors to balance this disparity, rural students are less able to access services both during the COVID-19 pandemic and when they return to in-school instruction.

Factors influencing learning virtually cause educational experts to worry that negative effects on learning will follow many students post-COVID-19. In rural schools however, school counselors faced high counselor to student ratios even before the pandemic which has played a part in college advisement for years. This disparity led some counseling scholars to refer particularly to rural students of color as an invisible population (Dobson 2018, 46). Compounding the problems in rural schools is the lack of "publically available, fine-grained data on rural regions" (Mueller et al. 2021, 2). The authors add that scholars, policymakers, and practitioners cannot use urban-centric data to understand and make recommendations for rural areas (Mueller et al. 2021, 2). More research is critical to understanding the issues connected to rural areas as a result of the COVID-19 pandemic and to how school counselors can offer the services they are trained for to students in need.

Providing Online Services for Students

The abrupt and in some cases lasting reduction or cancellation of resources and activities has an impact on the mental health of rural children around the world (de Figueiredo et al. 2021), and the rural USA is not exempt. Most notably, rural children are expressing that they are stressed alongside their parents and need help regulating their emotions, especially in the face of online bullying during remote instruction (McFayden et al. 2021, 80). Like instruction, counseling services have also shifted online to accommodate students who are learning from home (even if their school doors have re-opened). School counselors have to take on new roles during school reopening while struggling to learn how to incorporate new ethical standards in virtual and in-person formatting (American School Counselor Association 2020, 5). The increase in job responsibilities has interrupted school counselors' ability to connect to students during a time of great trauma (Pincus et al. 2020, 3). Harvard University and Boston College conducted a survey of 948 school counselors in 48 US states and Puerto Rico after the spring semester of 2020 which provided an early indication of school counselors' fatigue and burnout (Savitz-Romer 2020, 2). Nearly half of the counselors surveyed spent more time supporting students, as well as tending to their personal development and emotional needs since the start of the pandemic (Savitz-Romer 2020, 7). Two other areas of concerns are the lack of training and direction from the school district; 34% of rural counselors reported that they had no training since the start of the COVID-19 pandemic, half of the correspondents reported that they were not consulted by the district during contingency planning, and nearly one-fourth reported to have no communication from their regional school district since the start of the pandemic (Savitz-Romer 2020).

Even though little training or support is offered, school counselors must follow updated standards in practice in virtual settings (American School Counselor Association 2020, 5). School counselors in rural districts experience an alarming lack of support and data about students as only 43% of teachers were expected to check in with students during times of virtual schooling (Bond, Dibner, and Schweingruber 2020, 28). Nearly half of the counselors were asked to take more of an administrative task such as overseeing the school schedule and course scheduling during the start of COVID-19 (Savitz-Romer et al. 2020, 6). Lower than the national average, only 59.1% of school districts' plan in rural environments addresses students' socio-emotional learning (DeArmond, Chu, and Gundapaneni 2021, 3). This task is left to counselors as reported by the American School Counselor Association's *State of the Profession 2020* report (American School Counselor Association 2021). A survey of 7,000 American school counselors showed that the two biggest day-to-day challenges of school counselors in 2020 were having virtual access to students and providing counseling to students virtually (American School Counselor Association 2021, 8). School counselors desperately need support in the rural regions to provide proper care to their students.

Future Research and Conclusion

Future research should capture the effectiveness of the services offered to rural students in the face of these challenges. Likewise, the effects of access to information and technology should be further examined. For example, factors such as the origin of news sources affect health behavior with those consuming media produced in urban centers engaging in social distancing significantly more than those consuming media produced locally (Kim, Shepherd, and Clinton 2020). Misconceptions should be addressed for future pandemics. For instance, some students do enjoy online learning, with more introverted students favoring the online instruction. However, students do miss out on the more applied instructional activities (Kaden 2020, 8). Students in rural settings reported benefitting from social support through sharing their personal narratives of coping during quarantine, lockdown, and the pandemic in general. However, students reported struggling with the boundaries and privacy of online learning with their teachers and classmates being able to see into their homes. If we listen to the voices of the youth, we have more than enough areas of future inquiry.

Although schools responded as quickly as possible, future transitions should put routines in place sooner, especially for students receiving special education and English language learning (ELL) services (Ault et al. 2020, 193). This is an opportunity to challenge old systems that oppress students of color and other marginalized students and utilize technology for administrative tasks freeing up paraprofessionals for instructional tasks (Grooms and Child 2021, 15). Likewise, rural schools should collaborate across agencies to support students through wrap-around care and data-driven decision-making with parents and caregivers (Jameson et al. 2020, 186). Although the rural USA would like to move forward into the next academic year with COVID-19 behind us, it is uncertain if a similar public health crisis or pandemic should occur within our lifetimes. Learning from this pandemic will better inform educators on how to support rural children and help them transition into adulthood (Rowe et al. 2020, 220).

In conclusion, the lack of resources in rural education has further exacerbated childhood inequality in the USA in notable ways. The death toll and economic impact in terms of loss of jobs has left rural children with fewer adults within the family, school, and greater community systems to care and support them financially, emotionally, and physically. Quarantine and social isolation have reduced the number of social interactions for rural children, many of whom live in geographically remote areas. Because the digital divide delayed the rollout of remote instruction and because of the lack of professional development, rural students did not receive quality online instruction and may have disproportionately experienced learning loss. This especially puts ELL and students with disabilities (who are disproportionately students of color) at a greater disadvantage compared to their urban and suburban peers academically. Moving forward, educators will need to organize, advocate, and innovate to help rural students heal from trauma and meet their academic goals.

References

American School Counselor Association. 2019. *The ASCA National Model: A Framework for School Counseling Programs.* Alexandria, VA: ASCA.

American School Counselor Association. 2020. "School Reentry: The School Counselor's Role." *School Counseling: Standards in Practice.* www.schoolcounselor.org/getmedia/0034bb80-bd49-418c-9e17-d5bfdb5521da/SIP-School-Reentry.pdf.

American School Counselor Association. 2021. *ASCA Research Report: State of the Profession 2020.* www.schoolcounselor.org/getmedia/bb23299b-678d-4bce-8863-cfcb55f7df87/2020-State-of-the-Profession.pdf.

Ault, Melinda Jones, Ginevra Courtade, Sally A. Miracle, and Amanda E. Bruce. 2020. "Providing Support for Rural Special Educators During Nontraditional Instruction: One State's Response." *Rural Special Education Quarterly* 39 (4): 193–200. https://doi.org/10.1177/8756870520959653.

Bond, Enriqueta, Kenne Dibner, and Heidi Schweingruber. 2020. *Reopening K-12 Schools During the COVID-19 Pandemic: Prioritizing Health, Equity, and Communities.* Washington, DC: The National Academies Press. https://doi.org/10.17226/25858.

DeArmond, Micheal, Lisa Chu, and Padma Gundapaneni. 2021. "How Are School Districts Addressing Student Social-Emotional Needs During the Pandemic." *CPRE*, February 2021. www.crpe.org/sites/default/files/final_student_sel_needs_brief_2021.pdf.

de Figueiredo, Camila Saggioro, Poliana Capucho Sandre, Liana Catarina Lima Portugal, Thalita Mázala-de-Oliveira, Luana da Silva Chagas, Ícaro Raony, Elenn Soares Ferreira, Elizabeth Giestal-de-Araujo, Aline Araujo Dos Santos, and Priscilla Oliveira-Silva Bomfim. 2021. "COVID-19 Pandemic Impact on Children and Adolescents' Mental Health: Biological, Environmental, and Social Factors." *Progress* in *Neuro-Psychopharmacology and Biological Psychiatry* 106: 110171. https://doi.org/10.1016/j.pnpbp.2020.110171.

Dobson, Ashley. 2018. "Invisible Population." *Journal of College Admission* 238 (Winter): 44–7.

Dornauer, Mark, and Robert Bryce. 2020. "Too Many Americans are Living in the Digital Dark: The Problem Demands a New Deal Solution." *Health Affairs Blog*, October 28, 2020. https://doi.org/10.1377/hblog20201026.515764.

Dunn, Caroline G., Erica Kenney, Sheila E. Fleischhacker, and Sara N. Bleich. 2020. "Feeding Low-Income Children During the COVID-19 Pandemic." *New England Journal of Medicine* 382 (18): e40.

Edelman, Gilad. 2017. "A College Adviser in Every School." *Washington Monthly* 49 (9/10): 62–6.

Eisenberg, Ann, Lisa Pruitt, and Jessica Shoemaker. 2021. "5 Ways Biden can Help Rural America Thrive and Bridge the Rural-Urban Divide." *The Conversation*, January 21, 2021. https://theconversation.com/5-ways-biden-can-help-rural-america-thrive-and-bridge-therural-urban-divide-150610.

Gagnon, Douglas J., and Marybeth J. Mattingly. 2016. "Most US School Districts Have Low Access to School Counselors: Poor, Diverse, and City School Districts Exhibit Particularly High Student-to-Counselor Ratios." *Carsey Research* 108: 1–6. https://dx.doi.org/10.34051/p/2020.275.

Grooms, Ain A., and Joshua Childs. 2021. "'We Need to Do Better by Kids': Changing Routines in US Schools in Response to COVID-19 School Closures." *Journal of Education for Students Placed at Risk (JESPAR)* 26 (2): 1–22. https://doi.org/10.1080/10824669.2021.1906251.

Gross, Betheny, and Alice Opalka. 2020. *Too Many Schools Leave Learning to Chance During the Pandemic*. Washington: Center on Reinventing Public Education. www.crpe.org/sites/default/files/final_national_sample_brief_2020.pdf.

Gross, Betheny, Alice Opalka, and Padma Gundapaneni. 2020. "Getting Back to School: An Update on Plans from Across the Country." Washington: Center on Reinventing Public Education. www.crpe.org/sites/default/files/getting_back_to_school_brief.pdf.

Hansen, J. Andrew, and Gabrielle L. Lory. 2020. "Rural Victimization and Policing During the COVID-19 Pandemic." *American Journal of Criminal Justice* 45 (4): 731–42. https://doi.org/10.1007/s12103-020-09554-0.

Jameson, J. Matt, Sondra M. Stegenga, Joanna Ryan, and Ambra Green. 2020. "Free Appropriate Public Education in the Time of COVID-19." *Rural Special Education Quarterly* 39 (4): 181–92. https://doi.org/10.1177/8756870520959659.

Jensen, Lindsey. 2020. "Closing the Rural Opportunity Gap." In *Flip the System US: How Teachers Can Transform Education and Save Democracy,* edited by Michael Soskil, pp. 74–81. New York, NY: Routledge.

Kaden, Ute. 2020. "COVID-19 School Closure-Related Changes to the Professional Life of a K–12 Teacher." *Education Sciences* 10 (6): 165. https://doi.org/10.3390/educsci10060165.

Kamenetz, Anya. 2021. "New Data Highlights Disparities in Students' Learning in Person vs. Remotely." *MindShift*, March 24, 2021. www.kqed.org/mindshift/57595/new-data-highlight-disparities-in-students-learning-in-person-vs-remotely.

Kim, Eunji, Michael E. Shepherd, and Joshua D. Clinton. 2020. "The Effect of Big-City News on Rural America During the COVID-19 Pandemic." *Proceedings of the National Academy of Sciences* 11 (36): 22009–014.

Kuhfeld, Megan, and Beth Tarasawa. 2020. *The COVID-19 Slide: What Summer Learning Loss Can Tell Us About the Potential Impact of School Closures on Student Academic Achievement*. Portland, OR: Northwest Evaluation Association. www.nwea.org/content/uploads/2020/05/Collaborative-Brief_Covid19-Slide-APR20.pdf.

Kuhfeld, Megan, James Soland, Beth Tarasawa, Angela Johnson, Erik Ruzek, and Jing Liu. 2020. "Projecting the Potential Impacts of COVID-19 School Closures on Academic Achievement." EdWorkingPaper: 20–226. Annenberg Institute at Brown University. https://doi.org/10.26300/cdrv-yw05.

Lai, John, and Nicole O. Widmar. 2020. "Revisiting the Digital Divide in the COVID-19 Era." *Applied Economic Perspectives and Policy* 43 (1): 458–64. https://doi.org/10.1002/aepp.13104.

McFayden, Tyler C., Rosanna Breaux, Jennifer R. Bertollo, Kameron Cummings, Thomas H. Ollendick. 2021. "COVID-19 Remote Learning Experiences of Youth with Neurodevelopmental Disorders in Rural Appalachia." *Journal of Rural Mental Health* 45 (2): 72. https://doi.org/10.1037/rmh0000171.

Meyers, Laurie. 2020. "School Counseling in the Time of Coronavirus." *Counseling Today* 63 (4): 28–33.

Morton, Neal. 2020. "Counseling Kids During the Coronavirus: A Tough Job Made Even Tougher." *The Hechinger Report*, May 8, 2020. https://hechingerreport.org/counseling-kids-during-the-coronavirus-a-tough-job-made-even-tougher/.

Mueller, J. Tom, Kathryn McConnell, Paul Berne Burowc, Katie Pofahl, Alexis Merdjanoff, and Justin Farrel. 2021. "Impacts of the COVID-19 Pandemic on Rural America." *PNAS* 118 (1): 1–6. https://doi.org/10.1073/pnas.2019378118.

Nenga, Sandi K. 2021. "When Six Feet Feels Like Six Miles: Children's Images of Their Lives During the Pandemic." In *COVID-19 and Childhood Inequality*, edited by Nazneen Khan. London and New York: Routledge.

Oakland, Abby. 2020. "Minnesota's Digital Divide: How Minnesota Can Replicate the Rural Electrification Act to Deliver Rural Broadband." *Minnesota Law Review* 105: 429.

Parolin, Zachary, and Emma K. Lee. 2021. "Large Socio-economic, Geographic and Demographic Disparities Exist in Exposure to School Closures." *Nature Human Behaviour* 5: 522–8. https://doi.org/10.1038/s41562-021-01087-8.

Pincus, Robert, TeSaunda Hannor-Walker, Leonis Wright, and Judith Justice. 2020. "COVID-19's Effect on Students: How School Counselors Rise to the Rescue." *NASSP Bulletin* 104 (4): 251–6. https://doi.org/10.1177%2F0192636520975866.

Quintero, Diana, and Yuhe Gu. 2019. "Rural School Need Career Counselors, Too." *Brown Center Chalkboard from the Brookings Institute*, July 3, 2019. www.brookings.edu/blog/brown-center-chalkboard/2019/07/03/rural-schools-need-career-counselors-too/.

Richmond, Gail, Tonya Bartell, Christine Cho, Alix Gallagher, Ye He, Emery Petchauer, and Lucia Cardenas Curiel. 2020. "Home/school: Research Imperatives, Learning Settings, and the COVID-19 Pandemic." *Journal of Teacher Education* 71 (5): 503–4. https://doi.org/10.1177/0022487120961574.

Rowe, Dawn A., Erik Carter, Shimul Gajjar, Erin A. Maves, and Jennifer C. Wall. 2020. "Supporting Strong Transitions Remotely: Considerations and Complexities for Rural Communities During COVID-19." *Rural Special Education Quarterly* 39 (4): 220–32. https://doi.org/10.1177%2F8756870520958199.

Savitz-Romer, Mandy, Heather T. Rowan-Kenyon, Tara P. Nicola, Stephanie Carroll, and Laura Hecht. 2020. "Expanding Support Beyond the Virtual Classroom: Lessons and Recommendations from School Counselors During the COVID-19 Crisis." Harvard Graduate School of Education & Boston College Lynch School of Education and Human Development. www.gse.harvard.edu/sites/default/files/documents/School-Counseling-Covid-19-Report.pdf.

Shelton, Andrea J., and Emiel W. Owens. 2021. "Mental Health Services in the United States Public High Schools." *Journal of School Health* 91 (1): 70–6. https://doi.org/10.1111/josh.12976.

Simpson, Jenna Conan. 2020. "Distance Learning During the Early Stages of the COVID-19 Pandemic: Examining K-12 Students' and Parents' Experiences and Perspectives." *Interaction Design and Architecture(s) Journal—IxD&A* 46: 29–46. www.mifav.uniroma2.it/inevent/events/idea2010/doc/46_2.pdf.

The White House. 2021. "Fact Sheet: The American Jobs Plan." *White House*, March 31, 2021. www.whitehouse.gov/briefing-room/statements-releases/2021/03/31/fact-sheet-the-american-jobs-plan/.

Tran, Henry, Douglas Smith, and Emily Fox. 2018. *Perspectives of Potential and Current Teachers for Rural Teacher Recruitment and Retention*. University of South Carolina's Center for Innovation in Higher Education. http://static1.squarespace.com/static/5ab91858b40b9d3cf933b285/t/5c015b9f70a6ad937c9a29a7/1543592866678/SC%20Teacher%20Perspectives%20on%20RRI%20Final%20Draft%20rev2.pdf.

Turner, Chris. 2020. "'Children Are Going Hungry': Why Schools Are Struggling to Feed Students." *National Public Radio*, September 8, 2020. www.npr.org/2020/09/08/908442609/children-are-going-hungry-why-schools-are-struggling-to-feed-students.

USDA. 2020. "Rural Poverty & Well-Being." Accessed July 12, 2021. www.ers.usda.gov/topics/rural-economy-population/rural-poverty-well-being/.

Weber Handwerker, Elizabeth, Peter Meyer, Joseph Piacentini, Michael Schultz, and Leo Sveikauskas. 2020. "Employment Recovery in the Wake of the COVID-19 Pandemic." *Monthly Labor Review*, December 2020. www.bls.gov/opub/mlr/2020/article/employment-recovery.htm.

7 The Impact of Parental Burnout and Time with Children

Family Stress in a Large Urban City During COVID-19

Wendy Wagner Robeson and Kimberly D. Lucas

Families' abilities to address their children's needs were greatly challenged by the coronavirus disease 2019 (COVID-19) pandemic. Even before the pandemic, families were facing a losing battle of trying to keep their work from spilling over into their home lives (Nippert-Eng 1995; Williams and Boushey 2010). Families walked the fine line of balancing the ever-present needs of their children with the demands of their employers. Once the COVID-19 pandemic hit, work was physically pushed into the home for some families, while other families were pressed to continue to work with increased exposure to severe acute respiratory syndrome coronavirus 2 (SARS-CoV-2).

In the summer of 2020, researchers conducted focus groups and interviews over Zoom with 24 parents/guardians from Boston, Massachusetts who had at least one young child not yet enrolled in kindergarten to learn how families were handling work and child care issues during the pandemic. These mothers, fathers, and non-binary parents/guardians represented diverse family structures, including single-, two-parent, and extended family households; a multitude of races and cultures; and a cross-section of neighborhoods across the city. Of the participants, 79% were women, 80% were married or partnered, and 25% were required to be at their work site at the time of data collection, while another 13% were educators who were uncertain about the timeline and plan for their return to work. We did not systematically collect data on race or ethnicity, so our understanding of our sample in this regard comes from self-identification over the course of data collection. For the most part, families were grouped according to their self-identified employment situation (e.g., those working from home, some combination of going to a work site and work from home, needing to be at a work site (some referred to themselves as essential workers), and furloughed/unemployed).

Participants were asked to describe their child care and work arrangements prior to and during the COVID-19 pandemic. They talked about child care, work, and parenting while living through a pandemic. Despite the diversity within our sample, certain themes were still strongly pervasive across our participants' experience. We found that certain inequities by employment type and gender persisted in our sample. While all families worried about the

SARS-CoV-2 virus, some knew infected people and others saw the SARS-CoV-2 virus enter their own homes. Simultaneously, changes in work and care arrangements increased the stress of work–life balance for all families, although this manifested in different ways depending on employment type and family structure. Finally, the combined effects of increased fear and increased stress produced conditions of increased constraint and pressure. The effects of parental burnout were made concrete as participants described their process for seeking child care as the COVID-19 pandemic continued; shifts in preferences signal both the effects of fear and stress as well as potential futures for equitable structuring of child care systems.

Inequities Persist

The diversity of the sample of participants afforded us with rich experiences and it particularly underscored the salience of both employment type and gender in shaping the ways in which fear and stress were felt by parents/guardians. Here, we spend time discussing how these themes produced nuanced and important differences within our sample.

Disparities by Employment Type

Inequity experienced in Boston, by wealth and by gender, is noteworthy. While Boston is certainly not the only city in the country experiencing these types of inequities, the experience of wealth and gender disparity specific to Boston serves as a salient backdrop against which our findings are situated. It is well-documented (Munoz et al. 2015) that wealth disparities in Boston have produced two starkly different experiences of Boston: one where wealth, either gained or inherited, produces a stable foundation and one where lack of wealth means living in constant precariousness. Although unintentional, data from this project pointed to distinct differences in experiences, challenges, and needs by employment type.

Families with at least one parent/guardian who identified their employment situation as either "work from home" or a "combination of going to a work site and work from home" exhibited similar challenges and worries. Participants in these employment situations all began working from their homes in March 2020. While many had been told to prepare to re-enter their workplaces in the fall, several employers had already postponed reopening until January (or even June) of 2021, while other employers had yet to issue further notice. For these families, Zoom became an ever-present part of their lives, providing their employers, co-workers, and clients a window into their home lives as children, pets, and other family members sometimes made cameo appearances during work meetings. Because their children's child care or school had shut down as the COVID-19 pandemic hit, these families were attempting to fulfill their obligations to their employers from home while simultaneously caring for their children. Although income data was not collected, many of these parents/

guardians in these families worked jobs that likely placed their families in the upper-middle or upper income bracket (Pew Research Center 2015).

The second group we encountered included families with parents/guardians working at a site that required their physical presence. Because these families had to return to their work site, they risked losing their jobs or faced reduced hours if they did not have an alternate means of child care for their children as child care and schools had closed as the pandemic hit. This was difficult because although emergency child care was available for state-designated essential workers, other forms of child care did not reopen until the end of June 2020. Many of the parents/guardians in these families worked jobs that likely placed their families in the middle-income bracket that is both too high to qualify for social benefits but too low to live safely beyond the brink of poverty.

Uneven Distribution of Work Across Gender

Prior to the COVID-19 pandemic, gender was known to play a role in terms of distribution of housework, child care, and schooling within the home (Coltrane 1989; Walzer 1996; Williams and Boushey 2010). In Boston, the impact of this additional labor, also known as the "second shift" (Hochschild 1989), weighed heavily on women's ability to enter or re-enter the workforce (City of Boston Mayor's Office of Women's Advancement (MOWA) 2019). The COVID-19 pandemic exacerbated these gendered roles within heterosexual households (Heilman, Rosario Castro Bernardini, and Pfeifer 2020; Umamaheswar and Tan 2020) as well as a decline in women's employment due to lack of child care (Ewing-Nelson 2020; Heilman, Rosario Castro Bernardini, and Pfeifer 2020).

Among study participants, household and child care tasks similarly fell disproportionately on women. Working parents/guardians felt overwhelmed by additional child care and school responsibilities presented by the COVID-19 pandemic; however, in two-parent heterosexual families, working mothers in particular seemed to take on more of these responsibilities than their male counterparts. With children and adults at home more often than prior to the COVID-19 pandemic, moms took on more of the household planning and logistics, child-centered tasks, and household tasks. One mom working in the service industry shared that, "It's been the unofficial decision that I'll be home with the boys when work picks up more so dad can go back to work." Mothers discussed cutting back their work hours, switching to more flexible work, or simply quitting their jobs, citing their current juggling of the "second shift" with their own paid labor as untenable. A mom working as a teacher's assistant considered her options as she awaited information on whether her job would be remote, in-person, or hybrid in the fall, "... I know day care is really expensive, and it's kinda not worth my paycheck. So unless they [make my job remote], I might just stay home."

This is not to say that fathers did not contribute to household chores or carework, but that the bulk of the burden fell onto mothers (Heilman, Rosario Castro Bernardini, and Pfeifer 2020), and many of the mothers we spoke to were, similar to those surveyed by the Massachusetts Commission on the Status of Women (2020b), near or already at their "breaking point." Burnout is a real issue for working families, and the COVID-19 pandemic magnified gender inequities at home and at work. Women tend to be the "shock absorbers" of our society (Grose 2020), and so it is not surprising that moms have been exhausted by what was thought at first to be a few weeks, then a few months, and is now a way of life for the near future. This new reality could have a lasting effect on gender equity in the workplace for years.

Living in a New Reality

We began data collection while the COVID-19 pandemic was still very much a worldwide concern. As it was a once-in-a-lifetime occurrence, we wanted to learn more about how our families were handling their new reality. We found that our data produced themes that cross-cut the wide diversity of our participants. The way these themes affected families were sometimes different, but they remained a pervasive experience across all of our participants. Three themes centered on families' experience during the COVID-19 pandemic: families are worried and scared, families feel greater stress in balancing work and child care, and families feel increased constraint and pressure.

Families are Worried and Scared

When it comes to young children and child care, there is already plenty to worry about. Even before the COVID-19 pandemic hit, child care had already been deemed unaffordable and inaccessible for the majority of families, both in Boston and across the country (Morgan 1986; City of Boston Mayor's Office of Women's Advancement (MOWA) 2019). As the COVID-19 pandemic continued into the summer of 2020, families' fears seemed to compound; it is not surprising that fear of all kinds, but all centering on fear of the unknown, was a strong theme across all families' experiences.

Families fear becoming infected with SARS-CoV-2. Most families worried generally about the potential unknown effects of the virus on their immediate family members, and many participants discussed isolating themselves, with limited or no direct contact with others outside of their home. One mom who is a teacher shared her fears and anxieties:

> I have no desire to be in closed spaces for long periods of time. I see how anxious I get, and sometimes I can't breathe when I'm in a closed place for too long right now ... I'm not okay around a lot of people right now, and I'm not okay in closed spaces. I'm okay outside, and that's something new for me.

While only some participants discussed pulling their families into extreme isolation, participants commonly reported feeling anxious or stressed when considering potential interaction with people outside of their pod. The drastic onset of this anxiety or stress from adults could be felt throughout households: one parent discussed, "When I have that many people in this apartment, we're all going crazy." Even if children are not immediately concerned with coming into contact with the SARS-CoV-2 virus, the fact that the adults in their home are anxious or stressed permeates and casts a tenor over the entire household, a phenomenon researchers are describing as the "Hardship Chain Reaction" (University of Oregon 2020b).

Participants took as many precautions they could think of in the early days of March and April 2020, including limiting ventures to the grocery store and ceasing to visit relatives or friends. Some families expressed added concern because their children or other close relatives had conditions that placed them at elevated risk. One mom working in the service industry explained:

> just sickness-wise, and the fact that it's a virus that no one knows about and that whole scary factor of it adds a lot more unknowns to any situation, so you kind of look at: do you really want to go to that playground, how many kids are actually there? You talk to a kid about going somewhere and you're like, Oh wow that's like 30 kids over on that one play structure-- is that okay? Maybe 30's a lot, but three or four kids are using the same toddler sized play structure. Maybe we'll go to another place. That adult's not wearing a mask. Those kids don't wear a mask so maybe we shouldn't go there. That type of thing.

Some participants were worried about getting sick for reasons beyond unknown health effects. For example, a stay-at-home dad shared how fragile his family's work/care balance is:

> We're still a little hesitant to take [the kids] to playgrounds, just because [playgrounds] are generally pretty populated, and there's still a feeling of a germ situation. We don't necessarily think the kids would get sick, but if either of us [adults] got sick, it could be a really difficult situation watching the kids. And we're in tight enough quarters that if [my wife] got sick, I would and vice versa.

And, with more hanging in the balance, one foster parent feared that a positive diagnosis of COVID-19 in any family member might result in having a pending adoption denied.

Families feared exposure risk at work, at child care, or at school. In the early months of the pandemic, essential workers and others who had to physically return to their work sites were concerned about the lack of PPE at their work sites. Already fearful about the effects of COVID-19, these participants had no choice but to potentially expose themselves and their families by going to work. One mom working in a health care setting shared her routine:

> I come home, I strip naked in my front door because I see patients all day, and they come there with the paper saying they have COVID, and we still have to help them, but we don't have the protections that doctors have. They have the complete setup, we do not. We just have the masks and maybe gloves that we don't even have anymore. It was very scary. I could not hug my daughter when I came home, I just walked into the house, ran to the shower.

While our data were not precise enough to produce conclusions by race, we do know that prior work by Neely (2020) found that women of color disproportionately hold low-wage and essential jobs. The added fear of exposure at work likely also disproportionately affects families of color, making them even more vulnerable to raising young children in households where anxiety and stress pervade.

Similarly, all participants expressed concern about school and child care reopening, citing their concern about increased risk of exposure to their families. As one mom who was working from home shared the following:

> For us, we've been super closed off to everyone for the past four months. I feel like we've tried to be so careful and so insular that this—this feels like opening it up in such a big way. We've interacted with maybe three people, and now all of a sudden, our kid is going to be licking the same toys as how many other kids and how many other people they've interacted with. It's definitely breaking that bubble in a big way.

While the science was still in debate as to the severity of carriers and spread among young children, it is quite difficult to ensure that young children abide by social distance measures even part time (Hasteltine 2020). Many of the participants welcomed staying at home for the time being rather than returning to large office buildings and other work, child care, or school scenarios with more people. And while many participants worried about the various points of exposure, so, too, did their children. One participant mentioned that her toddler had started screaming, "Stay away from me people!" anytime they were outside and in proximity of others. In another family, a preschool-aged son shared that he missed his friends, asked many questions about death and dying, had trouble sleeping, and was plagued by monsters. The child's mental health and anxiety improved when he was back in child care for five weeks, but plummeted again when it ended.

Just as families were frightened for themselves and their family members contracting the SARS-CoV-2 virus, they also feared stagnation or even harm to children's growth and development in isolation. Besides fearing infection with SARS-CoV-2, participants also expressed alarm as to the possible harm to their children's mental health, socio-emotional development, and other aspects of their child's growth and development due to not being around other children and friends at child care or school. Participants cited examples of behaviors their children exhibited that they felt were worrisome. Some children's routines were disrupted: several participants noted that their children were watching more videos and had much more screen time than parents would have allowed prior to the COVID-19 pandemic, and one participant noted that his young daughter had "been staying up [late], and [her] whole schedule is upside down."

Families also noticed changes in their children's socio-emotional states. Some families began to experience attachment issues, with one father sharing that his two young children would scream for their mother whenever she was on Zoom or on the phone. Several families identified the need for their children to go back to child care so that they can interact with peers. One young child began asking about his mother's co-workers often seen over Zoom. This mother told us that she was worried that her son was "so desperate for other humans that he's just popping onto these Zoom calls and doesn't even know these people." Other families noticed that Zoom was not an appropriate replacement for in-person peer interaction; for example, one mom told us that her kindergarten-aged daughter stopped communicating when she had to attend school over Zoom.

Participants may not have had the jargon for it, but they all expressed an understanding that their children were missing something essential in staying home and away from their typical care or school situation. The stay-at-home dad mentioned above also noted that the lack of safe access to playgroups and other activities (e.g., story time at the library) has had an effect on his children's social development and his family's ability to provide experiences that help promote positive growth and development for his young children. These observations and related concerns over the effects of isolation on their children's growth and development complement statewide survey results demonstrating widespread concern that *not* attending child care would deprive young children of socialization and produce negative effects on young children's mental health (Strategies for Children 2020). An essential worker mom initially felt that emergency child care would include too many children, but now feels that she would put her four-year-old into emergency care if another shut-down occurs. She feels he needs to interact with others and that she would have no choice, for the sake of his growth and development, despite the germs. Our participants demonstrated that not having the needed socio-emotional experiences necessary for optimal development caused real harm to their children.

Families Feel Greater Stress in Balancing Work and Child Care

Families found it difficult to find balance between work life and home life during the COVID-19 pandemic as both worlds were turned upside down. Many participants felt that their employers did understand that working from home with young children would pose new and different challenges to productivity. This was true especially if their employers were also parents of young children. A teacher told us that her principal also had young children and was very understanding; she was asked to do her best given the circumstances.

Co-workers, other colleagues, and clients also seemed accommodating of young children invading (or regularly attending) Zoom meetings (one mom's child attended so often that she began calling him her "sidekick"). Participants felt that this blending of work and home helped humanize them and their home situation for their colleagues and clients, and it helped them better understand and have empathy for their peers' work/home situations. One work-from-home mom said:

> I actually like it when my kid interrupts calls [Zoom] when it's with people that I don't normally see. Especially when it's my boss' boss or senior leadership. This is what I'm dealing with. I know you all have kids that are in their teens or 20s, but I have a four-year-old literally climbing up my back, so this is why I'm not doing all the things I'm supposed to be doing. So it's a nice visual reminder.

Many employers seemed to understand that children would now be a presence throughout their employees' work day, but participants felt that their employers made few accommodations for this drastic disruption of the typical work day. Participants consistently cited the fact that they felt pressure to produce the same amount of work output as they did prior to the COVID-19 pandemic. Some participants, particularly those working from home in some capacity, noted that while their employers provided more flexibility in work hours and work days, the expectation of work output had not changed. A work-from-home mom told us:

> I think ... well, I know the work and output expectations are 100% the same if not more during all this. And it's kind of just like "Make it work." At my work at least people are advanced enough to not criticize if kids are around or that you hear kids, but the expectation is that you're working a full day.

An essential worker mom said that the attitude at her workplace felt like, "They're acknowledging that COVID is happening still, but at the same time they're just like, 'We want our job done.'"

Similar to respondents in a national survey of parents (Catalyst 2020), Bostonian participants feared losing their jobs for not producing as much output as peers who didn't have young children. They found ways to compensate for work or time lost, working early in the morning before children awakened, late into the night after children are asleep, or on weekends. Due to having young children in the home and no change in output expectations, work was often completed at the expense of sleep; time with their children, partner, or other family and friends; or personal time. One mom working from home describes how her child care decisions were fully colored by the inflexible expectations of her and her husband's jobs and how this, combined with having a young child in the home, became unsustainable:

I'm one of the ones who could keep my job, but I'm not working like I did before. So I have the constant fear that if I'm not focusing more on work, that I am at risk of losing my job. That's why I feel really pushed to send her back to day care, and that feels

really bad ... So now imagine all these families that you're now all of a sudden exposed to. We can control our environment, but we cannot control how the two teachers and the nine other families, what they're doing. That feels scary. It feels scary because if something happens, I feel like we could have continued what we're doing now. It's a matter of how much risk we want to take to feel that we are able to do our jobs ... But we feel that it's necessary because we want to keep our jobs. We just bought a house, there's a lot of financial responsibility ... It doesn't feel safe, but it also feels like we have to make sure we can pay our bills.

In a similar vein, another work-from-home mom described keeping a professional face for a particularly high-level work group:

My supervisors had been understanding, but I feel like it's navigating with other colleagues. How understanding or not are they going to be ... I don't want them to think I can't do this just because my kid is home with me. I feel like I have to be this certain person ... so that my ability to carry out a task isn't questioned.

Related to fear of job loss was fear of stature and capability that many women and people of color in our sample had to contend with. These findings corroborate results from a statewide survey that found that working parents worry that their job performance will suffer as they patch together child care arrangements (Strategies for Children 2020).

A few participants who happened to be decision-makers in their own organizations recognized that beyond the flexibility of working from home, work expectations might also need to shift. One mom working at a non-profit readjusted organizational expectations for her small staff (and herself), and she reported that this adjustment yielded a significant reduction in stress for herself as well as a better working environment for her small staff. A dad working from home and managing a small team cited his work culture as supporting him in recognizing that he and the workers he manages "don't really have the 8 hours or 40 hours a week that they had previously." This recognition has changed how he evaluated his staff (and how he is evaluated as well).

For essential workers at the beginning of the pandemic, and for participants whose work site reopened according to the state's reopening plan, there was no other choice but to return to their work sites to support their families. Because child care and school had shut down in the early days of the pandemic, these participants had to find a safe way to care for their children while they supported their families. Finding a safe and trusted place to care for their children was imperative for essential workers, who are largely women of color and also less likely to have a college degree, and who have also been disproportionately economically affected (Frye 2020; Misra 2020; Robertson and Gebeloff 2020). While some participants did have access to emergency child care as essential workers, not all who were required to return to work did.

Participants who had to return to their work site experienced compounded stress when their work site did not seem safe or prepared to deal with COVID-19. One essential worker mom described how her work culture affected her home life and child care decisions despite her worry and concern for her young children.

> They were kind of like, "You don't have to come in. Don't. But we really need you to come in when you can." ... I cannot lose my job right now, especially in my circumstances. Being the sole provider for my three kids, it's just not plausible for me to say, "No I can't do this." ... I go back to work in two weeks ... I would love to stay home and be safe, especially with them being so new—and being preemies ... They were born two months early.

For these participants, not only did they have to deal with the stress of finding care for their children while they were at work, but they also had to confront their fears around being infected.

Participants discussed their interest and intention to be good workers, but it was clear that the lack of accommodations from their employers made it difficult for them to feel that they were performing well. While participants whose employers allowed them to work from home felt stress around competing work and child care needs *within* their homes, participants whose employer required them to return to their work site felt stress around competing needs *because of the separation between* their work and child care needs. These stresses were no more and no greater than one another; they were simply different.

Families Feel Increased Constraint and Pressure

Their fears and employment constraints aside, Bostonian families were feeling constrained and pressured in ways different from their pre-COVID constraints and pressures. Too often, participants expressed feelings about not being a good parent/guardian and in the same breath, they expressed feelings about not being the employee they had been before the pandemic. One work-from-home parent encapsulated this quite well.

> The biggest challenge is just trying to work and parent at the same time. Nobody is meant to do that ... I can't be engaged with [my child] while I'm also working. It's really hard to do at the same time. "I want a snack or I need help to wipe my butt." Things like that come up that I need to help him with that I can't do. And I think it's hard for him to see me at home with him when he can't engage with me in that way. That's really hard on

him, it takes a toll on him I think … Right now, I'm working 9–2. But I do end up many nights working after he goes to bed. Which again, I'm exhausted and the work is not the right caliber of work. He goes to bed, I do dishes, and clean things up. And by the time I sit down, it's usually 9:30 or 10 that I'm sitting down at my computer to do work. This is not good for anybody. It usually takes me double the time to do that work, so it's really not efficient for me to work that late, but sometimes there's stuff that has to get done during that time. It's not great. It's not good. I feel like a bad employee and a bad parent at the same time.

As a national survey of parents found that,

> These parents are suddenly expected to be full-time care providers for their younger children, full-time teacher assistants and classroom managers for their older children, and in their spare time, full-time employees at their "day jobs" so that they can support their families' basic needs.
> (University of Oregon 2020a)

Another national survey estimated that parents were losing an average of eight hours of work per week trying to make this balance work (Finucane 2020). As already described, Bostonian families, regardless of type of employment, felt that they had to choose between being a good parent/guardian and being a good employee. With the limitation of only so many hours in the day (Heilman, Rosario Castro Bernardini, and Pfeifer 2020; Perelman 2020; Williams and Boushey 2010), the end result for all of our participants was feelings of inadequacy both as parents/guardians *and* as employees. Even over Zoom, we could see these feelings manifest in pained and anguished looks as participants described their inability to feel good in either of these roles; families felt that they had too much on their plate and were not able to give enough of themselves to their children *and* their work.

Families have been in a constant state of stress. Combined, families' fears and their rigid work responsibilities produced constraints against which they made decisions. Participants noted what these constraints, brought about by the COVID-19 pandemic, were doing to their own mental states. They explicitly expressed being stressed, worried and nervous, overwhelmed, and exhausted. Few people had found time for themselves in months. Participants described experiences consistent with findings from the Massachusetts Commission on the Status of Women's (2020b) survey, which reported that 80% of parents experienced significant to overwhelming stress. A mom working from home walked us through her work–life balancing act.

> It just feels like I'm working all the time to try and stay at an appropriate level of output for my job and the level I feel like I need to be producing at to really keep things moving along. It feels like if I take a break to … breastfeed and maybe can't do work, then it feels like I'm going to make up

> that time later whether I'm planning or, whether I just … [We were then interrupted by her baby.] This is what it's like all the time at work.

And a mom who is a service worker summed it all by saying the following.

> Life goal stuff—like going on a big family vacation—that's not even on the board anymore. Cause now it's let's get through the month. It's scary. Besides the obvious of sickness and all of that. The financial side of it … We have to have some humor with it because it's not only a sickness that has taken over and our child care is now completely changed and our way of taking care of our children is changed but the financial, our futures, our careers, everything. I feel like we're still in that Shake N Bake bag, and no one dumped us out yet.

This finding is particularly striking in light of recent national data demonstrating that families have experienced loss of emotional support during the pandemic (University of Oregon 2020a). In addition, national and statewide studies demonstrated that high levels of stress, anxiety, and depression were evident as early as August 2020 (Catalyst 2020; Gonzalez et al. 2020; Massachusetts Commission on the Status of Women 2020a). A separate national study made note that social distancing has a different emotional toll on women than on men (Heilman, Rosario Castro Bernardini, and Pfeifer 2020). Families are doing all they can to cope. Our Bostonian parents were experiencing burnout. An essential worker mom shared that she:

> sent [her kids] to [home state] to stay with my family … they stayed for a month and a half. Because … with my little one, because he'd been in the house all day, he was just having too much energy for me when I got home. I wasn't giving him the time that he needed for his school work or anything, so I just asked my family to take him so he could get the support he needed and I could get the support I needed without being overwhelmed and stressed.

In the same vein, a mom who is a service worker told us that she started taking anti-anxiety medication "because I was flipping out about every little thing." During a time when stress levels were on the rise due to the aforementioned fear of the SARS-CoV-2 virus, massive job loss, increased attention to anti-blackness and racial injustice, and climate disasters, lack of emotional support adds to the likelihood of the introduction of toxic stress into the home and, therefore, adverse effects on children's growth and development (Shonkoff and Phillips 2000).

The COVID-19 Pandemic, Families with Young Children, and Child Care Decisions

While we knew how important child care was prior to the COVID-19 pandemic, the onset of the pandemic has brought home the fact that child care is the bedrock upon which our society runs. Without child care, families cannot get to or focus on work, employees will not be as productive, and children may not receive the needed support for their optimal growth and development. Women's careers in particular are put at an even greater disadvantage in the absence of child care, as "child care is fundamentally about gender and race equity" (Asset Funders Network 2020), functioning as a means to mobility for women and women of color, and in turn, mobility for their children. Hence, the intersection of work life and home life was greatly affected during the COVID-19 pandemic with the lack of child care for so many families.

Participants told us about the child care arrangements they had prior to the pandemic, during the early months of the pandemic, and once child care programs began to reopen and schools were making plans. The kinds of child care participants used prior to the pandemic included center-based care, family child care, public or private school preschool programs, relative care, stay-at-home parents, and neighbors. We learned that families' fears had a deep influence on their decision to access available care and that families' perception of safety and their comfort with their selected child care was of paramount importance when they did decide to return to child care.

Fear Drives Changes in Accessing Care

Fear prevented families from accessing available care. Once the pandemic hit, nearly all participants took care of their children in their homes in response to the state of emergency declared by the Massachusetts governor on March 10, 2020. Some of our participants were classified by the Commonwealth as "essential workers," allowing them special access to emergency child care which was the only kind that was allowed to open during the first months of the pandemic. While emergency child care was set up rapidly and was free of charge, only one of our essential worker participants took advantage of the free emergency care at a family child care home. Other essential workers cited their fear of infection, not knowing how many other children would be present, or not having a relationship with their closest emergency child care provider. One essential worker mom explained her thought process:

> There was emergency day care open when it first started, before they figured it out at some point. However, they said that up to 40 kids can be in a center at the same time, and in my head I was like, "So what if 40 kids actually come, and how many adults are gonna be there? It's probably not safe. If you're telling us not to be around, then I'm not going to be around. So why send them there?"

While a national survey (Bipartisan Policy Center and Morning Consult 2020) found that essential workers had a hard time finding child care for their children, this was not the case in Boston, where emergency child care capacity peaked at 38% while it was available during the first months of the pandemic (MOWA, email to author, November 2020).

The top reasons parents cited for keeping children home were to minimize exposure to the SARS-CoV-2 virus for their children and concerns regarding cleaning and sanitation procedures. Into late summer, a few participants had either decided to homeschool their children or that one parent/guardian (in two-parent/guardian, heterosexual couples, this typically meant the mother) would stay home with the children while the other parent/guardian worked. These findings corroborated those from a statewide survey that found that, during the summer, 70% of families with school-age children considered keeping both school-age children and young children out of child care if they were working from home (MOWA, email to author, November 2020).

Other families did not have the option to keep a parent/guardian home. Participants from these families felt that they had no choice but to send their children to care, underscoring findings from a statewide study that found 37% of the respondents (and 40% of essential workers) in the Commonwealth expressed concern about leaving their children unattended because of a need to work (Massachusetts Commission on the Status of Women 2020b). A mom who is an essential worker described her current care situation: "Right now, my oldest son is 12. He's helping with his brother. His grandmother lives upstairs, so she checks in on them. So they're home right now during my work hours." Her experience echoed a finding from a statewide survey that 29% of families who had to return to work outside of the home considered having an older child watch a younger child while they worked (Strategies for Children 2020). As mentioned, the fear of infection that families felt in placing their children in group care alongside the need to physically go back to work placed these families in a position that produced feelings of inadequacy, both at home and at work.

A Basis of Trust is Necessary for Care Access

Families want child care that they feel comfortable with. Whether it was because they wanted to or because they had to, when families did utilize child care, they went to great lengths to ensure that they felt safe and comfortable with their choice, given their multiple fears and constraints. Participants who were able often looked to the familiar first. Community plays an imperative role for families, both in terms of child care and in terms of emotional support. Extended family, trusted neighbors, friends, church members, and other community members continued to provide child care relief into the COVID-19 pandemic, though in new ways and with new considerations. Some participants discussed moving out of state or moving their relatives in state for several months to be close to grandparents and other family members who, as part of a family's "pod," were thought to be more safe than non-pod child care options. Other participants, fearing for grandparents' health, drastically or completely cut down on their reliance on grandparents' help. Some participants discussed leaning on their local connections to find neighbors, friends, and church members who might help alleviate child care needs.

Some participants decided to return to their previous care arrangements immediately upon the state's reopening of child care. Others waited as long as they could but ultimately decided to return to their child care. These participants cited knowing and trusting their child care provider as a reason why they felt comfortable with their return. While some participants expressed worry about staff and other parents/families wearing masks and taking the necessary measures to keep everyone safe, having fewer children than was typical pre-pandemic helped ease fear. These fears were also being mitigated by the parallel fear and concern about young children's mental health and socio-emotional development. A mom who works for a non-profit organization brought her daughter immediately back to her family child care provider:

> I think it's because it's three families ... they know that we'll say that she's been sick. They know that nobody's gonna bring their kid if they're sick. We trust the other families; we trust the providers. Nobody's going if they're sick.

Participants who went back to their previous child care provider suggest that strong communication and trust between child care providers and all families were key.

Discussion

Child care and schools need to become places families recognize as partners in trying to craft a new reality that meets the needs of both parents/guardians and children. Families want what is best for their children and know that for their children's mental health, they need to be back with friends and other children so that their socio-emotional development is not muted or delayed. The COVID-19 pandemic has placed families under chronic stress, stemming from a number of factors, with many simply trying to get by day-to-day. We witnessed that many of our participants were on or over the edge of burnout from trying to both care for their children and meet their work-related demands. While it was known that in pre-pandemic times families were on the losing end of trying to balance their work lives with their home lives, the COVID-19 pandemic made their lives—and their children's lives—even more difficult. The fear, stress, and constraint presented by the COVID-19 pandemic were complicated by variation in employment type and family structure. Even choosing child care, which many parents did in the pre-pandemic days, was plagued by these new challenges brought by the COVID-19 pandemic.

Local, state, and federal government actors—as well as community organizations and other family supports—should consider new avenues to provide mental health, emotional, and trauma support to parents and families and address their fears while creating safety. This includes providing pathways for supporting young children's growth and development in the home, with their families, and in their communities. Families seemed to find their participation in the focus groups cathartic as they shared their stories with others who could empathize and relate. Likewise, local governments should identify a set of supports that can be deployed at the community, neighborhood, or cohort level to support families in finding ways to minimize or cope with chronic stress, to help identify where additional supportive services might be offered, and to provide families with the tools and resources for mitigating any additional future stress. It is imperative that families' fears about the SARS-CoV-2 virus be addressed with clear, consistent, and evidence-based communications and recommendations of a protocol regarding young children. These efforts can help reduce families' experiences of "too much" and reassure working families that they in fact are enough. The end result will be thriving families and healthy developmentally sound children.

References

Asset Funders Network. 2020. "Child Care and the Economy." Accessed July 12, 2021. https://assetfunders.org/event/child-care-and-the-economy/.

Bipartisan Policy Center and Morning Consult. 2020. "Bipartisan Center—Morning Consult Poll: Unemployment Insurance and Caregiving Responsibilities During COVID-19." *Bipartisan Policy Center,* July 23, 2020. https://bipartisanpolicy.org/blog/bipartisan-policy-center-morning-consult-poll-unemployment-insurance-and-caregiving-responsibilities-during-covid-19/.

Catalyst. 2020. "The Impact of COVID-19 on Working Parents." Accessed July 12, 2021. www.catalyst.org/research/impact-covid-working-parents/.

City of Boston Mayor's Office of Women's Advancement (MOWA). 2019. *Making Childcare Work.* Boston: Mayor's Office of Women's Advancement. www.boston.gov/sites/default/files/file/document_files/2019/10/final_report_on_child_care_in_boston_-_2019.pdf.

Coltrane, Scott. 1989. "Household Labor and the Routine Production of Gender." *Social Problems* 36 (5): 473–90. https://doi.org/10.2307/3096813.

Ewing-Nelson, Claire. 2020. *Four Times More Women Than Men Dropped Out of the Labor Force in September.* Washington, DC: National Women's Law Center. https://nwlc.org/resources/four-times-more-women-than-men-dropped-out-of-the-labor-force-in-september/.

Finucane, Martin. 2020. "Northeastern Researchers Find Lack of Child Care Has Been a Significant Challenge for Workers During the Pandemic." *The Boston Globe,* July 7, 2020. www.bostonglobe.com/2020/07/07/nation/northeastern-study-finds-child-care-has-been-challenge-workers-during-pandemic/.

Frye, Jocelyn. 2020. *On the Frontlines at Work and at Home: The Disproportionate Economic Effects of the Coronavirus Pandemic on Women of Color.* Washington, DC: Center for American Progress. www.americanprogress.org/issues/women/reports/2020/04/23/483846/frontlines-work-home/.

Gonzalez, Kathryn E., Emily C. Hanno, Jorge Cuartas, Stephanie M. Jones, Nonie K. Lesaux, Kerry Hofer, Amy Checkoway, and Barbara Goodson. 2020. *How Are They Faring? Impacts of the COVID-19 Pandemic on the Lives of Families and Young Children in Massachusetts*. Saul Zaentz Early Education Initiative, Harvard Graduate School of Education. https://zaentz.gse.harvard.edu/wp-content/uploads/2020/08/ELS@H-COVID-Report_-Parents_Final_2.pdf.

Grose, Jessica. 2020. "Mothers Are the 'Shock Absorbers' of our Society." *The New York Times*, October 14, 2020. www.nytimes.com/2020/10/14/parenting/working-moms-job-loss-coronavirus.html.

Hasteltine, William A. 2020. "New Evidence Suggests Young Children Spread COVID-19 More Efficiently than Adults." *Forbes*, July 31, 2020. www.forbes.com/sites/williamhaseltine/2020/07/31/new-evidence-suggests-young-children-spread-covid-19-more-efficiently-than-adults/#2b685c1e19fd.

Heilman, Brian, María Rosario Castro Bernardini, and Kimberly Pfeifer. 2020. *Caring Under COVID-19: How the Pandemic Is—and Is Not—Changing Unpaid Care and Domestic Work Responsibilities in the United States*. Boston: Oxfam and Washington, DC: Promundo-US. https://promundoglobal.org/resources/caring-under-covid-19-how-the-pandemic-is-and-is-not-changing-unpaid-care-and-domestic-work-responsibilities-in-the-united-states/.

Hochschild, Arlie Russell. 1989. *The Second Shift: Working Parents and the Revolution at Home*. New York, NY: Viking.

Massachusetts Commission on the Status of Women. 2020a. "Impact of COVID-19 and Related Policy on Massachusetts Women and Girls." Accessed July 13, 2021. www.mass.gov/files/documents/2020/04/21/MCSW%20COVID-19%20Report%20.pdf.

Massachusetts Commission on the Status of Women. 2020b. "Child Care and Education During COVID-19: A Report on the Economic and Social Impact on Women in Massachusetts." Accessed July 13, 2021. www.mass.gov/doc/mcsw-child-care-and-education-during-covid-19-report-october-2020/download.

Misra, Joya. 2020. "Nearly 3 in 5 US Moms Were in the Workforce Before the COVID-19 Pandemic—Is That Changing?" *The Conversation*, July 3, 2020. https://theconversation.com/nearly-3-in-4-us-moms-were-in-the-workforce-before-the-covid-19-pandemic-is-that-changing-141510.

Morgan, Gwen C. 1986. "Supplemental Care for Young Children." In *In Support of Families*, edited by Michael Yogman and T. Berry Brazelton, Chapter 9, pp. 156–170. Cambridge, MA: Harvard University Press.

Munoz, Ana Patricia, Marlene Kim, Mariko Chang, Regine O. Jackson, Darrick Hamilton, and William A. Darrity, Jr. 2015. "The Color of Wealth in Boston." Boston: Federal Reserve Bank of Boston. www.bostonfed.org/publications/one-time-pubs/color-of-wealth.aspx.

Neely, Megan Tobias. 2020. "Essential and Expendable: Gendered Labor in the Coronavirus Crisis." *The Clayman Institute for Gender Research*, Stanford University, June 3, 2020. https://gender.stanford.edu/news-publications/gender-news/essential-and-expendable-gendered-labor-coronavirus-crisis.

Nippert-Eng, Christena E. 1995. *Home and Work*. Chicago, IL: University of Chicago Press.

Perelman, Deb. 2020. "In the COVID-19 Economy, You Can Have a Kid or a Job. You Can't Have Both." *The New York Times*, July 2, 2020. www.nytimes.com/2020/07/02/business/covid-economy-parents-kids-career-homeschooling.html.

Pew Research Center. 2015. "The American Middle Class Is Losing Ground: No Longer the Majority and Falling Behind Financially." *Pew Research Center*, December 9, 2015. www.pewresearch.org/social-trends/2015/12/09/the-american-middle-class-is-losing-ground/.

Robertson, Campbell, and Robert Gebeloff. 2020. "How Millions of Women Became the Most Essential Workers in America." *The New York Times*, April 18, 2020. www.nytimes.com/2020/04/18/us/coronavirus-women-essential-workers.html.

Shonkoff, Jack P., and Deborah A. Phillips (Eds.). 2000. *From Neurons to Neighborhoods: The Science of Early Childhood Development*. Washington, DC: National Academy Press.

Strategies for Children. 2020. "COVID-19 Response—Parent Survey." Accessed July 12, 2021. www.strategiesforchildren.org/covid-19.html.

Umamaheswar, Janani, and Catherine Tan. 2020. "'Dad, Wash Your Hands': Gender, Care Work, and Attitudes Toward Risk During the COVID-19 Pandemic." *Socius* 6: 1–14. https://doi.org/10.1177/2378023120964376.

University of Oregon. 2020a. "RAPID-EC Study." Accessed July 14, 2021. https://medium.com/rapid-ec-project.

University of Oregon. 2020b. "A Hardship Chain Reaction." *University of Oregon*, July 20, 2020. https://medium.com/rapid-ec-project/a-hardship-chain-reaction-3c3f3577b30.

Walzer, Susan. 1996. "Thinking About the Baby: Gender and the Division of Infant Care." *Social Problems* 43 (2): 219–34. https://doi.org/10.2307/3096999.

Williams, Joan C., and Heather Boushey. 2010. *The Three Faces of Work-Family Conflict: The Poor, the Professionals, and the Missing Middle*. San Francisco, CA: Center for American Progress. https://cdn.americanprogress.org/wp-content/uploads/issues/2010/01/pdf/threefaces.pdf?_ga=2.73194000.261800572.1626117831-1189420461.1626117831.

Part 3

Unmasking Pandemic Agency

8 When Six Feet Feels Like Six Miles

Children's Images of Their Lives During the COVID-19 Pandemic

Sandi K. Nenga

In early 2020, news coverage of the coronavirus disease 2019 (COVID-19) global pandemic was dominated by the words and images of adults who were trying to understand the epidemiology of the severe acute respiratory syndrome coronavirus 2 (SARS-CoV-2) outbreak and chronicle the disruptive consequences of virus mitigation efforts. News coverage focused on hospitals overrun with COVID-19 patients, shuttered workplaces, empty streets, and the sudden switch to videoconferencing platforms. Attempts to slow the spread of the virus meant that schools closed or moved online, parents were either unemployed or working at home, and social gatherings with friends and family were cancelled. Although these changes clearly impacted children, many news stories focused on the experiences and perspectives of *adults* who suddenly and simultaneously had to fulfill the roles of worker, parent, teacher and playmate (see Robeson and Lucas 2021, this volume). As the COVID-19 pandemic continued into the 2020–21 school year, news stories featured adult educators, policymakers and parents worried that online and hybrid schooling models were stalling or even reversing kids' academic progress. One innovative photo essay asked children to draw what they missed from their lives before lockdown (Kyung-Hoon and Reuters Photographers 2020), but there was little attention paid to what *children* said about their daily lives *during* the COVID-19 pandemic.

Focusing on children's viewpoints aligns this chapter with the New Childhood Studies, which assumes that children have agency, that they are important to study in their own right and not just as future adults, and that childhoods vary along axes of inequality such as gender, race, class, disability, region, and era (Corsaro 2017; Prout and James 1990). One way that New Childhood Studies scholars minimize adult-centric interpretations and re-center the perspectives of young people inhabiting the social structure of childhood is to follow their lead on terminology: in this project and in prior literature, young people referred to themselves as kids rather than children (Taft 2019; Thorne 1993). From this point forward, I will use the term "kids" to describe the young people I studied both to align this chapter with the theoretical sensibilities of the new sociology of childhood and to amplify the kids' voices. This study also foregrounds the agency of kids by asking them to

DOI: 10.4324/9781003250937-12

articulate their own experiences of the COVID-19 pandemic through words and images. This analysis of kids' images is grounded firmly in the theoretical tradition of interpretive reproduction. Interpretive reproduction argues that kids borrow symbols, meanings, and routines from adults and other children, collectively refashion them to address their own concerns and values present in their peer cultures, and, in doing so, both recreate and change the larger society (Corsaro 1992, 2017). In this chapter, I pay particular attention to the ways that kids borrow and manipulate visual elements of the COVID-19 global pandemic to express their own concerns and values in drawings and photographs. Through their images, kids documented the ways the pandemic disrupted their norms and institutions, increased their anxiety and loneliness, and pushed them to explore new activities and means of connecting with friends.

Collecting Kids' Drawings and Photographs

In fall 2020, I designed and conducted a community-engaged learning and research project embedded in an undergraduate sociology course titled "Childhood and Youth." This project used participatory drawing (Literat 2013) and photovoice (Morojele and Muthukrishna 2016; Woodgate, Zurba, and Tennent 2017) methods to capture kids' perspectives on their daily lives during the COVID-19 global pandemic. Participatory visual methods offer several advantages when working with kids, including giving kids more time to reflect on complex concepts and produce nuanced images (Literat 2013). Drawing pictures and taking photographs also offer younger kids who may not be as verbal another means of expressing their ideas (Literat 2013).

After receiving approval from the university's institutional review board, we recruited 21 kids aged 6 to 16 years who lived in Texas by widely advertising the study on a university email list and smartphone app. Several university employees forwarded the study advertisement to parents in their social circles. Our participants typically included parents, relatives, friends, and/or neighbors who were university faculty, staff, and alumni, which meant that the kids in our study were likely from more educated and affluent families. The only demographic characteristic we asked for was age: the average age of the kids in this sample was 9.7 years. There was 1 six-year-old, 6 seven-year-olds, 2 eight-year-olds, 3 nine-year-olds, 1 ten-year-old, 1 eleven-year-old, 2 twelve-year-olds, 4 thirteen-year-olds, and 1 sixteen-year-old. Although we did not ask about race directly, the kids in our sample appeared to be White, Asian, Latinx, and biracial. All names in this chapter are pseudonyms; some participants wanted to choose their pseudonym as Padfoot did, some parents chose pseudonyms for their kids, and sometimes the college student chose the pseudonym. Because our participants referred to themselves, their fellow students, and their friends as "kids" (but never as "children"), I refer to our participants as "kids" as a means of centering their perspectives and voices (Taft 2019; Thorne 1993).

Once I obtained parental consent, I assigned each student in my college class to work with one kid. The college students met with the kids participating in the study via videoconferencing twice and asked kids for verbal assent at the beginning of both sessions. In the first session, the college student and the participant each drew a picture of "what their lives were like during the pandemic" and shared them with each other. We asked kids or their parents to send us the drawings as a scanned document, a texted photo, or a mailed hard copy. Before the second session, the college student asked their participant to take three photographs showing us what their everyday lives were like during the pandemic. To protect the confidentiality of others, we asked kids not to show anyone's face in their photographs. If kids did include faces, we blurred them out. For each drawing and photograph, we asked the kids during the interview what was in the image and why they chose to draw or photograph that specific image. The participatory drawing sessions typically lasted for 20 to 60 minutes, and the photovoice sessions lasted for 5 to 15 minutes. College students recorded the sessions and transcribed the kids' descriptions of their images. Because some kids shared more than one drawing and three photographs with us, there were a total of 94 images that illustrated what their lives were like during the pandemic.

As a community-engaged learning project and an ethical research project, it was important for us to ensure that kids benefitted from their participation. Many kids who were kept at home for online schooling had little opportunity to meet new people, and the two online sessions allowed them to meet and chat with a college student. Parents wrote to tell me that their kids' "moods were elevated" after each session and the kids were "excited" and "engaged" as they thought about which three pictures to take for the second session. After the conclusion of the second session, each college student handwrote a thank-you note on university stationery, enclosed two temporary tattoos, and mailed the card. Several parents told me that their kids were excited to receive mail and to wear the temporary tattoos. One participant put on her temporary tattoo and showed it to her friends at school, telling them she had received the tattoo for helping a college student with a "very important research project."

The college students and I used the kids' images and what they said about them to create an online museum exhibit titled "Childhoods During the Pandemic." Once the exhibit went live, I sent the link to each parent. One parent wrote to say that her kid wanted to see each image and read every single quote in the exhibit; she also noted that it helped her kid realize that she was not alone in her pandemic struggles. The project offered kids a chance to be part of something bigger than themselves. For this chapter, I conducted inductive qualitative data analysis on both the images and what the kids said about each image. I searched for emergent themes and patterns, frequently documenting my observations in coding memos (Gerson and Damaske 2021).

New Rules, New Procedures

Kids' drawings and photographs revealed that they were very aware of the COVID-19 pandemic and the many ways that their lives were changing. As stay-at-home orders were issued in many counties across Texas, kids were asked to follow new rules in public, at school, and in stores. Nearly every kid (18 of 21) produced an image documenting the new rules they had to follow because of the pandemic, highlighting their subjugated status.

Several kids either drew or photographed the masks, gloves, and hand sanitizer bottles which they were now required to use whenever they left their homes. Chase, age 8, photographed seven piles of color-coordinated cloth face masks laid out neatly on a countertop. He explained, "Those are all the masks my grandma made us to wear. We will have to wear all of those all the time, like at least 90 or 99 percent of the time, I think." Many of our participants who photographed masks noted that a family member had made them. It is possible that in the absence of face-to-face visits, the masks became tangible reminders that their remote family members cared about them. Some of our participants noted that the parents with whom they lived used the masks and hand sanitizer to keep them safe while facing the dangers of the pandemic. Allison, age 9, photographed a bottle of hand sanitizer because, as she explained, "My daddy and my mommy are always telling me to put hand sanitizer on." Creating images of their personal protective equipment simultaneously documented the new rules they had to follow and allowed kids to tell us that their families cared for them and worried about their safety.

Many of our participants were aware that methods for procuring food and supplies changed during the COVID-19 pandemic. To illustrate what his life was like since the pandemic began, Mason, age 7, drew the logo of a company known for shipping goods directly to people's homes and apartments. As the stay-at-home orders were issued, many affluent Texans rushed to stock up on food and supplies. Jake, age 8, was so impressed with his family's ability to buy in bulk that he drew a picture of "my overflowing pantry" which was a three-sided room completely filled with box shapes. When people did venture out to a grocery store, the experience changed dramatically because of physical distancing and disinfection strategies. Allison, age 9, drew a picture of the shopping experience at H-E-B (a major grocery retailer in Texas) from her perspective. On the left side of her drawing (see Figure 8.1), she, her younger brother, and her mother are wearing masks and standing on a circle with two dark ovals and the words "6 feet apart." The grocery stores had put down similar circles with footprint outlines where Allison drew ovals. The figure Allison drew to represent herself is asking "Mommy when can I take my mask off?" Another customer waits, bag in hand and mask on face, on a similar circle on the right side of the drawing. Between them are a hand sanitizer dispenser, a sign reading "thank you for practicing social distancing," and an empty shelf topped by a sign reading "disinfectant" which is covered by a "sold out" sticker. At the bottom of the drawing is a long arrow labeled "6 feet (6 miles)." The scale of Allison's drawing tells us something about what the grocery store looks like from a kid's perspective. The hand sanitizing dispenser, the sign thanking customers for social distancing, and the empty disinfectant shelves are all about as tall as she is, and they easily fit within the 6 feet between customers. Six feet apart to a small child may

When Six Feet Feels Like Six Miles 123

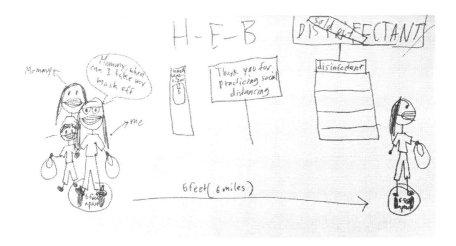

Figure 8.1 The grocery store by Allison (age 9).

literally feel farther apart than it does for adults; when two adults can determine a 6-foot distance by stretching out their arms so their fingertips just miss each other, two kids with shorter arms might stretch out their arms and see a wide gulf of empty space between them. As Allison said, "I drew the 6 feet apart, but it feels like 6 miles." Even as Allison documents the new way her family obtains food, her image highlights how much she values being physically close to and socially connected with others.

Many kids began to attend school online during the spring 2020 semester. When public schools partially reopened for in-person attendance in fall 2020, several students remained at home for part or all of the week. Our participants documented this seismic shift in their educational experiences in both drawings and photographs. Several kids took pictures of their computers and the workspaces they had created on tables and desks where they could do their online schoolwork. Julie, age 13, photographed her laptop computer sitting atop an old wooden desk. In the photograph, a white wall takes up the right half of the photograph and the laptop and wooden desk are on the left half of the image, tilting to the left. This de-centering and skewing of the laptop may reflect her ambivalent feelings about the computer. Julie explained,

> I do school on my computer, so I use it every day. It's very important. It's a big part of my life, which is kind of weird. The Wi-Fi is slow and my computer won't connect to it, which is really annoying.

Difficulties connecting to the Internet not only frustrated the kids with unreliable Wi-Fi and computers, but the students who were their classmates (see Arrastia-Chisholm, Grimes, and Kelley 2021 for more on the pandemic and digital divide). Padfoot's drawing illustrated his view of an online classroom: a five-by-five grid of boxes, 18 of which contain the words "vidio [sic] off." Padfoot, age 9, explained that he drew

> a zoom meeting. That's the teacher and she's saying "And then ..." That person is saying "I understand," then [another] said "I don't get it." ... I don't get to see many faces because they usually have their cameras off and I can't talk to them.

Several kids highlighted their inability to talk to friends during online school. Notably, the first image Penelope, age 12, drew to represent online school was the word "Friends" with a slash through it (see Figure 8.2). During the COVID-19 pandemic, online school for kids was characterized by technology use, the frustrations engendered by slow and unreliable Internet connections, and a decreased ability to interact with their classmates.

When some schools reopened partially or fully for in-person instruction in the fall, school was notably different because of new rules and procedures designed to reduce the transmission of the SARS-CoV-2 virus. Amelia's drawing of her in-person school experience featured a door, a table with a piece of paper on it, and a picture of a girl with a large head holding a pencil. Prominently drawn on the girl's face is a large blue triangle covering her mouth and nose; the blue triangle is almost as large as the girl's shirt. Amelia, age 6, explained, "It's me at school wearing my mask and doing a math problem." Amelia clearly associated masking with school and carried this theme into the photographs she took. One of her pictures was of a mask decorated to look like a cat nose and whiskers. Amelia told the college student interviewing her, "That's a mask and

Figure 8.2 In-person and online school by Penelope (age 12).

it reminds me of school because I wear masks mostly all day." Although Amelia's drawing did reference academic work, the visual dominance of the big blue triangle on her face highlights the centrality of masking in her school experience. Personal protective equipment and disinfection procedures also dominated other kids' images of in-person school. Penelope, age 12, painstakingly drew several images to illustrate what her in-person school experience was like: two masked stick figures with an arrow between them labeled "6 feet apart," a face mask, a bottle labeled hand sanitizer, a roll of paper towels, a spray bottle, and a round lunch table with plexiglass dividers on top and four miniature chairs. The chairs are so small that one fits underneath the leg of the table (see Figure 8.2). Penelope explained why she drew each item:

> We have assigned seating, distanced out for sure. Masks are a super big deal. If you show up to school without a mask, they have disposable masks. And then plexiglass between people in the lunchroom. It's definitely hard to hear the person next to you talking through the plexiglass, but you know, it works. And then paper towels and disinfectant spray quite a bit. They hand out paper towels and the teachers come and spray the tables and we have to wipe them down exiting every classroom, hand sanitizer on the way in and out of every classroom. We always have to put hand sanitizer on. They are very picky about that.

Anything related to physical distancing and disinfection are the largest elements of Penelope's drawing. The roll of paper towels and the spray bottle, for example, are taller than the lunch table. In contrast, anything that could facilitate social interaction is portrayed in miniature—like the four chairs where she might sit to talk with her friends through a plexiglass divider.

Signs of Struggle

For many kids, the global COVID-19 pandemic and virus mitigation procedures introduced new behavioral routines, heightened fears about death and loss, and increased social isolation (see Hunt and Rhodes 2022, this volume, for more about kids' increasing mental health challenges during the pandemic). Of the 21 kids in our project, 11 created images that expressed their fear, anxiety, sense of betrayal, frustration, boredom, and loneliness.

Because we recruited kids from university networks, our participants tended to come from middle-class and upper middle-class families. Most of our participants had parents or siblings with a college degree, reliable computers and Internet access, health insurance coverage, and relatives and friends who were able to work from home during the pandemic. Although at least one kid was quarantined with COVID-19 during data collection, no kids in this study mentioned experiencing the death of loved ones. Even so, a few kids expressed their knowledge of and anxiety about the potentially fatal consequences of COVID-19. Mason, age 7, took a picture of a three-dimensional Halloween skeleton dramatically flopped down on a bed "because people can die of coronavirus." Chase, age 8, drew on the imagery of a popular online game to process his ideas of the pandemic's death toll. In the online game *Among Us*, characters work together to complete tasks on a spaceship; one character who has been designated "the imposter" attempts to kill the other characters without revealing their identity. Chase drew a before and after picture of two characters from the game and he changed the spacesuit visors to look more like face masks with strings. In the first pane of his drawing labeled "Before covid19," the two characters walk toward the viewer. In the second pane titled "After covid19," one character continues walking toward the viewer while the bottom half of the second character lies on the ground in a pool of blood. Chase asked us to caption his drawing with the phrase: "COVID-19 was the imposter that killed a lot of people!" Chase creatively appropriated images and ideas from an online game that became popular during the pandemic to express his dismay about the number of people who died from COVID-19. Chase also expressed a sense of betrayal because the SARS-CoV-2 virus is secretly stalking and killing a lot of people, just like the imposter in the game.

Kids may have been acutely aware of the dangers the virus posed, in part, because many parents tried to keep their kids safe by keeping the kids at home all the time. One parent who contacted me to volunteer her kids for the study described them as "rarely leaving the confines of our front yard." Mason, age 7, drew a picture of a slide inside a circle with a slash through it to explain why he could not leave his house to go to a playground. To illustrate what their lives were like at home, kids took pictures of their refrigerators, their toaster ovens, their snack stashes and favorite toys. Their worlds had shrunk to a daily trek between bedroom, kitchen, and the table or desk where they did online school. Jimmy, age 12, photographed a couch with a pillow and blanket on it; the couch filled the frame so that a mere inch of wall and floor surrounded it. Jimmy explained that his couch portrait represented his days of "sitting on the couch and eating a lot of snacks and watching TV." PB, age 10, drew his living room. The drawing features a tiny figure in a red shirt and blue pants alone in a living room. He is dwarfed by a large TV and large pieces of living room furniture. There is a row of pictures hanging from a shelf above the couch, a plant in a pot, and two windows, one of which has an abstract plant in it. Text above the tiny figure reads, "I have nothing better to do except watch TV because I really can't come out of the house." While they stayed home, household items took on outsized importance and became large elements in their images.

School became another site where kids revealed they were struggling with academics, boredom, and loneliness. Some kids struggled with the academic work online, as did Jimmy, age 12, whose drawing featured a face glaring at a laptop screen with a giant F on it. "The face in the center is me being angry at online school," he stated. Even kids who earned high grades complained that their classes had become too easy, boring, or frustrating when the tech failed. More commonly, kids who made the switch to online schooling told us that online school added to their social isolation. Recall that Padfoot's drawing of online school featured 18 of 25 boxes with the words "vidio off" [sic]. Being schooled at home matters, Allison, age 9, told us because "there's no recess and you don't get to talk to anybody at lunch." Addison, age 11, drew a picture of her kitchen table where she and her brother sat to do schoolwork. As she described the school setup, Addison noted, "I haven't seen my friends in a while, but school's been okay." Similarly, while discussing his photograph of a desk and computer, Ryan, age 12, noted,

> I picked this because I am at-home school, like I'm not going-in school, so I'm not seeing my friends a lot. I feel like I've been really affected by COVID because I'm not seeing all of my friends, and I'm in my room 90% of the day just working on my computer.

Kids' face-to-face interactions with friends in school are critical for the creation and maintenance of peer cultures where kids learn trust and collaboration, experience group solidarity, develop a sense of inclusion and belonging, practice conflict resolution, and form identities (Crosnoe 2000; Corsaro 2017; García-Sánchez 2017; McDonnell 2017). Interacting with supportive friends is critical for kids' emotional and social well-being (Traylor et al. 2016). The lack of face-to-face interaction with friends during the global COVID-19 pandemic was one of the most common sources of sadness and loneliness identified by our participants.

New Ways to Connect and Spend Time

Nearly all the kids in this study (18 of 21) created images that documented their new methods for spending time and connecting with their friends. They used several activities to structure their days and address at least some of the boredom and isolation they experienced during the COVID-19 pandemic.

To fill their days, kids spent more time on solitary activities such as drawing, crafting, playing with toys, building with interlocking blocks, reading, exercising, and practicing instruments. In response to our request for a drawing that showed us what their lives were like during the pandemic, several kids drew pictures that looked like a collage of small items. For example, Abigail, age 16, drew a saxophone, a computer, a DVD, a paintbrush and artist palette, a pillow, a snack stash, and the logos for a gaming company and a social media platform. Each item, she explained, represented something she did frequently in her room during the pandemic. Other kids intensified their solitary outdoor activities. Ryan, age 12, explained that during the pandemic he went fishing more often because he could not see his friends and because fishing calmed him when he felt stress. He created a drawing of a fish wearing a surgical mask (see Figure 8.3). "The reason I drew this picture," he said,

> was because I went fishing a lot and with COVID we have to wear masks. Recently I went fishing and I caught a fish that I have never seen in Texas

Figure 8.3 Masked Guadalupe Bass fish by Ryan (age 12).

before called the Guadalupe Bass. I put a mask on it because it's COVID and we have to wear masks everywhere just to be safe.

The fish became his companion during the pandemic and gave him a sense of peace. Ryan expressed his desire to protect the fish by giving the Guadalupe Bass a surgical face mask to wear.

As kids were spending more time at home, pets and siblings became their most significant interaction partners and important sources of play, greetings, and affection. One participant, Grace, age 9, featured her three dogs in her drawing and all three of her photographs. Grace noted that she spent a lot of time playing with her dogs outside and pointed out that one dog "has this super loud bark that he does to say good morning." Other kids offered up pictures of them petting and cuddling cats and dogs. If they had siblings, kids created images which documented the ways they spent time with siblings. Layla, age 7, took a picture of Halloween decorations on a fireplace. "I made those decorations with my sister. I like making things with my sister," she said. Noah, also 7 years old, took a picture of his bicycle because "me and my sister bike around the square for a while and then we come back home." Kids reported taking walks and playing games with their siblings more during the pandemic.

Siblings and pets, however, can never take the place of friends. When they discussed their images of online school, our participants routinely pointed out how much they missed their friends (see Padfoot, Penelope, Allison, Addison, and Ryan above). The kids with access to technology used chat rooms, phones, and gaming systems to communicate with friends while in-person schooling was suspended. Kids clearly valued these forms of communication because they made drawings and took photographs that prominently featured this technology. Padfoot, age 9, took a picture that consisted solely of his handheld gaming device lying on a wood table because "I play it with my friends a lot and we talk on Discord." Padfoot's gaming device in combination with a chat room allowed him to engage in collaborative play and group communication with his friends during the stay-at-home orders. Julie, age 13, drew only the outline of a smartphone with a cord for headphones attached to it because "that's what I use all the time now to talk to my friends." In contrast to the collage of activities others drew, Julie's single-object drawing reinforced how important the phone was for allowing her to connect with her friends. Guillermo, age 13, took a photo of a gaming console and a portion of the monitor screen above it to show us what his life was like while he was quarantined with COVID-19. "That's where I spent most of my nights with my friends, and it was like the only voice-to-voice communication with them. During quarantine that was one of my only sources of fun." Kids' images of phones, computers, and gaming consoles represented a source of amusement, entertainment, and most importantly, voice-to-voice communication with their friends in the absence of face-to-face interaction.

Conclusion

Months after the stay-at-home orders were first issued in 2020, journalists began reporting that the virus mitigation efforts were profoundly affecting kids' educational progress. Parents, policymakers, and educators worried that the 2020–21 school year might be a "lost year" in which kids showed no progress or even "pandemic learning loss." The social and emotional consequences of the pandemic for kids were acknowledged, but mostly because they were important for understanding kids' academic performance: "We also know that far too many students have suffered from isolation, making it harder to focus on traditional school tasks" (Penuel and Schultz 2021). Standardized test scores suggested the COVID-19 pandemic was exacerbating educational inequalities and putting low-income Black and Latino students even further behind their affluent White peers (Reilly 2020). However, accounts focusing on academics centered *adults'* concerns about the effects of the pandemic on kids while pushing *kids'* perspectives on the COVID-19 global pandemic to the margins.

This project attempted to re-center kids' voices and views on the pandemic. Although a few kids expressed frustration with online learning, their images focused less on learning loss and more on the social and emotional consequences of the COVID-19 pandemic. The most commonly expressed sentiment by kids in this study was that they missed in-person visits with friends and family. The relative size and position of objects in their images, as well as what they said about them, revealed the centrality and importance of interacting face-to-face. The kids' desire to see their friends was not simply a shallow desire to have fun. The virus mitigation efforts that restricted kids' social interactions made it difficult for kids to maintain their peer cultures, which are critical sites for social development and sources of emotional well-being (Crosnoe 2000; Corsaro 2017; García-Sánchez 2017; McDonnell 2017; Traylor et al. 2016). Kids' drawings and photographs also expressed the emotional consequences of the pandemic: their sadness, fear, boredom, anxiety about death, and sense of betrayal. It is important to point out that the kids I studied experienced these emotions even though they and their relatives were less likely to become severely ill and die; anxiety, anger, fear, and grief were likely even more prominent emotions for kids living in Indigenous, Black, Latinx, and working-class communities that experienced higher morbidity and mortality rates. Adult-centric accounts of kids' experiences during the COVID-19 pandemic, which focus primarily on academic deficits, risk misidentifying the socio-emotional sources of kids' distress as well as the resources kids need to survive the pandemic and thrive afterward.

Despite the social and emotional challenges they faced during the pandemic, many of the kids in this study exhibited hope and resilience. Kids used their images to remind themselves of a better future at the end of the pandemic. As Chase, age 8, said when talking about his picture of piles of masks: "I can't wait for this pandemic to be over, for us all to go back and be together with everyone again!" When asked to draw a picture that showed us what his life was like during the pandemic, Logan, age 13, drew an image that captured the past, present, and future. On the left, in the past, a cartoon figure stood in front of a house on a hill saying, "See you soon!" In the middle, a rain cloud hovered over a body of water with scuba divers and fish in it. On the right, the same cartoon figure stood on the hill, in front of a house and under a shining sun while calling out "Welcome back!" Logan explained his picture by stating the following:

> The left side is [a theme park] before coronavirus, and everyone's happy and it's wonderful. This in the middle is coronavirus, and it's like we fell underwater and it's not as good, and there's a cloud right here above it. The rain is coronavirus and the sun is when it's all better again. We are trying to swim back to [the theme park] over here on the right which
> is good again.

Logan's drawing showed how he creatively appropriated elements of popular culture to place his own struggles on a timeline. He remembered a happier past when people interacted face-to-face and said things like "see you soon." Then, he expressed his current sadness and loneliness by drawing the COVID-19 pandemic as a rain which created a lake and turned people into underwater SCUBA divers who were cut off from and unable to communicate with others. Logan then noted this phase was a temporary disruption, just one stage on a journey which would lead to a place where people welcomed each other back to dry land and sunshine. Once there, they could begin to interact in-person once again. In this hoped-for future when the COVID-19 pandemic was over, perhaps for kids six feet would no longer feel like six miles.

Acknowledgments

I would like to thank the following students who helped collect data for this project: Miriam Arzoumanian, Annie Bass, Olivia Brooks, Mackenzie Follis, Jennifer Garcia, Katie Henderson, Camryn James, Lovely Lopez, Katherine Maykopet, Kevin Neal, Natalie Owen, Natasha Perez-Krause, Erica Pineda, Ayala Porat, Emma Rhode, Luisa Rivera, Kathryn Rorer, Megan Schlab, Darby Stowers, and Caroline Warms. I gratefully acknowledge Kathryn Gold Hadley and Nazneen Khan for their helpful comments on this chapter.

References

Arrastía-Chisholm, Lee Edmondson Grimes, and Heather M. Kelley. 2021. "COVID-19 Realities and Misconceptions for Rural PK-12 Students: Implications from Rural Education Research." In *COVID-19 and Childhood Inequality,* edited by Nazneen Khan. London and New York: Routledge.

Corsaro, William A. 1992. "Interpretive Reproduction in Children's Peer Cultures." *Social Psychology Quarterly* 55 (2): 160–77. https://doi.org/10.2307/2786944.

Corsaro, William A. 2017. *The Sociology of Childhood,* 5th edition. Los Angeles: Sage.

Crosnoe, Robert. 2000. "Friendships in Childhood and Adolescence: The Life Course and New Directions." *Social Psychology Quarterly* 63 (4): 377–91. https://doi.org/10.2307/2695847.

García-Sánchez, Inmaculada M. 2017. "Friendship, Participation, and Multimodality in Moroccan Immigrant Girls' Peer Groups." *Sociological Studies of Children & Youth* 21: 1–31. https://doi.org/10.1108/S1537-466120160000021003.

Gerson, Kathleen, and Sarah Damaske. 2021. *The Science and Art of Interviewing.* New York: Oxford University Press.

Kyung-Hoon, Kim, and Reuters Photographers. 2020. "Children's Drawings from Lockdown Show the World What They Miss Most." *Reuters*, June 15, 2020. https://widerimage.reuters.com/story/childrens-drawings-from-lockdown-show-the-world-what-they-miss-most.

Literat, Ioana. 2013. "'A Pencil for Your Thoughts': Participatory Drawing as a Visual Research Method with Children and Youth." *International Journal of Qualitative Methods* 12 (1): 84–98. https://doi.org/10.1177/160940691301200143.

McDonnell, Susan. 2017. "Speaking Distance: Language, Friendship and Spaces of Belonging in Irish Primary Schools." *Sociological Studies of Children & Youth* 21: 33–53. https://doi.org/10.1108/S1537-466120160000021004.

Morojele, Pholoho, and Nithi Muthukrishna. 2016. "'My Journey to School': Photovoice Accounts of Rural Children's Everyday Experiences in Lesotho." *Gender & Behaviour* 14 (3): 7938–61.

Penuel, William, and Katherine Schultz. 2021. "A Better Way to Make Sense of Pandemic 'Learning Loss.'" *The Washington Post*, March 25, 2021. www.washingtonpost.com/education/2021/03/25/a-better-way-to-look-at-pandemic-learning-loss/.

Prout, Alan, and Allison James. 1990. "A New Paradigm for the Sociology of Childhood? Provenance, Promise and Problems." In *Constructing and Reconstructing Childhood: Contemporary Issues in the Sociological Study of Childhood*, edited by Allison James and Alan Prout, pp. 7–34. London: The Falmer Press.

Reilly, Katie. 2020. "The Learning Gap Is Getting Worse as Schools Rely on Remote Classes, Especially for Students of Color." *Time*, December 8, 2020. https://time.com/5918769/coronavirus-schools-learning-loss/.

Robeson, Wendy Wagner, and Kimberly D. Lucas. 2021. "The Impact of Parental Burnout and Time with Children: Family Stress in a Large Urban City During COVID-19." In *COVID-19 and Childhood Inequality*, edited by Nazneen Khan. London: Routledge.

Taft, Jessica K. 2019. *The Kids Are in Charge: Activism and Power in Peru's Movement of Working Children*. New York, NY: New York University Press.

Thorne, Barrie. 1993. *Gender Play: Girls and Boys in School*. New Brunswick, NJ: Rutgers University Press.

Traylor, Amy C., Javonda D. Williams, Jennifer L. Kenney, and Laura M. Hopson. 2016. "Relationships Between Adolescent Well-Being and Friend Support and Behavior." *Children & Schools* 38 (3): 179–86. https://doi.org/10.1093/cs/cdw021.

Woodgate, Roberta L., Melanie Zurba, and Pauline Tennent. 2017. "Worth a Thousand Words? Advantages, Challenges and Opportunities in Working with Photovoice as a Qualitative Research Method with Youth and their Families." *Forum: Qualitative Social Research* 18 (1): 126–48. https://doi.org/10.17169/fqs-18.1.2659.

9 The COVID-19 Pandemic

Childhood Inequalities Unmasked in the Caribbean

Aldrie Henry-Lee

Introduction

"We are not living our childhood," commented a 12-year-old Syrian girl (Save the Children 2020). Indeed, the coronavirus disease 2019 (COVID-19) pandemic has altered childhood; an estimated 99 percent of children, globally—or more than 2.3 billion children—live in one of the 186 countries that have implemented some form of restrictions due to COVID-19 (Save the Children 2020). Although children are less likely to become infected with severe COVID-19 illness, containment measures to reduce the spread of the pandemic have disproportionately affected them. A global study carried out by Save the Children (2020) assessing 46 countries revealed the following statistics.

- Eighty-six percent of respondents revealed that COVID-19 has impacted their access to healthcare, medicine and medical supplies;
- Less than 1 percent of children from poor households said that they had access to the Internet for distance learning;
- Eighty-two percent of poor households reported a loss of income;
- Thirty-two percent of households had a child, caregiver, parent, or caregiver report violence in the home.

It is already evident that the pandemic will have a significant impact on children's rights to adequate provision, protection, and participation. Disadvantaged prior to the pandemic, the virus will reverse all gains that poorer households may have made; children living in poverty will find themselves being left further behind in meeting the UN2030 Agenda, which includes equitable access to child prosperity.

The theory of endangerment, which builds on Bronfenbrenner's (1979) work, is highly applicable to understanding the impacts of the pandemic on children in the Caribbean as they face endangerment in all institutions in society. As Henry-Lee states (2020):

> Children of the SIDs in the Caribbean are an endangered species; at risk in private and public spaces. Child endangerment is the process of exposing

the younger generation to risks such as inadequate provision of basic necessities, insufficient protection, and insufficient facilitation of opportunities for child participation. Endangerment takes place by both primary and secondary agents of socialization and at the macro, meso and micro levels.

(41)

Building on the theme of endangerment, this chapter examines the impact of the pandemic on childhood in the Caribbean. Specifically, this chapter examines the impact of COVID-19 in five selected Caribbean countries: Barbados, Jamaica, Haiti, St. Lucia, and Trinidad and Tobago. These countries have varying population sizes, levels of human development (as measured by the HDI value and rank), and poverty levels. Four research questions are addressed throughout the chapter. First, what has been the impact of the virus on socialization in the family? Second, how have changes in the education sector affected childhood in these countries? Third, how has the pandemic affected physical education (PE) and recreational activities? Fourth, what is the future of childhood in the Caribbean?

To further explore these questions, both primary and secondary data were reviewed and analyzed. The secondary data included presentations made by children at the 15th Annual Caribbean Child Research Conference held in November 2020. A content analysis of the presentations was conducted to determine the impact of the pandemic on the children in the Caribbean. The voices and perspectives of these children are integrated throughout the discussion of key findings. Other secondary data include the reports of non-profit and other agencies and scholarly literature on the status of children during the pandemic. Primary data include survey data that was collected from a convenience sample of 55 PE teachers from both primary and secondary level schools. Data analysis revealed that the current pandemic has increased the endangerment of childhood in the Caribbean and has exacerbated childhood inequalities in these societies.

The Regional Context

Colonized by the English, Dutch, Spanish, and French, the Caribbean form a group of islands more than 2,000 miles (3,200 km) long, separating the Gulf of Mexico and the Caribbean Sea, to the west and south, from the Atlantic Ocean, to the east and north (Clarke and Brereton n.d.). Barbados, Haiti, Jamaica, St. Lucia, and Trinidad and Tobago were chosen because they represent various levels of human development, racial diversity, and social structures.

Barbados reports the highest level of human development (0.814) as measured by the UNDP's (2021) Human Development Index (HDI) (see Table 9.1). Haiti is the poorest country in the Caribbean. While the Black population accounts for more than 50 percent in other countries, in Trinidad and Tobago, Black people only represent 34.2 percent of the population. Inequality (measured as Gini coefficients) is high in all countries, with Haiti reporting the highest

Table 9.1 Basic socioeconomic indicators for selected Caribbean countries

	Barbados	Haiti	Jamaica	St. Lucia	Trinidad and Tobago
Population ('000)[1]	288	11,521	2,968	185	1,405
Average economic growth (last five years) (2019)[10]	−0.096	−1.682	0.7	1.729	−0.003
Contribution of main industry to GDP[11]	17 (2020)	22.1 (2017)	59.33 (2019)	75.18 (2019)	55.11 (2018)
Debt to GDP ratio[3]	134.09 (2020)	54.36 (2020)	101.33 (2020)	59.98 (2018)	45.12 (2019)
Homicide rate (per 100,000 inhabitants)[3]	9.8 (2018)	6.7 (2018)	47.4 (2019)	21.4 (2018)	28.2 (2020)
Total unemployment rate[3]	10.94	13.92	7.95	20.15	2.8
Male unemployment (2019)[9]	9.87	10.91	5.83	14.09	3.46
Female unemployment (2019)[9]	10.35	16.25	9.94	17.18	3.48
Youth unemployment rate (2020)[3]	31.58	31.21	22.41	44.38	6.5
Poverty rate[2]	17 (2017)	59 (2019)	12.6 (2018)	18.4 (2019)	20 (2017)
Gini coefficient[4]	0.32	0.61	0.35	0.51	0.39
Child poverty rate[8]	32 (2010)	25 (2007)	25 (2020)	36.7 (2006)	28.9 (2017)
GDP per capita (US$) (2019)[6]	18,148.24	1,272.49	5,582.26	11,611.42	17,397.98
HDI value (2019)[7]	0.814	0.510	0.734	0.759	0.796
HDI rank (out of 189 countries) (2020)[7]	58	170	101	86	67
Life expectancy rate (2018)[5]	79	63.66	74.37	76.06	73.38
Primary school enrollment[12]	100 (2019)	114 (1998)	85 (2019)	102 (2019)	106 (2010)
Secondary school enrollment[13]	103 (2019)	18 (1986)	85 (2019)	90 (2019)	86 (2004)
Transition rate to Grade 5[14]	100 (2019)	38 (1986)	92.84 (2018)	91.98 (2018)	72.13 (2010)

(continued)

Sources:
[1] Country Meters (2021).
[2] Barbados—Naitram (2020).
   Haiti—UNICEF (2020b).
   Jamaica—Smith (2020).
   St. Lucia—World Bank (2021).
   Trinidad & Tobago—Index Mundi (2021).

Table 9.1 Cont.

3 Statista (2021).
4 Caribbean Development Bank (2018).
  http://worldpopulationreview.com/countries/gini-coefficient-by-country/ https://data.worldbank.org/indicator/SI.POV.GINI?locations=BB-JM-HT-LC-TT UNDP. (2016). Caribbean Human Development Report.
5 https://data.worldbank.org/indicator/SP.DYN.LE00.IN?locations.
6 https://data.worldbank.org/indicator/NY.GDP.PCAP.CD?locations.
7 http://hdr.undp.org/en/countries.
8 www.unicef.org/easterncaribbean/media/1176/file/child-poverty-in-the-eastern-caribbean-area-2017.pdf.
  https://borgenproject.org/child-poverty-in-jamaica/.
  https://research-information.bris.ac.uk/ws/portalfiles/portal/189194365/Final_report_in_English.pdf www.undp.org/content/dam/unct/caribbean/docs/SitAN%20Trinidad%202018%20WEB%20(1).pdf.
9 www.theglobaleconomy.com.
10 https://data.worldbank.org/indicator/NY.GDP.MKTP.KD.ZG?locations.
11 Barbados—https://pubdocs.worldbank.org/en/438851586546174000/mpo-brb.pdf.
  Haiti—www.indexmundi.com/haiti/economy_profile.html.
  Jamaica—www.statista.com/statistics/527157/share-of-economic-sectors-in-the-gdp-in-jamaica/.
  St Lucia—www.statista.com/statistics/730757/share-of-economic-sectors-in-gdp-in-saint-lucia/.
  Trinidad—www.statista.com/statistics/728953/share-of-economic-sectors-in-the-gdp-in-trinidad-and-tobago/.
12 https://data.worldbank.org/indicator/SE.PR.M.ENRR?locations.
13 https://data.worldbank.org/indicator/SE.SEC.ENRR?locations.
14 Barbados—http://uis.unesco.org/en/country/bb.
  Haiti—http://documents1.worldbank.org/curated/en/823841468035508642/pdf/WPS7175.pdf.
  Jamaica—http://uis.unesco.org/en/country/jm.
  St Lucia—http://uis.unesco.org/en/country/lc.
  Trinidad—www.indexmundi.com/facts/trinidad-and-tobago/school-enrollment.

level at 0.61 (World Population Review 2021). Child poverty rates are also high, ranging from 36.7 percent in St. Lucia to 25 percent in Haiti and Jamaica (UNDP 2021).

All five countries have ratified the Convention of the Rights of the Child (CRC). Only Haiti does not have a youth policy. Haiti and St. Lucia do not have any policies to reduce violence against children and neither of them have a Child Care and Protection Act. St. Lucia allocates the largest proportion of its budget to health and education (see Table 9.2). The impact of the pandemic on childhood in the Caribbean is discussed using examples from these five countries. Across all countries, the impact of the pandemic on children has been deleterious.

Containment and Societal Disruption

A secondary school student in Trinidad and Tobago stated, "COVID-19 is like an unwelcome visitor that invites themselves over and refuses to leave." The measures used to reduce to the spread of the virus have affected all societies and social groups, and to children, it seems they "refuse to leave." Lockdowns and curfews have contracted economic activities. The COVID-19 pandemic has already inflicted a high cost on populations around the world (OECS 2020). Preliminary assessments suggest that the economic impact of COVID-19 is likely to be more severe than the 2008 Global Financial Crisis and more pronounced in developing countries (OECS 2020).

The majority of Haitians earn their livelihoods through informal work, such as fishing, direct services, or street vending, and a ban on such activities would not only be difficult to impose, it could also cripple household incomes. In fact, a 20 percent reduction in household consumption could push another million people into poverty and 2.5 million into extreme poverty (Global Volunteers St. Lucia n.d.). The impact of the pandemic was vividly portrayed by a primary school student from Trinidad and Tobago who stated, "My Dad lost his job as a driver. Without money, you cannot have food, clothing, education, health and shelter." Children with disabilities, street children, children of inmates, and children in State Care are further isolated during the pandemic.

Impact on the Family: Childhood Under Lockdown

The family is the primary agent of socialization whose functions include reproduction, love and nurturing; emotional and economic support of its members; socialization; informal education; and consumption of society's goods and services. Researchers have highlighted the uniqueness and diversity of Caribbean families reflecting "different socioeconomic pressures as well as multi-ethnic value systems" (McKenzie and McKenzie 1971). There are several variations of the family in the Caribbean which include nuclear, common law (consensual union), visiting—matrifocal, female-headed, single parent, extended, grandmother-headed, sibling, and other variations. The pandemic has had a

Table 9.2 Legal and policy contexts

	Date Convention on the Rights of the Child ratified (CRC)[1]	Youth policy	Policy to reduce violence against children	Child Care and Protection Acts[7]	% of budget spent on health and education[8]
Barbados	9 Oct. 1990	Yes[2]	Yes	Yes (1991)	21.96 (2020)
Haiti	8 June 1995	No (draft 2011)[3]	No	No	19.68 (2020)
Jamaica	14 May 1991	Yes[4]	Yes	Yes (2004)	31.90 (2020)
St. Lucia	16 June 1993	Yes[5]	No	No	29.4 (2020)
Trinidad and Tobago	5 Dec. 1991	Yes[6]	Yes	Yes (2012)	13.6 (2020)

Sources:

[1] United Nations Treaty Collection (1989).
[2] Ministry of Family, Culture, Sports, and Youth, Barbados (2011).
[3] Youthpolicy.org (2021a).
[4] Youth Innovation Centre (2021).
[5] The Commonwealth (2021).
[6] Youthpolicy.org (2021b).
[7] Sawyers (2015).
[8] Country Economy (2021).

grave economic impact on households and families in the Caribbean. For example, in the poorest country, Haiti, the UN Environment Programme (2020) noted that even before the pandemic, almost 59 percent of the Haitian population were living in poverty; 23.8 percent were living in extreme poverty and more than 60 percent were unable to meet their basic needs. They warned that poorer households have even fewer options and that coping with the pandemic may have long-term negative impacts including decreasing household food supply, depleting savings, or alienating families and children from their social networks.

Even before the pandemic, children and adolescents represented a highly vulnerable group in both the USA and the Caribbean. The current pandemic threatens family life and livelihoods. With the loss of parental income, children are at risk of increased poverty, food insecurity, loss of education, and increased physical and emotion violence (ECLAC-UNICEF 2020). It is also evident that the pandemic has caused a reorganization of the family's roles and functions. This reorganization has impacted the quality of childhood during the pandemic. As one child from St. Lucia stated, "Everything has changed from the way I like it and the way that I enjoyed it."

In Haiti, the poorest country in the Caribbean, the impact has been very severe. According to UNICEF's (2020a) revised Humanitarian Response Plan, 4.1 million Haitians (nearly 40 per cent of the Haitian population) are estimated to be food insecure. The same report estimates that the number of children suffering from acute malnutrition has risen to 167,000 and over 2.2 million persons are estimated to require emergency health care, including 1 million children and 315,000 pregnant women. UNICEF's (2020b) Humanitarian Report similarly notes that COVID-19 has put greater pressure on the livelihoods of vulnerable families and further exacerbated existing humanitarian needs. Children are at heightened risk of abuse, exploitation, and violence, while economic shutdowns, physical distancing, and confinement measures also pose serious threats to children's health, well-being, and protection.

Leslie (2020) noted that the pandemic has affected parent–child relationships. She noted that demand for parents to secure additional resources to facilitate children's online learning may leave such families frustrated and could interfere to some degree with parent–child bonding. Leslie (2020) also opined that the type of family structure is also a key contributor to the quality of the parent–child relationship in that nuclear families may fare better than single-parent households, as additional responsibilities can be shared. Leslie (2020) believes that it highlights that the merits of extended families have come into focus during the pandemic.

The children themselves have expressed the way that life has become stressful. "We cannot laugh loudly. If we tried to play, we would be shouted out at to stop making noise or it is too early for that," commented a secondary school student from Trinidad and Tobago. Similarly, another student from Trinidad and Tobago remarked, "Even our dog gets in trouble when he barks." Table 9.3 examines the causes and effects of family tensions during the pandemic. There

Table 9.3 Family tensions—causes and effects

Types	Causes	Potential effects
Child to parent	Frustration of having to stay indoors. Not seeing friends and being unable to play outside the house Lack of understanding of why this is happening (especially younger children) Uncooperative behavior and arguing with parents	Anger and verbal abuse directed at children Physical disciplining of children Violence against children
Parent to child	Loss of patience caused by child behavior Difficulty in adapting to being at home, supporting online learning and managing other competing demands Frustration and anxiety caused by decrease in family incomes, having to find food and pay rent	
Parent to parent	Stress due to more time at home together Loss of self-esteem due to unemployment Reduced incomes and fear of uncertainty	Domestic violence witnessed by children with consequent negative impacts
Parental absence (after relaxation of lock down)	Unattended children left at home as the parent leaves to work or search for employment Older children having to care for younger siblings	Child neglect Lack of control over online time, thereby reducing learning and increasing vulnerability to online predators Delinquent behavior Absence from school

Source: UNICEF (2020a, 15).

are a variety of tensions: child to parent, parent to child, and parent to parent. When the lockdowns and curfews relaxed, some children were left unattended at home as parents left for work or search for employment. The poorer the households, the more deleterious the impact.

Some families suffer from a multiplicity of vulnerabilities. A recent study revealed that poor and female-headed households have been the worst-affected victims of the coronavirus pandemic in the Caribbean, making them, paradoxically, the greatest casualties of the economic fallout of the containment measures geared toward their survival (Daley Jonielle 2021). Loss of jobs during the pandemic has affected female-headed households more negatively. While more male households suffered temporary lay-offs, more female-heads of households were hit by permanent time off from work, as female-dominated jobs were most affected by the COVID-19 (Daley Jonielle 2021).

There is little research on the impacts of the pandemic on grand-families (families in which children are raised by grandparents). However, news media have reported that there are more than 2.7 million American children growing up in grand-families (Trinidad Express 2021). Grandparents (usually older folks) are told to stay inside and remain socially and physically distant. However, if they are the sole caregivers of the children in the household, it is extremely difficult to adhere to these health protocols. If they fall sick, the children are further disadvantaged.

Illness of parents/guardians/breadwinners affects children, emotionally and economically. For those whose parents/guardians became infected with COVIID-19, they have to bear the effects of the quarantining of their sick relatives: physical and emotional distance; no hugs, kisses, or interaction. Some children have to be removed from the homes of their sick parents; causing disruption in their lives. The younger the children are, the less likely they are to understand these actions. Some children will feel neglected and shunned. One child from Turks and Caicos stated, "COVID-19 ripped family members apart from each other." The poorer the households, the more difficulty to enact the health protocols for sick household members.

During the pandemic, the family assumed additional functions normally carried out by other institutions. Family members became responsible for supervising school work, implementing recreational activities for their members, and in some cases fulfilling their religious needs. While there were some positive effects on the family during the containment measures (e.g., more family integration), there were some major damaging effects as discussed in this section.

Children in another Caribbean island are facing a double jeopardy: the pandemic and a natural disaster. The volcano in St. Vincent erupted in early April 2021 caused families living in the northern part of the island to evacuate to other parts of the country and other islands. They were mandated to take only their essential items and documents. Evacuation causes mental and psychological problems for children. They miss the comfort of their homes and familiar environments. Poorer families face increased food insecurity and uncomfortable accommodation. The volcanic ash caused water and electricity to be disconnected.

The School: Virtual Socialization

School before the pandemic was usually a physical building with teachers in front of students, formally teaching them valuable information which was supposed to facilitate entry into the labor market. Known as the secondary agent of socialization, the school is seen as one of the most valued social institutions in society. The pandemic disrupted schooling as we knew it as reflected in the following remark from a secondary school student from Trinidad and Tobago:

> Close your eyes and imagine back when you were a child in school with all the resources at your disposal; the school library, the textbooks, notebooks filled with scribbles as the teacher directs in front, writing on the white boards and then just like that, imagine the transition to your room where there is unstable wifi connection and the teacher only exists as a static filled voice coming through the monitor that you have been staring at for the last five hours.

In a world in which formal education is increasingly valued, negative impacts to education increasingly penetrate other social spheres (Davies and Mehta 2013).

Developing Kimberlé Crenshaw's work on intersectionality, Tefera, Powers, and Fischman (2018) assert that there are dynamic and complex ways that race/ethnicity, citizenship, ability, age, and religion shape individual identities and social life. They claim that complex demographic, social, economic, and cultural transformations shape educational processes and outcomes. There were significant inequalities in education before the pandemic. Children from wealthier households had access to better quality education. These inequalities have been intensified due to the containment measures implemented because of the pandemic.

Even in Barbados, with the highest level of human development, social inequalities were exposed during the pandemic and school closures resulted in unequal outcomes for children in Barbados. Naitram (2020) noted that Barbados does not boast a full penetration of Internet access, resulting in inequitable access to online learning, and there are at least 4,000 students who do not have appropriate access to devices needed for online learning. In Jamaica, the inadequate access to devices was severe. "Some households have one phone, one tablet, one computer and more than one child. How will all of the children attend online school?," asked a secondary school student from Jamaica.

Naitram (2020) further warned that the long summer holidays would widen the educational inequalities between students with high-income and low-income background. While the wealthier children can be assisted to "catch up" through paid summer educational activities, children from poorer homes do not have this luxury. The longer the school closures in Barbados, the more severe the learning consequences (Naitram 2020). School closures also increased food insecurity. During face-to-face instruction, the Government of Barbados' School Meals Department provides low-cost lunches for primary school students. Students from low socioeconomic backgrounds do not have access to these lunches during the period of online learning and closed schools.

One of the functions of school is to provide opportunities for socialization with friends. Children speaking at a Caribbean Child Conference in November 2020 noted that during school closures, "Children cannot build relationships with their friends" (primary school student from Barbados) and that, "We have not seen our closest friends for months (primary school student from St. Lucia). Boys and girls are impacted differently by school closures and the pandemic has deepened gender inequalities. Table 9.4 provides some of the gender

Table 9.4 Gender inequalities in education

Inequalities in access to, and completion of, secondary school. Although girls outperform boys in terms of secondary school completion, the reasons as to why girls and boys drop out of school are gendered.	**Gender segregation in curricular areas continues to be predominant.** While the percentage of girls who reach the basic level in reading and writing is higher than that of men, it is lower in relation to science and mathematics.
Early pregnancy, marriage/union, a higher burden of caregiving on girls, and inadequate access to menstrual supplies and WASH infrastructure impact their school attendance, performance, and completion.	**Violence in and around schools occur,** including gender-based violence. However, not all schools have formal, established referral pathways, or competencies within school staffing, to address GBV disclosures.
In LAC, of all adolescents, **27.5% of girls neither study nor work** compared to 14.5% of boys. While general time use data shows girls more represented in care work, 2016 data showed boys more represented in paid labor.	Gender, ethnicity, and household income affect access to technology **digital literacy**, with girls from rural, poorest quintiles and indigenous households more affected.

Source: UNICEF and LACRO (2020).

inequalities exacerbated by COVID-19 in the Caribbean region. Girls are more at risk of being victims of violence and dropping out of school to take care of sick relatives or smaller children at home.

It is evident that the issues of race and ethnicity still plague our Caribbean societies. Persons with lighter skin and the browner complexion still receive better treatment in the society (Kelly and Bailey 2018), and children are aware of how their physical appearance can affect what they gain from the educational process. A secondary student in Jamaica noted, "The texture of your hair determines how well you are attended to in class." The disadvantages experienced by "blacker" children will be intensified during this pandemic.

Sagewam (2020) noted that gender inequality is further accentuated when one considers that single female-headed households with more than four children are among the poorest in St. Lucia. The closure of schools due to the advent of the COVID-19 pandemic forced education providers worldwide to move their services online. Teachers, students, and other education personnel were compelled to adapt quickly and develop skills to remain relevant in these unprecedented times. UNICEF (2020a) noted that 4 million children have been missing out on their education because of school closure due to COVID-19, especially in urban areas such as Port-au-Prince, Cap Haïtien, and Cayes. As a result, over 70 percent of school children lost a complete school year. The same report stated that many children risk falling far behind in their learning and those who were already vulnerable may never return to school. The report also revealed that school closures entailed the interruption of access to other important basic services provided by schools such as school feeding, water, sanitation, hygiene, recreational programs, and pedagogical and psychosocial support.

For some children, school is a haven from violence at home. Isolated at home, a UNICEF/CAPRI (2020) study found that many children were more frustrated and at a greater risk of abuse since the onset of the pandemic. The Child Protection and Family Services Agency (CPFSA) noted a reduction in the number of reported cases of child abuse in March 2020 (Russell 2021). The decline in cases may be due to school closures and lack of access to mandatory reporters. When children are at school, their teachers and guidance counselors are better able to identify suspected cases. During face-to-face classes, the teachers and the guidance counselors can note changes in behavior and follow-up to confirm suspected cases of child abuse.

The quality of childhood in St. Lucia has deteriorated because remittances have reduced; this decline has disproportionately affected poorer households and will accelerate the growth of income inequality in St. Lucia (Martial 2021), particularly for specific groups. Already disadvantaged prior to COVID-19, the vulnerability of migrant children in Trinidad and Tobago was magnified during the pandemic. UNICEF (2020c) reported that during a registration exercise in 2019, 19,000 migrants were registered, comprising 16,500 adults and 2,400 children under the age of 17 in Trinidad and Tobago. UNICEF (2020c) noted that migrant children are at a heightened risk of abuse, neglect, violence, exploitation, and psychological distress due to disruptions in family and community connections, challenges in accessing education, limited opportunities for play and socialization, and lack of support services. Given the illegal status of many of their parents, the effects of long-term unemployment will be more deleterious on migrant children.

Another very vulnerable group, children with disabilities, have been further marginalized with the switch to online learning (see Sharma 2021, this volume). Beyond these inequities, equal access does not mean the quality of learning is the same. Even when all children have their devices and have stable access to the Internet, the homes in which some children live are not conducive to learning. Additionally, children have different learning styles. For many each day is a struggle to keep with the curriculum and their assignments. Perhaps, this secondary student from St. Lucia sums it up best: "COVID-19 causes us to learn for a day and not for life."

Impact on Physical Exercise and Leisure

Containment measures have reduced physical exercise and mobility. Fearon (2020) described the impact of the lockdowns on the student athletes who would normally have to deal with balancing academic and athletic obligations. The pandemic has increased their challenges as they need to try to stay fit at home, keep up with their academic studies, work and deal with all the disappointments of postponement and cancellations of sport activities. Children are at risk of obesity. A primary school student from Turks and Caicos noted, "We are eating junk food out of boredom." High levels of child obesity are already reported for children in the Caribbean (Mumena et al. 2018). Staying home for such long periods is expected to result in an increased number of cases of child obesity.

Fearon (2020) warns of the long-term effects of this pandemic on student athletes as they grapple to make adjustments to their future in sports. Some teachers are experiencing a mix of emotions during this time, miss the physical contact with students, and believe the subject of PE is losing its identity as a consequence of the current situation (Varea and Gonzalez-Calvo 2020). Data collected from 55 PE teachers in Jamaica revealed that only 31 percent of them were coping well or very well with COVID-19 (Table 9.5). The pandemic has elevated the stress levels that teachers experience as they are forced to work more hours, and navigate an unfamiliar remote environment, made worse by frequent technical problems (Zalaznick 2021). Only 6 percent were able to continue classes in person (some had very small classes), while only 56.4 percent of them were able to successfully continue their classes online. Unstable connectivity and inadequate access to the Internet by teachers and students resulted in 87 percent of children encountering problems while conducting online classes.

Prior to the pandemic, there was great emphasis on academic rather than on PE and the focus on the latter diminished during the pandemic. If data was limited on the telephone devices, parents would opt to provide their children access to the academic subjects. Some teachers complained that they had not seen their children online since their schools closed.

"We are missing playing together on the monkey bars at schools, running and playing soccer, running to catch the swing," lamented a primary school

Table 9.5 Findings from primary data collected from 55 PE teachers (N=55)

Responses	%
How are you coping with COVID-19?	9
• Very well	23
• Well	53
• Neither well or badly	11
• Badly	4
• Very badly	
Classes were suspended	94
Successfully hosted PE classes online	56.4
Encountered problems while conducting online classes	87.0

Source: Author's study.

student from Turks and Caicos. The lack of exercise has long-term negative effects on children. One primary school student from Barbados noticed this, stating, "Children are eating and eating and getting fatter." There is no doubt that the lack of play, exercise, and sport will have a deleterious effect on all children everywhere.

What Does it all Mean?

"COVID-19 caused a big hole in our social life," said a primary school student, highlighting that the effects of these social and other impacts of the pandemic on children have been traumatic and will be long term. Much research has highlighted the impact of adverse childhood experiences on the quality of childhood (e.g. Burke et al. 2011).

This chapter sought to answer the following research questions:

1 What has been the impact of the virus on socialization in the family?
2 How have changes in the education sector affected childhood in these countries?
3 How has the pandemic affected physical education and recreational activities?
4 What is the future of childhood in the Caribbean?

The research questions were answered using secondary data from previous studies and the primary data from 55 PE teachers and an analysis of the presentations by children on an online Caribbean child conference held in November 2020. The focus was on five Caribbean islands which were selected because their diversity provides a robust understanding of the impacts of COVID-19 on children. Table 9.6 provides a summary of some of the main findings of this study.

Analysis of both secondary and primary data revealed that the primary agent of socialization, the family, was drastically affected by the pandemic. The poorer the families, the worse the impact. The family assumed the role of other agents of socialization, for example, the school. Parents/guardians and adult relatives are now in charge of supervision of the educational processes for their children. The added pressures of loss of income, close proximity in the home during curfews and lockdowns, and working at home while supervising children caused much emotional stress. Tensions increased and relationships among family members became strained. Poorer families had the added burdens of food insecurity and inadequate access to health care. Some children were exposed to increased violence with girls being more at risk. There were a few positive effects of the containment measures: more interaction with family members and doing educational assignments and playing together. However, the findings show that the quality of childhood deteriorated and the vulnerability of children in poorer families was increased.

For children, the greatest disruption in their lives resulted from school closures. Prior to the pandemic, physical presence at school was beneficial for the

Table 9.6 Summary of main findings of this study

Action	Some effects	Long-term implications for quality of childhood
No more hugs, especially from parents who are frontline workers and grandparents who are infected with COVID-19 and taking care of their grandchildren	Isolation, loneliness	Difficulty connecting and showing affection
Physical distancing	Social integration reduced	Social relationships may deteriorate
School closures	• Disruptions to education • Falling behind in education • Family takes over supervising education • Reduced access to school feeding programs for children from poorer households • No access to school officials to report violence at home • Closure of child-friendly spaces for children to play	• Unequal educational performance outcomes: • Unequal access to higher education • Unequal educational outcomes • Implications for labor market (e.g. unemployment, underemployment) • Increased food insecurity • Traumatized children with mental health problems
Lockdowns with family	**Positive:** Improved relationship among family members **Negative:** • Increased family tensions • Increased exposure to violence, especially for girls	Children from poorer families "left behind" socially, economically, and psychologically. Some children are more vulnerable than others, for example, children with disabilities, street children, children in conflict with the law, children whose parents have migrated or are imprisoned and those in State care.

Source: Author's summary.

majority of children. The main function of this secondary agent of socialization is the formal transmission of knowledge. However, for the children interviewed, the "social interactive" function was the significant loss due to school closure. While they lamented the connectivity issues and the transmission of knowledge via an electronic scene, it was the interaction with their friends—eating and playing together—that they missed the most. Online school was now mostly a burden with both teachers and children having difficulty adjusting to the new norm. Children from poorer families, those from the rural areas and children with disabilities suffered from a multiplicity of risks with reduced income, food insecurity, and unstable and limited access to the Internet.

Another function of the school which has not been sufficiently highlighted in the literature is the provision of recreational activities. Most schools provide formal PE. This break from the more academic subjects is both therapeutic and healthy. The children at the child conference predicted an increase in obesity among children due to the reduction in physical exercises.

School closures resulted in the reduction in quality of PE. Exercises could not be assessed properly by the teachers. Poorer households are more likely to make their children skip their PE classes. With limited data on their electronic devices, given the choice between using the data for academic subjects and PE, the preference would be to skip the PE. The latter is considered less important than other subjects such as English, mathematics, and science.

The Future of Caribbean Childhood

"I am not certain about the future yet. Nobody knows if we'll survive this pandemic. We should hope for the best." This remark from a primary school student from Barbados captures that children, like their parents, are uncertain about the future. This pandemic has disrupted social life as we know it. Children from poorer families are more at risk than their wealthier counterparts. The world will never be the same. If and when the pandemic is over, resocialization will be necessary. New norms may develop. Socialization behind masks has taken its toll and de-masking will require some adjustments. Will persons easily move to being socially and physically closer? Hugs and shaking hands may not automatically reclaim their prominence. Washing and sanitizing hands at home and at school will be the new "norm."

In the future, we must accommodate a childhood that provides opportunities for children to speak. The Caribbean Child Research Conference held in November 2020 provided indisputable evidence that children can express themselves clearly and know what can be done to improve their childhood. Child agency must be encouraged and developed. Gender, age, and residence-specific opportunities must be made available to children who want to speak. This would mean that the adage "children must be seen and not heard" is permanently discarded. No longer must a child say, "The children are talking but are they listening to us?" (primary school student, Trinidad and Tobago).

Disaster risk management strategies are of paramount importance as the current volcanic eruption in St. Vincent and the Grenadines has underscored. Natural disasters are particularly devastating to children, often resulting in their removal from a stable and comfortable environment to shelters with strangers and increased risk of violence, especially for girls. With the increased likelihood of natural disasters, we need to prepare survival kits for children so that their childhood will not be adversely affected.

During the pandemic, the roles of the family and the school merged. Supervision of school work (especially for younger children) was relegated to the family. When this pandemic is over, the school will not return to its pre-COVID-19 functionality. The school will expect increased involvement from parents in the education of the children. Some parents may continue the intense involvement in their children's schooling, while others will quickly disengage and attempt to return to a pre-COVID-19 situation. Both scenarios present a period of adjustment, de-socialization, and re-socialization.

Online education will retain some prominence post-COVID-19 in the Caribbean. It is easily conceivable that blended approaches of face-to-face and online delivery modes will be more in use than before the pandemic. Efforts need to be made to ensure that children from poorer households are not disadvantaged. To guarantee that their childhoods are not negatively affected, governments will need to ensure that all children everywhere have access to stable and good-quality Internet. For those who still struggle with online learning, remedial online classes should be provided. In keeping with an intersectionality approach to development, targeted gender-residential-age-specific online learning should be implemented. Language, racial, and cultural differences must be accounted for in the development of curriculum and online pedagogy. What is clear is that schools must be opened as quickly as possible as their functions cannot be adequately carried out by any other agent of socialization.

It is evident that a high-quality childhood depends on the functioning of the family, school, and all social institutions. Disruptions like the pandemic highlight how chaotic social processes will become when social beings are mandated to maintain physical distancing, lockdown at home and carry out all their responsibilities in one place for an extended period of time.

References

Bronfenbrenner, Urie. 1979. *The Ecology of Human Development: Experiments by Nature and Design.* Cambridge, MA: Harvard University Press.

Burke, Nadine J., Julia L. Hellman, Brandon G. Scott, Carl F. Weems, and Victor G. Carrion. 2011. "The Impact of Adverse Childhood Experiences on an Urban Pediatric Population." *Child Abuse & Neglect* 35 (6): 408–13. https://doi.org/10.1016/j.chiabu.2011.02.006.

Caribbean Development Bank. 2018. "Country Economic Review 2017 Barbados." *Caribbean Development Bank,* March 23, 2018. https://issuu.com/caribank/docs/barbados_cer_2018_final/5.

Clarke, Colin Graham, and Bridget M. Brereton. n.d. "West Indies Island Group, Atlantic Ocean." *Britannica.* Accessed April 18, 2021. www.britannica.com/place/West-Indies-island-group-Atlantic-Ocean/Colonialism.

Country Economy. 2021. "General Government Expenditure." Accessed April 19, 2021. https://countryeconomy.com/government/expenditure.

Country Meters. 2021. "Population of the World and Countries." Accessed April 19, 2021. http://countrymeters.info/.

Daley, Jonielle. 2021. "COVID Household Care Slashes Womens' Incomes." *The Gleaner*, April 21, 2021. https://jamaica-gleaner.com/article/lead-stories/20210421/covid-household-care-slashes-womens-incomes.

Davies, Scott, and Jal Mehta. 2013. "Educationalization." In *Sociology of Education: An A-to-Z Guide*, edited by James Ainsworth, 229–30. Thousand Oaks, CA: Sage Publications, Inc. http://dx.doi.org/10.4135/9781452276151.n126.

ECLAC-UNICEF. 2020. "COVID-19 Report. Social Protection for Families with Children and Adolescents in Latin America and the Caribbean. An Imperative to Address the Impact of COVID-19." Accessed April 17, 2021. www.cepal.org/sites/default/files/publication/files/46490/S20 0 0 7 44_en.pdf.

Fearon, Shanari. 2020. "How Student Athletes in Jamaica are Coping with the Coronavirus Outbreak." *Times Higher Education*, April 6, 2020. www.timeshighereducation.com/student/blogs/how-student-athletes-jamaica-are-coping-coronavirus-outbreak.

Global Volunteers St Lucia. n.d. "COVID-19 Update: Impacts on St Lucian Life." Accessed April 18, 2021. https://globalvolunteers.org/covid-19-update-impacts-st-lucian-life/.

Henry-Lee, Aldrie. 2020. *Endangered and Transformative Childhood in Caribbean Small Island Developing States*. Palgrave Macmillan. https://doi.org/10.1007/978-3-030-25568-8.

Index Mundi. 2021. "Population Below Poverty Line." Accessed April 19, 2021. www.indexmundi.com/g/g.aspx?c=td&v=69.

Kelly, Monique D. A., and Stanley R. Bailey. (2018). "Racial Inequality and the Recognition of Racial Discrimination in Jamaica." *Social Identities* 24 (6): 688–706. https://doi.org/10.1080/13504630.2017.1381835.

Leslie, Shakira. 2020. "Has COVID-19 Worsened or Improved Jamaican Family dynamics?" *Global Voices*, May 27, 2020. https://globalvoices.org/2020/05/27/has-covid-19-worsened-or-improved-jamaican-family-dynamics/.

Martial, Zoe. 2021. "What Is the Impact of COVID-19 on Small Island Developing States? A Case Study on Income Inequality in Saint Lucia." The Centre for Evidence-Based Medicine. Accessed April 18, 2021. www.cebm.net/2021/01/what-is-the-impact-of-covid-19-on-small-island-developingstates-a-case-study-on-income-inequality-in-saint-lucia/.

McKenzie, Herman, and Hermione McKenzie. 1971. "Sociology and the Caribbean Family." Unpublished Paper. Mona. Department of Sociology, University of the West Indies.

Ministry of Family, Culture, Sports and Youth, Barbados. October 2011. "The National Youth Policy of Barbados." Accessed April 19, 2021. www.barbadosparliament.com/htmlarea/uploaded/File/Policy/2012/National%20Youth%20Policy%20Buildbooklet.pdf.

Mumena, Walaa A., Isabella Francis-Granderson, Leroy E. Phillip, and Katherine Gray-Donald. 2018. "Rapid Increase of Overweight and Obesity Among Primary School-aged Children in the Caribbean; High Initial BMI Is the Most Significant Predictor." *BMC Obesity* 5: 4. https://doi.org/10.1186/s40608-018-0182-8.

Naitram, Simon. 2020. "Barbados: COVID-19 HEAT Report. Human and Economic Assessment of Impact." UNDP, UNICEF and UN Women Eastern Caribbean. Accessed April 18, 2021. www.undp.org/content/dam/barbados/docs/heat-reports/covid-19-heat-report/COVID19%20HEAT%20Report%20%20Human%20and%20Economic%20 Assessment%20of%20Impact%20-%20Barbados.pdf.

OECS. 2020. *COVID-19 and Beyond: Impact Assessment and Responses*. Saint Lucia: OECS. https://drive.google.com/file/d/1W7QTdbTTzNB-4CtOZeYmHYB2CoEy3-rS/view.
Russell, Jessica. February 2021. "February 2021: Update on Children's Rights in Jamaica." Our Colourful Voices. Accessed April 19, 2021. http://nuestravozacolores.org/eng/february-2021-update-on-childrens-rights-in-jamaica/.
Sagewam, Indera. 2020. "Saint Lucia. COVID-19 HEAT Report. Human and Economic Assessment of Impact." UNDP, UNICEF and UN Women Eastern Caribbean. Accessed April 18, 2021. www.humanitarianresponse.info/sites/www.humanitarianresponse.info/files/assessments/human-and-economic-assessment-of-impact-heat-report_-_saint lucia.pdf.
Save the Children. 2020. "Protect a Generation. The Impact of COVID-19 on Children's Lives." Accessed April 18, 2021. www.savethechildren.org/content/dam/usa/reports/emergency-response/protect -a-generation-report.pdf.
Sawyers, Kisha. 2015. *Child Rights in the Caribbean: An Annotated Bibliography*. West Indies: Caribbean Child Development Centre, University of West Indies, Open Campus. www.open.uwi.edu/sites/default/files/docs/Child%20Rights%20in%20the%20Caribbean_0.pdf.
Sharma, Rachana. 2021. "The Impact of COVID-19 on Children with Thalassemia and Their Families in India." In *COVID-19 and Childhood*, edited by Nazneen Khan. New York and London: Routledge.
Smith, Alecia. 2020. "Poverty Rate Fell by 40 Percent in 2018." *Jamaica Information Service*, June 25, 2020. https://jis.gov.jm/poverty-rate-fell-by-40-per-cent-in-2018/.
Statista. 2021. "Statistics." Accessed April 19, 2021. www.statista.com/.
Tefera, Adai A., Jeanne M. Powers, and Gustavo E. Fischman. March 2018. "Intersectionality in Education: A Conceptual Aspiration and Research Imperative." *Review of Research in Education* 42 (1): vii–xvii. https://doi.org/10.3102/0091732X18768504.
The Commonwealth. 2021. "Reviewing the National Youth Policy of St. Lucia." Accessed April 19, 2021. https://thecommonwealth.org/project/reviewing-national-youth-policy-saint-lucia.
Trinidad Express. 2021. "How the Pandemic Is Impacting Children and Families." *Trinidad Express*, March 10, 2021. https://trinidadexpress.com/online_features/community_cares/how-the-pandemic-is-impacting-children-and-families/article_12bfa467-c9b0-5b7d-8d6a-23b907f11a17.html.
UN Environment Programme. 8 July 2020. "Supporting Haiti's COVID-19 Response." Accessed April 18, 2021. www.unep.org/news-and-stories/story/supporting-haitis-covid-19-response.
UNDP. 2021. "Global Human Development Indicators." Accessed April 19, 2021. http://hdr.undp.org/en/countries.
UNICEF. 2020a. "Revised Humanitarian Response Plan." Humanitarian Action for Children. Accessed April 18, 2021. www.unicef.org/media/76481/file/2020-HAC-LACRO-revised-2.20.pdf.
UNICEF. 2020b. "UNICEF Haiti Humanitarian Situation Report No. 1: 1 January–30 June 2020." Accessed April 18, 2021. https://reliefweb.int/report/haiti/unicef-haiti-humanitarian-situation-report-no-1-1-january-30-june-2020.
UNICEF. 2020c. "The Impact of COVID-19 on Migrant Children in Trinidad and Tobago." UNICEF, August 31, 2020. https://reliefweb.int/report/trinidad-and-tobago/impact-covid-19-migrant-children-trinidad-and-tobago.

UNICEF/CAPRI. 2020. "The Impact of the COVID-19 Pandemic on Children in Jamaica." Accessed April 19, 2021. www.unicef.org/jamaica/reports/effect-covid-19-pandemic-jamaican-children-preliminary-results.

UNICEF and LACRO. 2020. "Impact of COVID-19 on Gender and Education." *UNICEF and LACRO*, June 2, 2020. Accessed August 15, 2021. https://es.unesco.org/sites/default/files/ms_shelly_n._abdool-zerezeghi_unicef_lac_regional_office.pdf.

United Nations Treaty Collection. 1989. "Convention on the Rights of the Child." Accessed April 19, 2021. https://treaties.un.org/Pages/ViewDetails.aspx?src=TREATY&mtdsg_no=IV-11&chapter=4&clang=_en.

Varea, Valeria, and Gustavo González-Calvo. 2020. "Touchless Classes and Absent Bodies: Teaching Physical Education in Times of Covid-19." *Sport, Education and Society*. https://doi.org/10.1080/13573322.2020.1791814.

World Bank. 2021. "St. Lucia." Accessed April 19, 2021. http://pubdocs.worldbank.org/en/681431582655269212/mpo-lca.pdf.

World Population Review. 2021. "Gini Coefficient by Country 2021." Accessed April 19, 2021. https://worldpopulationreview.com/country-rankings/gini-coefficient-by-country.

Youth Innovation Centre. "National Youth Policy 2017–2030." Accessed April 19, 2021. www.youthjamaica.com/content/national-youthpolicy#:~:text=Jamaica's%20National%20Youth%20Policy%20was,pursue%20and%20achieve%20their%20goals.&text=Jamaica's%20youth%20are%20intelligent%2C%20ambitious%20and%20eager%20to%20succeed%20in%20life.

Youthpolicy.org. 2021a. "Fact Sheet. Haiti." Accessed April 19, 2021. www.youthpolicy.org/factsheets/country/haiti/.

Youthpolicy.org. 2021b. "The Government of the Republic of Trinidad and Tobago National Youth Policy." Accessed April 19, 2021. www.youth policy.org/national/Trinidad_Tobago_ 2004_ National_Youth_ Policy.pdf.

Zalaznick, Matt. 2021. "Stress Tops Reasons Teachers Quit. COVID Has Made Matters Worse." District Administration, February 22, 2021. https://districtadministration.com/stress-teachers-quit-before-during-covid-pandemic-salary/.

10 Risk-Taking Among Older Youth at the Outset of the COVID-19 Pandemic in the USA

Marie C. Jipguep-Akhtar, Denae Bradley, and Tia Dickerson

On January 30, 2020, the Director General of the World Health Organization (WHO) declared the coronavirus disease 2019 (COVID-19) outbreak a Public Health Emergency of International Concern (PHEIC) (World Health Organization 2020). A primary purpose of a PHEIC statement is to limit the public health and societal impacts of emerging and recurring disease risks (Durrheim, Gostin, and Moodley 2020) such as COVID-19. To achieve this goal, the WHO recommended that the public should engage in good hygiene practices such as wearing face masks and washing hands with warm water and soap, staying at home, practicing physical distancing, and carefully handling purchased products as effective COVID-19 preventive measures (Henning-Smith, Tuttle, and Kozhimannil 2021; Kaushik, Agarwal, and Gupta 2020). For most people, adhering to these recommendations required transforming the ways in which we organize ourselves socially and in our daily routines (Figueiredo et al. 2021), developing new health habits, and adopting behaviors unfamiliar and incompatible with our existing habits and norms (Brossard et al. 2020a). Public health officials declared that any behavior that conflicted with these measures could increase the spread of COVID-19, therefore representing a health risk (Keinan, Idan, and Bereby-Meyer 2021).

The COVID-19 outbreak sparked renewed interest in risk-taking behavior among young people. This is in great part because, as asymptomatic carriers of the coronavirus, young people may have contributed significantly to early community spread and increased mortality rates among older and vulnerable populations in Wuhan, China. Between January and December 2020 in the United States of America (USA), COVID-19 disease was the underlying or contributing cause of 377,883 deaths, with rates highest among those above 85 years (Ahmad et al. 2021). During that time, however, COVID-19 incidence was highest among persons aged 30 or younger who accounted for the largest proportion of total COVID-19 cases (>20%). They were also more likely to transmit the virus than others (Boehmer et al. 2020; Lockerd Maragakis 2020). This suggests that the risk of becoming sick with COVID-19 is age-specific (Franzen and Wöhner 2021).

Like childhood, the coming-of-age period is a sensitive window for upholding health behaviors that contribute to present and future health

DOI: 10.4324/9781003250937-14

quality (Institute of Medicine and National Research Council 2015). Given that pandemics will emerge more often, spread more rapidly, kill more people (Dziba et al. 2020) and also that mitigation requires the adoption of new health-promoting behaviors (Brossard et al. 2020b) especially among young people, it is important to develop a better understanding of their risk-taking during pandemics. We draw on survey data collected during the initial weeks of social distancing in the USA (Christensen and Magnusson 2020b) to examine risk-taking among young people at the start of the COVID-19 pandemic. In particular, we examine the associations of perceived health status, COVID-19 knowledge, anxiety over COVID-19, and trust in institutions to risk-taking. We also explore the effects of race and gender on risk-taking. Our analysis of COVID-19-specific risk-taking among young people is couched in the propositions of the Health Belief Model (HBM).

HBM is an expectancy value model that contextualizes behavior in terms of how severe an individual perceives a threat, their susceptibility to the threat, whether they feel empowered to meet the threat and the benefits or barriers they may encounter while meeting the threat (Carico, Sheppard, and Thomas 2021; Hochbaum, Rosenstock, and Kegels 1952). It has been adapted to examine long- and short-term health behaviors, including sexual risk behaviors and the transmission of human immunodeficiency virus/acquired immunodeficiency syndrome (HIV/AIDS) (Denison 1996). HBM is a very applicable and flexible model for investigating risk-taking among young people in the context of a pandemic. Of relevance to the present study are postulates that health behaviors result from perceived disease risk and motivation or cues to action (Jipguep 2001). In accordance with these propositions, it is expected that COVID-19 knowledge, anxiety over COVID-19, perceived health status, and trust in institutions will have direct effects on risk-taking among young people. It is also proposed that demographic attributes, namely, gender and race, will also influence COVID-19 risk-taking.

Risk-Taking Among Young People in the Context of a Pandemic

The coming-of-age milestone, the period of life between ages 10 and 24, is an important stage of the lifecourse. It is the neurological, physical, and emotional transition point in time when individuals are especially susceptible to engaging in risk behaviors (National Academies of Sciences and Medicine 2020; UNICEF 2011). This includes eating poorly, being physically inactive, and smoking, which are typically associated with disease and premature death (Centers for Disease Control and Prevention 2020b; Lindberg et al. 2000; Woolf and Laudan 2013). For these reasons, there continues to be much speculation that older youth lack the competence to recognize, assess, and appropriately judge risk (Institute of Medicine and National Research Council 2001). This has never been more true than in the context of the COVID-19 pandemic.

Shortly after the pandemic began, the WHO declared that children and youth are vulnerable to severe acute respiratory syndrome coronavirus 2 (SARS-CoV-2), noting that they could suffer from severe disease, die, and that their lives and the lives of others depend on their decisions to protect themselves (Aylward 2020). Social and behavioral scientists have substantively furthered our pre-COVID-19 understanding of risk-taking among older youth. From their contributions, we know that young people engage in a wide range of risky behaviors that their older peers shun, and at an enormous cost (Tymula et al. 2012). They drive faster, take part in more dangerous sexually and criminally risky behaviors, and their mortality and morbidity rates are 200% greater than their younger peers (Reyna and Farley 2006; Tymula et al. 2012). We also know that knowledge of a disease such as COVID-19, risk of contracting or being harmed by an illness-causing virus, trust in the government, desire to protect others, moral obligation to comply with preventive measures, and use of immunosuppressants is associated with adherence to preventive measures among young people (Aerts et al. 2020; Ferrer et al. 2018; Nivrette et al. 2021; Yang et al. 2020). Furthermore, we know that healthy behaviors learned early in life are more likely to be maintained during adulthood and that health-promoting behaviors aid in preventing or delaying chronic or life-threatening disease (Frech 2012).

Recently published research found that during a pandemic, disease-transmitting behaviors are shaped by low awareness of disease severity (which may result from contradictory or unclear public messaging) and perceptions of low personal risk (O'Connell et al. 2021). Gender and emotional responses such as fear of infection, disease, or anxiety have also been linked to health preventive behaviors during pandemics (Keinan, Idan, and Bereby-Meyer 2021). A few studies have in fact shown that men exhibit lower rates of preventive behavior adoption against COVID-19, including handwashing, social distancing, use of masks, and proactively seeking effective medical help. There is also evidence that because they are more knowledgeable about the symptoms of COVID-19 disease, women seem to be more aware of the risk they face (Bronfman et al. 2021; Bwire 2020; Howard 2021). Other research demonstrates that compared to younger people, older individuals are more likely to practice healthy behaviors in general, and within epidemics in particular (Barari et al. 2020; Callaghan 2005; Kim and Crimmins 2020; Small et al. 2013). Research suggests that media (e.g., television and Internet) has a profound influence on young people's views of themselves and some media content has also been linked to risky behavior in this group (D'Arcy 2004). From the start of the pandemic, government and public health officials relied on the media to educate the public with what was known about SARS-CoV-2 and the health behaviors that can reduce individual-level risk and curtail the spread of COVID-19 (Anwar et al. 2020; Gollust, Lantz, and Ubel 2009; Zhao et al. 2020). In this regard, the media assumed a public health role (Strazewski 2020).

When the COVID-19 outbreak began, healthcare and public health organizations suggested greater adherence to lifestyle modifications will greatly delay the spread of the disease (Carico, Sheppard, and Thomas 2021). However, research shows that throughout the pandemic, young people engaged in behaviors that increased the risk of SARS-CoV-2 transmission. Such behaviors included leaving the home and venturing into public spaces for nonessential reasons and maintaining insufficient distance (less than 6 feet) from others in public settings (Centers for Disease Control and Prevention 2020a; Hutchins et al. 2020; O'Connell et al. 2021). This led public health officials and scholars to surmise that older youth may believe they were invulnerable (Institute of Medicine and National Research Council 2001) to coronavirus. All the while, high levels of anxiety were observed among young adults during the early stages of the COVID-19 pandemic in the USA (Reading Turchioe et al. 2021). Thus, for older youth, it is plausible that adhering to COVID-19 preventive measures may be more challenging than breaking them as they may interfere with maintaining an active social life (Knies 2012; Patton et al. 2016; Tymula et al. 2012). In other words, failing to adhere to COVID-19 preventive measures may form important risk behaviors.

Yet, researchers have sought explanations about how to promote universal adherence to public health mandates and foster general engagement in disease-preventing behaviors during pandemics. Several studies demonstrate that COVID-19 infection rates among older adults are associated with young people's willingness to adapt their health behaviors (Karan 2020; Lunn et al. 2020; Sohrabi et al. 2020). This may be due, in great part, to the fact that COVID-19 redefined risk-taking in such a way that previously benign behaviors that young people regularly engage in, such as getting together with friends and family, going out for a drink, or traveling, are now risky behaviors (Braun 2020; Kahl 2020). The central question we addressed is whether self-perceived health status, knowledge of COVID-19, anxiety over COVID-19, and trust in the media were associated with risk-taking at the start of the COVID-19 pandemic.

Data and Methods

Data, Sample, and Measures

This study is based on data from the anonymous cross-sectional Internet survey of *Political and Personal Reactions to COVID-19 during Initial Weeks of Social Distancing in the United States*. The survey gathered political and personal reactions to COVID-19 during the initial weeks of social distancing among 1,030 adults who resided in the USA on March 31, 2020. Questions assessed political ideology, scientific trust, and media consumption, as well as attitudes, anxieties, impacts, and knowledge related to COVID-19. The survey also collected mental health and demographic information (Christensen et al. 2020). Data collection procedures for the survey are fully described online and the data are publicly accessible at the Inter-University Consortium for Political and Social Research (ICPSR) website (Christensen and Magnusson 2020a).

We identified respondents between ages 18 to 24 (N=124). This age group has been conceptualized as late adolescence by Sawyer and colleagues (Sawyer et al. 2018) in their landmark article on *The Age of Adolescence*. Nearly three-fifths (59.7%) were 18 to 21 years of age, 44.4% self-identified as female, 48.4% were White, and 61.6% were non-White. Approximately 80% had knowledge that the SARS-CoV-2 virus "is thought to spread mainly from person-to-person through the inhalation of respiratory droplets produced when an infected person coughs or sneezes." More than 84% understood "one can contract COVID-19 (Coronavirus) by touching infected surfaces and then touching your nose or mouth" (Christensen and Magnusson 2020a).

The main outcome of this study, *COVID-19 risk-taking*, was operationalized as whether respondents engaged in COVID-19 preventive behaviors at the start of the pandemic. It is a composite index constructed from ten questions that assessed "the extent to which [participants] changed [their] social contact and out-of-home routines/behaviors in response to COVID-19 (Coronavirus)." Specifically, participants were asked about communicating and having face-to-face contact with others, including relatives who live nearby, close friends, colleagues, work friends, and strangers. They were also asked about going to restaurants/bars, grocery and retail stores, work, and traveling outside their living area. Answer choice selections were "much less than usual," "somewhat less than usual," "about the same as usual," "somewhat more than usual," "more than usual," and "not applicable." The resulting scale had a reliability score of .827, with values ranging from 12 to 24. Higher values signified higher COVID-19 risk-taking.

Independent variables included demographic characteristics (race and gender), self-reported health status, knowledge of COVID-19, anxiety over COVID-19, and trust in the media. *Gender* (male versus female) was derived from a survey item that asked participants to confirm their gender identity as male, female, transgender, or other. A dichotomous measure of *Race* (white versus non-white) was evaluated based on a question that categorized respondents into White, Black/African American, Asian, American Indian, or Alaska Native, Native Hawaiian or Pacific Islander, and/or Other, including multiple races.

Knowledge of COVID-19 was computed from participants' responses to three questions that measured knowledge of COVID-19. The first two questions asked whether (1) coronavirus is spread mainly from person to person through the inhalation of respiratory droplets produced when an infected person coughs or sneezes or (2) infection with SARS-CoV-2 virus results from touching infected surfaces followed by one's nose or mouth. Response options were "true," "false," or "I don't know." The third question asked about the seasonal flu and coronavirus. Respondents were asked to identify which of the two is deadlier, or whether they were "about the same in terms of risk of dying." The final score was dichotomized into low and high knowledge of COVID-19. *Self-reported health status* captured participants' perceptions of their own health status. Participants were asked what they would about their general health. Responses were measured on a four-point Likert scale with four options: "poor," "fair," "very good," and "excellent."

Trust in the media was evaluated with the following question: "In general, I trust the news media to deliver impartial news." Participants were asked whether they "strongly agreed," "agreed," "somewhat agreed," "neither agreed nor disagreed," "somewhat disagreed," "disagreed," or "strongly disagreed." *Anxiety over COVID-19* is an index that reflects participants' fears over a very young family member, a healthy adult family member, an elderly family member, or themselves contracting COVID-19. With values ranging from low to high, this four-item scale has an internal consistency reliability score of .857.

Results

Our analyses considered gender, race, perceived health status, knowledge of COVID-19, anxiety over COVID-19, and trust in the media as predictors of risk-taking among older youth in the context of the pandemic. Descriptive statistics for study variables, including multi-item measures of COVID-19 knowledge, anxiety, and risk-taking, are presented in Table 10.1. Participants were, on average, 21 years of age. More than three-fifths (62.9%) reported high knowledge of COVID-19. They also reported relatively high levels of self-perceived health ($M=3.59$; range=1–5) and trust in the media ($M=3.82$; range=1–5). Levels of COVID-19 anxiety ($M=4.36$; range=1–7) were slightly high and COVID-19 risk-taking ($M=24.8$; range=12–54) was low among respondents.

Correlation analyses (see Table 10.2) yielded respectable associations between COVID-19 anxiety and risk-taking ($r=-.342$, $p<.01$) and trust in

Table 10.1 Descriptive statistics and reliability scores for study variables

Variables	n	%	M	SD	Range	α	Number of items
Gender							
Male	68	54.8					1
Female	55	44.4					
Race							
White	60	48.4					1
Non-white	64	51.6					
COVID-19 knowledge							
Low	46	37.1					4
High	78	62.9					
Age			20.84	1.88	18–24		1
Self-perceived health			3.59	1.02	1–5		1
Trust in the media			3.82	.97	1–5		1
COVID-19 anxiety			4.36	1.60	1–7	.857	4
COVID-19 risk-taking			24.80	9.61	12–54	.827	10

Risk-Taking Among Older Youth   159

Table 10.2 Correlation coefficients for study variables

Variables	1	2	3	4	5	6	7	8	9	10	11	12	13	14	15	16
1. Race	1	.187**	.033	-.063*	.018	-.116**	.699**	.187**	.164**	.219**	.079*	.937**	.923**	.953**	.844**	.041
2. Gender		1	-.096**	-.007	.108	.015	.587**	.927**	.916**	.962**	.845**	.150**	.185**	.107**	.141**	-.180**
3. Self-perceived health			1	-.067*	.013	-.071*	-.030	.166**	-.112**	-.124**	-.069	.259**	.012	-.029	.003	.015
4. COVID-19 knowledge				1	.055	-.145**	-.022	-.030	.284**	-.020	-.080*	-.076*	.198**	-.005	-.097**	-.071*
5. COVID-19 anxiety					1	-.229*	.116	.056	.101	.307**	.021	-.016	-.024	.300**	-.038	-.342**
6. Trust in the media						1	-.103**	.022	-.037	.009	.365**	-.124**	-.136**	-.067	.229**	.005
7. Gender x Race							1	.559**	.529**	.801**	.407**	.626**	.659**	.757**	.571**	-.071*
8. Gender x Self-perceived health								1	.836**	.901**	.790**	.229**	.179**	.079*	.148**	-.181**
9. Gender x COVID-19 knowledge									1	.915**	.733**	.126**	.250**	.099*	.103**	-.170**
10. Gender x COVID-19 anxiety										1	.843**	.152**	.221**	.626**	.179**	-.103*

(continued)

Table 10.2 Cont.

Variables	1	2	3	4	5	6	7	8	9	10	11	12	13	14	15	16
11. Gender x Trust in the media											1	.059	.063*	.051	.192**	-.155**
12. Race x Self-perceived health												1	.855**	.901**	.777**	.042
13. Race x COVID-19 knowledge													1	.899**	.754**	.031
14. Race x COVID-19 anxiety														1	.826**	.022
15. Race x Trust in the media															1	.034
16. COVID-19 risk-taking																1

*p<.05 **p<.01 (one-tailed).

the media (r=−.229, p<.05). Modest yet statistically significant relationships were also detected between trust in the media and race (r=−.116, p<.01) as well as COVID risk-taking (r=−.180, p<.01). Additional but small correlations emerged between COVID-19 risk-taking and the interactions of gender and self-perceived health (r=−.181, p<.01), gender and knowledge (r=−.170, p<.01), gender and COVID-19 anxiety (r=−103, p<.05), and gender and trust in the media (r=−.155, p<.01). Minor correlations were found between race and COVID-19 knowledge (r=−.063, p<.05), gender and self-perceived health (r=−.096, p<.01), and the interaction of race and gender (r=−.071, p<.05).

A three-stage hierarchical multiple regression (HMR) was performed to fit the outcome measure (COVID-19 risk-taking) by gender, race, self-perceived health, knowledge of COVID-19, anxiety over COVID-19, trust in the media, and their respective interactions. Diagnostic tests showed very little missing data (less than 2%), no multicollinearity, and that all assumptions for HMR were met. Table 10.3 presents the main results of our analysis. Model 1 is the baseline model, which exclusively contains the control variables and serves to evaluate the added explanatory value of the independent variables. Model 2 adds the direct effects of the four independent variables and Model 3 includes the effects of the interaction terms.

Model 1 explained a small amount of the variance in COVID-19 risk-taking among older youth (R^2=.045). Gender was found to have a direct effect on COVID-19 risk-taking, which indicates that being male is associated with a .215-point increase in COVID-19 risk-taking (β=−.215, p<.05). Model 2 assessed the direct effect of self-perceived health, knowledge of COVID-19, anxiety over COVID-19, and trust in the media on COVID-19 risk-taking (Table 10.3). The study findings revealed that when these independent variables were included, the prediction model produced a statistically significant increase in the variance explained in COVID-19 risk-taking over and above that of race and gender (R^2=.151, p<.01). Within Model 2, COVID-19 anxiety emerged as the sole significant predictor of COVID-19 risk-taking (β=−.320, p<.01). Its potency nullified the influence of gender and suppressed the expected effects of race, self-perceived health, COVID-19 knowledge, and trust in the media. This suggests that for a one unit decrease in COVID-19 anxiety, COVID-19 risk-taking increases by .320 points. The inclusion of the interaction terms in the model was accompanied by a statistically significant increase in predicted variation (R^2=.203, p<.05). Within Model 3, COVID-19 anxiety (β=−.352 p<.05) and the interaction of gender and knowledge (β=.733, p<.05) predicted COVID-19 risk-taking.

This study offers three meaningful insights about risk-taking among older youth at the beginning of the COVID-19 pandemic. First, being male is associated with higher risk-taking compared to being female. Second, experiencing little fear over a very young family member, a healthy adult family member, an elderly family member, or oneself contracting SARS-CoV-2 is associated with increased COVID-19 risk-taking. Third, males and females differ significantly on risk-taking based on their knowledge of COVID-19.

Table 10.3 Hierarchical regression analyses for variables predicting COVID-19 risk behavior

	Model 1			Model 2			Model 3		
	B	SE B	β	B	SE B	β	B	SE B	β
Race	.342	.260	.123	.308	.254	.111	2.306	1.880	.831
Gender	-.600	.261	-.215★	-.517	.275	-.186	-1.001	1.968	-.359
Self-perceived health				-.026	.132	-.019	.210	.253	.154
COVID-19 knowledge				.126	.248	.044	-.041	.409	-.014
COVID-19 anxiety				-.108	.030	-.320★★★	-.119	.048	-.352★
Trust in the media				.015	.073	.019	.041	.131	.054
Gender x Race							-.460	.623	-.153
Self-perceived health x Race							-.274	.283	-.358
COVID-19 knowledge x Race							-.717	.546	-.463
COVID-19 anxiety x Race							.018	.070	.093
Trust in the media x Race							.010	.161	.064
Self-perceived health x Gender							-.160	.292	-.192
COVID-19 knowledge x Gender							1.191	.533	.733★
COVID-19 anxiety x Gender							-.026	.070	-.136
Trust in the media x Gender							-.050	.162	-.078
Constant	1.546			2.814			2.191		
R^2	.045			.151			.203		
R^2 change	.045			.106			.051		

★p<.05 ★★p<.01 (two-tailed).

This is because the interaction of gender and knowledge has a statistically significant effect on COVID-19 risk-taking. Knowledge modifies the relationship between gender and risk-taking such that increased knowledge marginally reduces risk-taking among males compared to females.

Discussion

The COVID-19 outbreak imposed critical health and safety behavior modifications for people of all ages (Vale et al. 2020). Early in the pandemic, young people were cast as healthy, active, "socially worthy" but "risky" agents who deliberately engaged in behaviors that risked their health and that of others (Cook et al. 2021). Thus, reaching and convincing them to follow COVID-19 preventive measures was identified as a key challenge in controlling the pandemic (Groot Kormelink and Klein Gunnewiek 2021). However, prior analyses have not examined the extent to which young people changed their social contact and out-of-home routines in response to the COVID-19 pandemic. In spite of this, identifying sociodemographic and other groups more or less likely to follow public health recommendations and mandates were touted as vital to slowing and stopping the spread of COVID-19 (Hearne and Niño 2021).

The two most important findings that emerged from this study are related to gender. First, we observed that gender had a negative direct effect on COVID-19 risk-taking. Second, we found that COVID-19 knowledge had a minimal effect on risk-taking among males compared to females. These results agree with previous reports that COVID-19 risk-taking is higher among men and lower among women. They allude to adherence to preventive behaviors as lower among women because they are more knowledgeable about the disease, its symptoms, and the risk associated with SARS-CoV-2 infection (Bronfman et al. 2021; Bwire 2020; Howard 2021). While results also support a recent study showing that women were more likely to engage in health preventive behaviors than men, they sharply deviate from assertions that age is generally unrelated to voluntary compliance behaviors (Clark et al. 2020). Several studies have examined factors associated with nonadherence to preventive behaviors such as social distancing during the COVID-19 pandemic (Hills and Eraso 2021). The majority did not identify a relationship between gender and risk-taking or nonadherence to preventive behaviors. However, our results put forward the notion that gender (being male or female) explains, at least in part, the influence of knowledge on COVID-19 risk-taking. This suggests the effect that knowledge on risk-taking may not be fully understood without accounting for gender, especially among older youth. In all, these results offer that knowledge has an important effect on young men's health risk-taking behavior, which in turn may be key for their risk and vulnerability to disease (Duncan, Schaller, and Park 2009). For these reasons, we must probe whether gender is an important mechanism for preventive health behaviors among males, and also the ways in which it may intersect with other social factors to produce disparities in disease, knowledge attitudes, and behaviors. Indeed, scholars, the world over, have been highly concerned with how beliefs in male norms inform negative behavioral health outcomes among young men (Heilman, Barker, and Harrison 2017).

Bearing this in mind, examining how masculinity and gender norms shape the health behaviors of older male youth is critical, particularly during pandemics.

The other key finding that emerged from this study pertains to the relationship between race and COVID-19 risk-taking. Unlike Hearne and Niño (2021) who found that Blacks, Latinas/os, and Asians were more likely to report wearing a mask in response to the coronavirus than Whites, this study found no association between race and risk-taking. Hearne and Niño (2021) also determined that, at the beginning of the pandemic, White men were least likely to wear a mask. Our results suggest that, by itself, race does not have an effect on COVID-19 risk-taking among older youth. This may be explained by the fact that 62.9% of participants reported high COVID-19 knowledge.

The present study extends research on risk-taking among older youth when individuals are especially susceptible to engaging in risk behaviors. Study results suggest that young people changed their behaviors in response to the COVID-19 pandemic. Most respondents reported having less face-to-face contact with family members who live nearby, close friends, colleagues, work friends, and strangers, engaging in increased virtual communication. They also refrained from traveling and going to restaurants/bars, grocery and retail stores, or work. These findings challenge representations that young people think that COVID-19 is not a potentially severe disease for them and that they underestimate the probability of getting the disease (Commodari and la Rosa 2020). This holds true even for those whose self-perceived health was high. In fact, perceived health status did not predict risk-taking, which raises question about the assertion that young people may think that they are invulnerable (Institute of Medicine and National Research Council 2001) to coronavirus.

Findings also indicate that COVID-19 anxiety was high among study respondents. As expected, lower anxiety over coronavirus was associated with increased risk-taking early in the pandemic. This is consistent with the findings of Wang and Zhao (2020) which suggested that young people exhibited high anxiety because of the COVID-19 outbreak. Our results also echo prior evidence that the COVID-19 outbreak produced anxiety in young people (Kujawa et al. 2020). Although respondents expressed personal concern over contracting COVID-19, a greater percentage reported that they would be scared if a family member (elderly, healthy adult, or younger person) contracted COVID-19. More respondents reported anxiety over others becoming ill with COVID-19. This suggests that they were concerned about the health of others during the pandemic. We also found that lower COVID-19 anxiety was associated increased risk-taking among male respondents and that non-White participants reported significantly higher COVID-19 anxiety compared to their White counterparts.

Conclusion

What is clear from our research is that at the start of the pandemic, risk-taking was higher among males coming-of-age and among those who reported lower anxiety over COVID-19. Also evident is that not all young people engage in behaviors that put their and the lives of others at risk. Claims that young people's choices have an effect on the trajectory of the pandemic (Mackley and Henry 2020) may therefore distort their role in mitigation. This suggests that specific subgroups, not all young people (Tetreault et al. 2021), may have engaged in higher risk-taking when the COVID-19 pandemic began. Young Black and Hispanic men and women are more at risk than their White counterparts due to long-standing racial health inequities and social determinants of health that leave them more vulnerable (Lockerd Maragakis 2020). Our findings point to gender and race being more than markers for classifying and comparing health behaviors and outcomes; they may interact with other social factors to structure adherence or nonadherence to preventive health behaviors among older youth.

Notwithstanding, our study comes with several limitations. We used secondary cross-sectional data. Given that the pandemic has evolved, and preventive measures were politicized, analyses of repeated cross-sectional or longitudinal data would have allowed for assessing and comparing risk-taking among older youth and other population groups over time. Our study sought to understand the risk behaviors of coming-of-age youth within the context of pandemics. Perceived health was associated with anxiety over COVID-19 among the young people in our sample. This suggests that COVID-19 anxiety is related more to perceived health than it is by age, although mortality rates are closely tied to being older. Despite a positive correlation between gender and trust in the media, the latter did not significantly predict risk-taking. This may be indicative of high media skepticism among young people. Our results indicate that the relationships of gender, race, self-reported health status, trust in the media, and anxiety over COVID-19 to risk-taking among young people is complex. These findings are important for the present study as well as for understanding behavior modification among young people when health and other natural crises arise.

References

Aerts, Céline, Mélanie Revillaid, Laetitia Duval, Krijn Paaijmans, Javin Chandrabose, Horace Cox, and Elisa Sicuri. 2020. "Understanding the Role of Disease Knowledge and Risk Perception in Shaping Preventive Behavior for Selected Vector-Borne Diseases in Guyana." *PLoS Neglected Tropical Diseases* 14 (4): 1–19. https://doi.org/10.1371/journal.pntd.0008149.

Ahmad, Farida B., Jodi A. Cisewski, Arialdi Miniño, and Robert N. Anderson. 2021. "Provisional Mortality Data—United States, 2020." *MMWR Surveillance Summaries* 70 (14): 519–22. https://doi.org/10.15585/mmwr.mm7014e1.

Anwar, Ayesha, Meryem Malik, Vaneeza Raees, and Anjum Anwar. 2020. "Role of Mass Media and Public Health Communications in the COVID-19 Pandemic." *Cureus*, September. https://doi.org/10.7759/cureus.10453.

Aylward, Bruce. 2020. "COVID-19 Virtual Press Conference." www.who.int/docs/default-source/coronaviruse/transcripts/covid-19-virtual-press-conference---18-august.pdf?sfvrsn=c93ccc39_2.

Barari, Soubhik, Stefano Caria, Antonio Davola, Paolo Falco, Thiemo Fetzer, Stefano Fiorin, Lukas Hensel, Andriy Ivchenko, Jon Jachimowicz, and Gary King. 2020. "Evaluating COVID-19 Public Health Messaging in Italy: Self-Reported Compliance and Growing Mental Health Concerns." *MedRxiv*. https://doi.org/10.1101/2020.03.27.20042820.

Boehmer, Tegan K., Jourdan DeVies, Elise Caruso, Katharina L. van Santen, Shichao Tang, Carla L. Black, Kathleen P. Hartnett, et al. 2020. "Changing Age Distribution of the COVID-19 Pandemic—United States, May–August 2020." *MMWR. Morbidity and Mortality Weekly Report* 69 (39): 1404–9. https://doi.org/10.15585/mmwr.mm6939e1.

Braun, Emily. 2020. "'COVID-19 Exhaustion': Sociologist Explains Risky Behaviors." *Spectrum News*, June 16, 2020. www.baynews9.com/fl/tampa/coronavirus/2020/06/18/sociologist-explains-covid-19-exhaustion-why-people-take-more-risks.

Bronfman, Nicolás, Paula Repetto, Paola Cordón, Javiera Castañeda, and Pamela Cisternas. 2021. "Gender Differences on Psychosocial Factors Affecting COVID-19 Preventive Behaviors." *Sustainability* 13 (11): 6148. https://doi.org/10.3390/SU13116148.

Brossard, Dominique, Wendy Wood, Robert Cialdini, and Robert M. Groves. 2020a. *Encouraging Adoption of Protective Behaviors to Mitigate the Spread of COVID-19. Encouraging Adoption of Protective Behaviors to Mitigate the Spread of COVID-19*. National Academies Press. https://doi.org/10.17226/25881.

———. 2020b. *Encouraging Adoption of Protective Behaviors to Mitigate the Spread of COVID-19. Encouraging Adoption of Protective Behaviors to Mitigate the Spread of COVID-19*. National Academies Press. https://doi.org/10.17226/25881.

Bwire, George M. 2020. "Coronavirus: Why Men Are More Vulnerable to Covid-19 Than Women?" *SN Comprehensive Clinical Medicine* 2 (7): 874–76. https://doi.org/10.1007/S42399-020-00341-W.

Callaghan, Donna. 2005. "Healthy Behaviors, Self-Efficacy, Self-Care, and Basic Conditioning Factors in Older Adults." *Journal of Community Health Nursing* 22 (3): 169–78.

Carico, Ronald Ron, Jordan Sheppard, and C. Borden Thomas. 2021. "Community Pharmacists and Communication in the Time of COVID-19: Applying the Health Belief Model." *Research in Social and Administrative Pharmacy*. Elsevier Inc. https://doi.org/10.1016/j.sapharm.2020.03.017.

Centers for Disease Control and Prevention. 2020a. "Social Distancing, Quarantine, and Isolation: Keep Your Distance to Slow the Spread." May 6, 2020. www.cdc.gov/coronavirus/2019-ncov/prevent-getting-sick/social-distancing.html.

———. 2020b. "2019 Youth Risk Behavior Surveillance System (YRBS) Results and Data Available Now." August 27, 2020. www.cdc.gov/healthyyouth/data/yrbs/index.htm.

Christensen, Sarah R., and Brianna M. Magnusson. 2020a. "Political and Personal Reactions to COVID-19 During Initial Weeks of Social Distancing in the United States." May 8, 2020. https://doi.org/10.3886/E119629V1.

———. 2020b. "Political and Personal Reactions to COVID-19 During Initial Weeks of Social Distancing in the United States." Ann Arbor, MI: Inter-University Consortium for Political and Social Research [Distributor]. August 3, 2020. www.openicpsr.org/openicpsr/project/119629/version/V1/view.

Christensen, Sarah R., Emily B. Pilling, J.B. Eyring, Grace Dickerson, Chantel D. Sloan, and Brianna M. Magnusson. 2020. "Political and Personal Reactions to COVID-19 During Initial Weeks of Social Distancing in the United States." *PLoS One* 15 (9 September): e0239693. https://doi.org/10.1371/journal.pone.0239693.

Clark, Cory, Andrés Davila, Maxime Regis, and Sascha Kraus. 2020. "Predictors of COVID-19 Voluntary Compliance Behaviors: An International Investigation." *Global Transitions* 2 (January): 76–82. https://doi.org/10.1016/J.GLT.2020.06.003.

Commodari, Elena, and Valentina Lucia la Rosa. 2020. "Adolescents in Quarantine During COVID-19 Pandemic in Italy: Perceived Health Risk, Beliefs, Psychological Experiences and Expectations for the Future." *Frontiers in Psychology* 11 (September): 2480. https://doi.org/10.3389/fpsyg.2020.559951.

Cook, Peta S., Cassie Curryer, Susan Banks, Barbara Barbosa Neves, Maho Omori, Annetta H. Mallon, and Jack Lam. 2021. "Ageism and Risk During the Coronavirus Pandemic." In *The COVID-19 Crisis: Social Perspectives*, pp. 207–18. Taylor & Francis. https://doi.org/10.4324/9781003111344-22.

D'Arcy, Jan. 2004. "Media Influences in Young People's Lives." *The Canadian Child and Adolescent Psychiatry Review = La Revue Canadienne de Psychiatrie de l'enfant et de l'adolescent* 13 (1): 2. www.ncbi.nlm.nih.gov/pubmed/19030145.

Denison, Julie. 1996. "Behavior Change—a Summary of Four Major Theories: Health Belief Model AIDS Risk Reduction Model Stages of Change Theory of Reasoned Action." Arlington, VA. https://pdf.usaid.gov/pdf_docs/PNABZ712.pdf.

Duncan, Lesley A., Mark Schaller, and Justin H. Park. 2009. "Perceived Vulnerability to Disease: Development and Validation of a 15-Item Self-Report Instrument." *Personality and Individual Differences* 47 (6): 541–46. https://doi.org/10.1016/J.PAID.2009.05.001.

Durrheim, David N., Laurence O. Gostin, and Keymanthri Moodley. 2020. "When Does a Major Outbreak Become a Public Health Emergency of International Concern?" *The Lancet Infectious Diseases*. Lancet Publishing Group. https://doi.org/10.1016/S1473-3099(20)30401-1.

Dziba, Luthando, Isabel Sousa Pinto, Judith Fisher, and Katalin Török. 2020. "IPBES Workshop on Biodiversity and Pandemics." https://ipbes.net/sites/default/files/2020-10/IPBES%20Pandemics%20Workshop%20Report%20Executive%20Summary%20Final.pdf.

Ferrer, Rebecca A., William M.P. Klein, Aya Avishai, Katelyn Jones, Megan Villegas, and Paschal Sheeran. 2018. "When Does Risk Perception Predict Protection Motivation for Health Threats? A Person-by-Situation Analysis." *PLoS One* 13 (3): e0191994. https://doi.org/10.1371/journal.pone.0191994.

Figueiredo, Camila Saggioro de, Poliana Capucho Sandre, Liana Catarina Lima Portugal, Thalita Mázala-de-Oliveira, Luana da Silva Chagas, Ícaro Raony, Elenn Soares Ferreira, Elizabeth Giestal-de-Araujo, Aline Araujo dos Santos, and Priscilla Oliveira Silva Bomfim. 2021. "COVID-19 Pandemic Impact on Children and Adolescents' Mental Health: Biological, Environmental, and Social Factors." *Progress in Neuro-Psychopharmacology and Biological Psychiatry* 106 (March): 110171. https://doi.org/10.1016/j.pnpbp.2020.110171.

Franzen, Axel, and Fabienne Wöhner. 2021. "Coronavirus Risk Perception and Compliance with Social Distancing Measures in a Sample of Young Adults: Evidence from Switzerland." *PLoS One* 16 (2 February): e0247447. https://doi.org/10.1371/journal.pone.0247447.

Frech, Adrianne. 2012. "Healthy Behavior Trajectories Between Adolescence and Young Adulthood." *Advances in Life Course Research* 17 (2): 59–68. https://doi.org/10.1016/j.alcr.2012.01.003.

Gollust, Sarah E., Paula M. Lantz, and Peter A. Ubel. 2009. "The Polarizing Effect of News Media Messages About the Social Determinants of Health." *American Journal of Public Health* 99 (12): 2160–67. https://doi.org/10.2105/AJPH.2009.161414.

Groot Kormelink, Tim, and Anne Klein Gunnewiek. 2021. "From 'Far Away' to 'Shock' to 'Fatigue' to 'Back to Normal': How Young People Experienced News During the First Wave of the COVID-19 Pandemic." *Journalism Studies,* June 2021. https://doi.org/10.1080/1461670X.2021.1932560.

Hearne, Brittany N., and Michael D. Niño. 2021. "Understanding How Race, Ethnicity, and Gender Shape Mask-Wearing Adherence During the COVID-19 Pandemic: Evidence from the COVID Impact Survey." *Journal of Racial and Ethnic Health Disparities,* January 2021: 1–8. https://doi.org/10.1007/S40615-020-00941-1.

Heilman, Brian, Gary Barker, and Alexander Harrison. 2017. "THE MAN BOX." Washington, DC and London. https://promundoglobal.org/resources/man-box-study-young-man-us-uk-mexico-key-findings/.

Henning-Smith, Carrie, Mariana Tuttle, and Katy B. Kozhimannil. 2021. "Unequal Distribution of COVID-19 Risk Among Rural Residents by Race and Ethnicity." *Journal of Rural Health.* Blackwell Publishing Ltd. https://doi.org/10.1111/jrh.12463.

Hills, Stephen, and Yolanda Eraso. 2021. "Factors Associated with Non-Adherence to Social Distancing Rules During the COVID-19 Pandemic: A Logistic Regression Analysis." *BMC Public Health 2021* 21 (1): 1–25. https://doi.org/10.1186/S12889-021-10379-7.

Hochbaum, Godfrey M., Irwin M. Rosenstock, and Stephen Kegels. 1952. *Health Belief Model.* Washington, DC: US: Public Health Service.

Howard, Matt C. 2021. "Gender, Face Mask Perceptions, and Face Mask Wearing: Are Men Being Dangerous During the COVID-19 Pandemic?" *Personality and Individual Differences* 170 (February): 110417. https://doi.org/10.1016/J.PAID.2020.110417.

Hutchins, Helena J., Brent Wolff, Rebecca Leeb, Jean Y. Ko, Erika Odom, Joe Willey, Allison Friedman, and Rebecca H. Bitsko. 2020. "COVID-19 Mitigation Behaviors by Age Group—United States, April–June 2020." *MMWR. Morbidity and Mortality Weekly Report* 69 (43): 1584–90. https://doi.org/10.15585/mmwr.mm6943e4.

Institute of Medicine and National Research Council. 2001. "Perceptions of Risk and Vulnerability." In *Adolescent Risk and Vulnerability: Concepts and Measurement,* edited by Baruch Fischhoff, Elena O. Nightingale, Joah G. Iannotta, and Institute of Medicine and National Research Council, pp. 15–49. National Academies Press (US). https://doi.org/10.17226/10209.

———. 2015. *Investing in the Health and Well-Being of Young Adults. Investing in the Health and Well-Being of Young Adults.* National Academies Press. https://doi.org/10.17226/18869.

Jipguep, Marie C. 2001. "Assessing the Importance of Awareness and Related Factors on the Adoption of Non-Risky Health Behaviors: A Focus on the Republic of Cameroon." Doctoral dissertation, Howard University.

Kahl, Colin. 2020. "TECH FIT 4 EUROPE: The Geopolitics of COVID-19 (EU Policy Blog)." *Microsoft Corporate Blogs*, 2020. https://blogs.microsoft.com/eupolicy/2020/11/06/covid-19-global-pandemic-or-existential-crisis/.

Karan, Abraar. 2020. "To Control the Covid-19 Outbreak, Young, Healthy Patients Should Avoid the Emergency Department." *BMJ* 368: m1040. https://doi.org/10.1136/bmj.m1040.

Kaushik, Manish, Divya Agarwal, and Anil K Gupta. 2020. "Cross-Sectional Study on the Role of Public Awareness in Preventing the Spread of COVID-19 Outbreak in India." *Postgraduate Medical Journal*, Published Online First (September 2020). https://doi.org/10.1136/postgradmedj-2020-138349.

Keinan, Ruty, Tali Idan, and Yoella Bereby-Meyer. 2021. "Compliance with COVID-19 Prevention Guidelines: Active vs. Passive Risk Takers." *Judgment and Decision Making* 16 (1): 20–35.

Kim, Jung Ki, and Eileen M. Crimmins. 2020. "How Does Age Affect Personal and Social Reactions to COVID-19: Results from the National Understanding America Study." *PLoS One* 15 (11 November): e0241950. https://doi.org/10.1371/journal.pone.0241950.

Knies, Gundi. 2012. "Life Satisfaction and Material Well-Being of Children in the UK." Accessed August 15, 2021. www.iser.essex.ac.uk.

Kujawa, Autumn, Haley Green, Bruce E Compas, Lindsay Dickey, and Samantha Pegg. 2020. "Exposure to COVID-19 Pandemic Stress: Associations with Depression and Anxiety in Emerging Adults in the United States." *Depress Anxiety* 37: 1280–88. https://doi.org/10.1002/da.23109.

Lindberg, Laura Duberstein, Scott Boggess, Laura Porter, and Sean Williams. 2000. "Teen Risk-Taking: A Statistical Portrait." *Urban Institute*. https://aspe.hhs.gov/sites/default/files/private/pdf/72851/TeenRiskTaking.pdf.

Lockerd Maragakis, Lisa. 2020. "Coronavirus and COVID-19: Younger Adults Are at Risk, Too." *Johns Hopkins Medicine*, December 1, 2020. www.hopkinsmedicine.org/health/conditions-and-diseases/coronavirus/coronavirus-and-covid-19-younger-adults-are-at-risk-too.

Lunn, Peter D., Cameron A. Belton, Ciarán Lavin, Féidhlim P. McGowan, Shane Timmons, and Deirdre A. Robertson. 2020. "Using Behavioral Science to Help Fight the Coronavirus." *Journal of Behavioral Public Administration* 3 (1). https://doi.org/10.30636/jbpa.31.147.

Mackley, Michael, and Henry Annan. 2020. "Youth Have an Important Role to Play in Fighting the COVID-19 Pandemic—Healthy Debate." *HealthyDebate*, April 29, 2020. https://healthydebate.ca/2020/04/topic/youth-fighting-pandemic/.

National Academies of Sciences and Medicine. 2020. *Promoting Positive Adolescent Health Behaviors and Outcomes: Thriving in the 21st Century*, edited by Robert Graham and Nicole F. Kahn. Washington, DC: The National Academies Press. https://doi.org/10.17226/25552.

Nivette, Amy, Denis Ribeaud, Aja Murray, Annekatrin Steinhoff, Laura Bechtiger, Urs Hepp, Lilly Shanahan, and Manuel Eisner. 2021. "Non-Compliance with COVID-19-Related Public Health Measures Among Young Adults in Switzerland: Insights from a Longitudinal Cohort Study." *Social Science and Medicine* 268 (January): 113370. https://doi.org/10.1016/j.socscimed.2020.113370.

O'Connell, Katherine, Kathryn Berluti, Shawn A. Rhoads, and Abigail A. Marsh. 2021. "Reduced Social Distancing Early in the COVID-19 Pandemic Is Associated with Antisocial Behaviors in an Online United States Sample." *PLoS One* 16 (1 January): e0244974. https://doi.org/10.1371/journal.pone.0244974.

Patton, George C., Susan M. Sawyer, John S. Santelli, David A. Ross, Rima Afifi, Nicholas B. Allen, Monika Arora, et al. 2016. "Our Future: A Lancet Commission on Adolescent Health and Wellbeing." *The Lancet* 387 (10036): 2423–78. https://doi.org/10.1016/S0140-6736(16)00579-1.

Reading Turchioe, Meghan, Lisa v. Grossman, Annie C. Myers, Jyotishman Pathak, and Ruth Masterson Creber. 2021. "Correlates of Mental Health Symptoms Among US Adults During COVID-19, March–April 2020." *Public Health Reports* 136 (1): 97–106. https://doi.org/10.1177/0033354920970179.

Reyna, Valerie F., and Frank Farley. 2006. "Risk and Rationality in Adolescent Decision Making: Implications for Theory, Practice, and Public Policy." *Psychological Science in the Public Interest, Supplement* 7 (1): 1–44. https://doi.org/10.1111/j.1529-1006.2006.00026.x.

Sawyer, Susan M., Peter S. Azzopardi, Dakshitha Wickremarathne, and George C. Patton. 2018. "The Age of Adolescence." *The Lancet Child & Adolescent Health* 2 (3): 223–28. https://doi.org/10.1016/S2352-4642(18)30022-1.

Small, Gary W., Prabha Siddarth, Linda M. Ercoli, Stephen T. Chen, David A. Merrill, and Fernando Torres-Gil. 2013. "Healthy Behavior and Memory Self-Reports in Young, Middle-Aged, and Older Adults." *International Psychogeriatrics* 25 (6): 981.

Sohrabi, Catrin, Zaid Alsafi, Niamh O'Neill, Mehdi Khan, Ahmed Kerwan, Ahmed Al-Jabir, Christos Iosifidis, and Riaz Agha. 2020. "World Health Organization Declares Global Emergency: A Review of the 2019 Novel Coronavirus (COVID-19)." *International Journal of Surgery* 76: 71–6. https://doi.org/10.1016/j.ijsu.2020.02.034.

Strazewski, Len. 2020. "How News Media Is Filling Public Health Role During COVID-19 | American Medical Association | American Medical Association." *American Medical Association,* September 16, 2020. www.ama-assn.org/delivering-care/public-health/how-news-media-filling-public-health-role-during-covid-19.

Tetreault, Eleanor, Andreas A. Teferra, Brittney Keller-Hamilton, Shreya Shaw, Soliana Kahassai, Hayley Curran, Electra D. Paskett, and Amy K. Ferketich. 2021. "Perceived Changes in Mood and Anxiety Among Male Youth During the COVID-19 Pandemic: Findings from a Mixed-Methods Study." *Journal of Adolescent Health* 0 (0): 1–7. https://doi.org/10.1016/j.jadohealth.2021.05.004.

Tymula, Agnieszka, Lior A. Rosenberg Belmaker, Amy K. Roy, Lital Ruderman, Kirk Manson, Paul W. Glimcher, and Ifat Levy. 2012. "Adolescents' Risk-Taking Behavior Is Driven by Tolerance to Ambiguity." *Proceedings of the National Academy of Sciences of the United States of America* 109 (42): 17135–40. https://doi.org/10.1073/pnas.1207144109.

UNICEF. 2011. "The State of the World's Children 2011 | Publications | UNICEF UK." | Publications | UNICEF UK." February 2011. Accessed August 15, 2021. www.unicef.org/reports/state-worlds-children-2011.

Vale, Michael T., Jennifer Tehan Stanley, Michelle L. Houston, Anthony A. Villalba, and Jennifer R. Turner. 2020. "Ageism and Behavior Change During a Health Pandemic: A Preregistered Study." *Frontiers in Psychology* 11 (November). https://doi.org/10.3389/fpsyg.2020.587911.

Wang, Chongying, and Hong Zhao. 2020. "The Impact of COVID-19 on Anxiety in Chinese University Students." *Frontiers in Psychology* 11 (May): 1168. https://doi.org/10.3389/fpsyg.2020.01168.

Woolf, Steven H., and Aron Laudan. 2013. "Individual Behaviors." In *U.S. Health in International Perspective: Shorter Lives, Poorer Health*, edited by Steven H. Woolf and Aron Laudan, pp. 138–54. Washington, DC: National Academies Press (US). www.ncbi.nlm.nih.gov/books/NBK154472/.

World Health Organization. 2020. "COVID-19 Public Health Emergency of International Concern (PHEIC) Global Research and Innovation Forum." February 12, 2020. www.who.int/publications/m/item/covid-19-public-health-emergency-of-international-concern-(pheic)-global-research-and-innovation-forum.

Yang, Xin Yu, Rui Ning Gong, Samuel Sassine, Maxime Morsa, Alexandra Sonia Tchogna, Olivier Drouin, Nicholas Chadi, and Prévost Jantchou. 2020. "Risk Perception of COVID-19 Infection and Adherence to Preventive Measures Among Adolescents and Young Adults." *Children* 7 (12): 311. https://doi.org/10.3390/children7120311.

Zhao, Erfei, Qiao Wu, Eileen M. Crimmins, and Jennifer A. Ailshire. 2020. "Media Trust and Infection Mitigating Behaviours During the COVID-19 Pandemic in the USA." *BMJ Global Health* 5 (10): 3323. https://doi.org/10.1136/bmjgh-2020-003323.

Index

academic achievement gap *see* education
adolescence *see* youth
adverse childhood experiences 5, 37
ACEs *see* adverse childhood experiences
age: age and COVID-19 transmission 153
agency 5, 7–8, 119–31
American Indian children *see* Indigenous children
anti-Asian discrimination 25, 27
anxiety 75, 77, 104, 125
Asian children 17, 20–1, 23, 26–7, 60, 77, 120

Barbados 134–5, 142
Biden Administration 89
Black children 1–2, 16–26, 47, 75–8, 80–1, 129–30, 134, 143, 164–5

Caribbean 8, 133–49
childcare 99–114
chronic illness 6, 17–18, 21, 63, 65, 155
Convention on the Rights of the Child (CRC) 51
cyber-bullying 93

delta variant *see* variants
depression 75
diabetes 18, 60
digital divide 88–90, 93–4, 124
disability: children with a disability 2, 15, 58–69, 82, 119
Discord 39, 129

education: access to online 24, 36–7, 93–4; inequality 24–5, 143; learning loss 25–6, 91; LGBTQ+ discrimination and affirmation in 36–7; physical education 145–6; special education 94; *see also* rural education
essential workers 18, 107–8
eviction 48

exercise 144–6
eugenics 6, 13–15, 22

food insecurity 20–21, 139
friends 126–7

Galton, Sir Francis 13
gender and sexual minority children and youth *see* LGBTQ+ children
gender inequality *see* inequality

Haiti 134–5
HBM *see* Health Belief Model
health: physical 21, 78, 144–5; risk 2; *see also* mental health
Health Belief Model 154
high-speed internet *see* Wi-Fi
Hispanic children *see* Latinx children
homeless children *see* homelessness
homelessness 2, 6, 35, 45–53, 77
hospitalization 2, 17
housing insecurity 1–2, 20
human rights 6; children's human rights 51–2

incarceration *see* juvenile detention
India 6, 58–69
Indigenous children 2; boarding schools 14
inequality: economic 20–3; educational 6–7, 23–8, 143; health and illness 1–2, 13, 16–20; racial 1–2, 6, 13–28; gender and sexual 6, 35–40, 143, 155
interpretive reproduction 5, 7, 119–20
intersectionality 15–16, 119, 142
isolation 24, 38, 58, 75–6, 81, 95, 102, 104–5, 124–9, 139–41, 147

Jamaica 134–5
juvenile detention 7, 13, 18–19, 80–2
juvenile justice *see* juvenile detention

Kane, Imani 4

Lareau, Annette 1
Latinx children 1–2, 16–23
LGBTQ+: children 2, 6; discrimination 35–40; support for 37–8; youth 6, 35–40
learning loss *see* education
lockdown *see* isolation

masks 4–5, 8, 24, 68, 103–4, 113, 122–5, 127–8, 130, 148, 153, 155, 164
mental health: diagnoses in children/youth 27, 75; access to services and treatment 7, 25, 48, 75–84, 89, 92–3; LGBTQ+ 35–38; impacts 20–1, 23, 67, 75, 91, 93, 104–5, 135; trauma-informed 7
Morgan, Dykota 3
mortality 2–3, 16–18, 153
multisystem inflammatory syndrome (MIS-C) 17, 47

nationalism 14, 16
neoliberalism 17
new sociology of childhood *see* interpretive reproduction

obesity 17–18, 145, 148
older youth *see* youth
online learning: shift to 5; access to 5, 24, 90–4, 123–5, 141–5; *see also* education

parental burnout and stress 7, 77, 99–114
parents: fear 102–8; impact on 7, 99–114; parental loss 22–3; working 18, 88–9
parent-child relationships 7, 37–8, 139–40
participatory drawing 7, 120
people with disabilities (PWD) 58–9; *see also* disability
pets 128
photovoice 7, 120
physical education (PE) 145
physical distance *see* social distance
policy 49
poor children *see* poverty
poverty 20–1, 23, 25, 46–8, 50, 52–3, 88, 90–1, 101, 133–9
probation 76, 78, 80–1
Progressive Era 14, 20

racial capitalism 14, 18, 20–1, 28
racial inequality *see* inequality
recreation 8, 68, 134, 141, 144, 148

remote learning *see* online learning
reproductive justice 5–6, 13–16, 18
resilience 5, 8, 28, 38
risk-taking 8, 153–65
Ross, Loretta 15
rural education 7, 88–95

school-based mental health services *see* mental health
school resource officers 25
Sinophobia 27; *see also* anti-Asian discrimination
social determinants of health 17
social distance 35, 119–31, 153–6
stay-at-home order 122, 129
sterilization 14–15
stimulus payments 18, 21–2
St. Lucia 134–5
stratified reproduction 15

telehealth 78
tele-mental health 76
telework *see* work from home
thalassemia 6, 58–69
theory of endangerment 133
trauma 76, 92; trauma-informed care *see* mental health
Trinidad and Tobago 134–5
Trump Administration 21
Trump, Donald 21, 25, 27

unequal childhoods 1
unemployment 140
urban children 99–114

vaccines: hesitancy 2, 19, 21; Pfizer 3; inequity 2–3, 17, 19–20, 46; rates 19–20
variants: B.1.1.7 2; delta 2–3, 17, 19, 21
violence: domestic 47, 49, 75–6, 91, 133, 137–9, 144, 147; gender-based 143, 146, 148; racial violence 78
virtual communities 38–9
virtual school *see* online learning

WHO *see* World Health Organization
Wi-Fi 5, 24, 49, 82, 89, 123–5
work and family 47, 99–114
work from home 18, 107, 99–114, 125
World Health Organization 153, 155

Zoom 37–9, 92, 99–100, 105–6, 109, 124

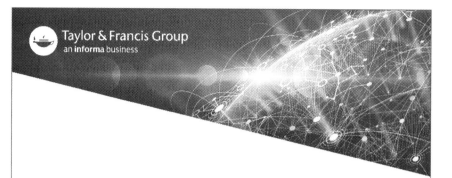

Printed in the United States
by Baker & Taylor Publisher Services